3 Classic

Legal Fictions
A Series of Cases from the Classics

More Legal Fictions
A Series of Cases from Shakespeare

Final Legal Fictions
A Series of Cases from Folk-Lore and Opera

Reported by
A. LAURENCE POLAK
B.A. (HONS. CLASSICS) LOND.,
A SOLICITOR OF THE SUPREME COURT

and

Illustrated by
DIANA PULLINGER

INDIAN ECONOMY REPRINT 2006

Universal
Law Publishing Co. Pvt. Ltd.

Indian Economy Reprint 2006

ISBN : 81-7534-361-3

Published by
UNIVERSAL LAW PUBLISHING CO. PVT. LTD.
C-FF-1A, Dilkhush Industrial Estate,
(Opp. Hans Cinema, Azadpur) G.T. Karnal Road,
Delhi-110033
Tel: 011-27215334, 27438103, 42381334
Fax: 011-27458529
E-mail *(For sales inquiries)*: sales@unilawbooks.com
Website: www.unilawbooks.com

Originally published by
STEVENS & SONS LIMITED, U.K.

All rights reserved.
No part of this publication may be reproduced, stored in a retrieval system, or transmitted in any form or by any means, electronic, mechanical, photocopying, recording, or otherwise without the prior permission of the publishers.

Printed in India at Taj Press, New Delhi

CONTENTS

I

Legal Fictions
A Series of Cases from the Classics

II

More Legal Fictions
A Series of Cases from Shakespeare

III

Final Legal Fictions
A Series of Cases from Folk-Lore and Opera

I
LEGAL FICTIONS

TAKING IN A LEDA

See page 17.

LEGAL FICTIONS
A Series of Cases from the Classics

ACKNOWLEDGMENTS

All the judgments here reproduced were first published, over a period of several years, in the pages of *Law Notes*, and I am glad to have this opportunity of acknowledging the great debt I owe to the Editors of that journal, particularly Mr. L. Crispin Warmington and Mr. H. G. Rivington, whose friendly help and criticism have given me so much encouragement at all times, and by whose courtesy publication in book form has been facilitated. I also desire to acknowledge the kindness and advice I have received from my present publishers and also from my old colleague, A. Goodman, Esq., LL.M.(Lond.), LL.B.(Cantab.), a Solicitor of the Supreme Court, who has made many helpful suggestions.

But *melius est petere fontes*, and I gratefully do so by coupling together the names of Frederick A. Wright, Esq., M.A. (Cantab.), sometime Professor of Classics in the University of London, my affectionate mentor and guide through the asphodel fields of Hellenic culture, and of Ernest Royalton-Kisch, Esq., M.C., M.A., LL.B. (Cantab.), a Solicitor of the Supreme Court, my old friend and principal, who first afforded me a foothold on the rugged paths of English law. To their joint early help and guidance is primarily due whatever of merit these pages may contain.

HAMPSTEAD, A. L. P.
October, 1945.

TO MY FATHER AND MOTHER
IN FILIAL AFFECTION
THIS BOOK IS DEDICATED

CONTENTS

		Page
Acknowledgments		5
Author's Apologia		8
AMPHITRYON *v.* AMPHITRYON	(P.D.A.)	13
DAEDALUS *v.* DAEDALUS AND SON, LTD.	(K.B.D.)	23
EURYSTHEUS *v.* HERCULES	(K.B.D.)	33
Re GOLDEN FLEECE, LTD.	(H.L.)	45
In re IARBAS' AND DIDO'S CONTRACT	(Ch.D.)	57
MENELAUS *v.* HELEN AND PARIS	(P.D.A.)	67
MINOS *v.* THESEUS	(K.B.D.)	77
PHEMIUS *v.* ULYSSES	(C.A.)	87
PLUTO *v.* CHARON	(Ch.D.)	99
REX *v.* PERSEUS	(C.C.A.)	109
Table of Cases Cited		117
Table of Statutes		118
Index		119

AUTHOR'S APOLOGIA

THE author of a new book, like the Speaker-elect in a new House of Commons, is nowadays expected to make a traditional show of reluctance at being dragged from his chosen obscurity into the full glare of the public eye. So much has this become the fashion, that it seems in these days almost indecent to rush into print without analysing and explaining one's motives.

Perhaps the main fascination of the law as a study and career consists in the opportunities it presents of observing the vagaries of the actors upon the human stage in their most diverse activities, of here and there entering upon the scene, a *deus ex machinâ*, to set them back upon the path from which they have strayed, and to provide an edifying and satisfactory *dénouement*.

Why, then, should the action of the play be limited to conventional and contemporary situations? The English system of law—and, indeed, any system worthy the name—must pride itself on being able to deal with *all* situations, however unusual or complex; no tangle should be suffered to defy unravelling by the deft fingers of a High Court Judge.

If it be objected by any reader that the intrusion into these pages of an undue element of the marvellous is a violation of the Aristotelian unities and a defect in good taste, I would reply with the maxim *omne ignotum pro mirabili*. The fact that there is no known case in the Reports of an action for personal injuries inflicted by a

Minotaur, or of a company meeting attended by a Centaur (who might well have graced the chair with a happy blend of humanity and horse-sense), is no evidence against the possibility of such occurrences arising at some future time. And as in the law, so in war. When Alice met the White Knight and, upon observing a mousetrap among the accoutrements of his steed, remarked: "It isn't very likely there would be any mice on the horse's back," the White Knight replied: "Not very *likely*, perhaps; but, if they *do* come, I don't choose to have them running all about!" Therein, I submit, he exhibited that spirit of resourcefulness, that open mind, that receptiveness to the possibility of all eventualities, which every lawyer, and every soldier, should cultivate. "You see," went on the White Knight, after a pause, "it's as well to be provided for *everything*." How often in the course of legal practice, no less than during a brief and undistinguished period of service as a gunner officer in the recent war, have I fancied myself cast in the *role* of the White Knight! With what weight of legal equipment, accoutrements, emergency rations, defensive and offensive weapons, do we drape ourselves before entering upon the battles of the law! Most of them are never used at all, but we have to keep them oiled, cleaned, polished and at the "ready"—just in case. "It's as well to be provided for *everything*."

Finally, in the minds of those who still preserve the saving grace of the child, who see "the glory and the freshness of a dream" in all around them, there may arise a vague resentment at the barbarous and brutal lopping or stretching of the beautiful figures of ancient Hellas to fit the Procrustean bed of English legal procedure. To all such I would observe that such incongruity serves but to show off the delicate tracery of the old in bolder relief against the flat background of the new. How should we appreciate the divine grace and majesty of the Homeric gods without the contrast of the everyday domestic life in the home of Penelope? And if a great thinker like Plato could clothe his purest, coldest philosophical abstractions in the voluptuous warmth of Hellenic myth and legend—beauty and wisdom in one— why should not the cold light of legal learning shine from the English Bench upon the passions and the motives of the heroes and heroines of old? We shall but respect the former the more for its perspicacity, and sympathise the more with the latter as human beings like ourselves.

SWEARING A FOREIGN WITNESS

PROBATE, DIVORCE AND ADMIRALTY DIVISION (DIVORCE).
AMPHITRYON v. AMPHITRYON AND JUPITER.
Husband and wife—Husband's absence on service—Evidence of non-access—Wife's evidence contrà—*Paternity of child born during wedlock—Impersonation of husband by divine co-respondent—Rape—Criminal Law Amendment Act, 1885, s. 4—Wife not guilty of adultery—Judicature Act, 1925, s. 188—Co-respondent a foreign sovereign—Lack of Jurisdiction.*

AN unusual set of circumstances was disclosed in this dissolution suit in which judgment was delivered by the President in the following terms:

" In this suit Squadron-Leader Amphitryon, of 'The Lodge,' Thebes, petitions for dissolution of his marriage on the ground of the adultery of his wife, Alcmene, with Mr. Jupiter, who is said to reside at 'The Mount,' Olympus. The petitioner cites Mr. Jupiter as co-respondent, and asks for damages against him.

" The respondent by her answer denies the adultery. She denies that there have been acts of intimacy between herself and the co-respondent, whom she alleges she has never met; alternatively, she pleads that if any such acts took place they were not voluntary on her part, but took place in circumstances amounting to rape.

" The co-respondent appears only under protest to claim immunity from the jurisdiction of the Court on the ground that, as a foreign sovereign, he cannot be impleaded in a civil action.

"It appears from the petition that the parties were married some four years ago, and cohabited together at Thebes and other places. There is living one child of the marriage, Hercules, born last year, whose paternity is in issue in these proceedings.

"The story disclosed by the evidence is both uncommon and complex. Squadron-Leader Amphitryon is an officer who has rendered distinguished service in the Air Force for a number of years. Two years ago he was detailed to take part with his squadron in a punitive expedition against the Taphians, and departed, by air, at the end of January, leaving his wife behind in Thebes.

"Up to this point there is no controversy between the parties. The principal conflict of evidence arises on the question of access or non-access by the husband on the material dates. Here at once the Court has been brought up against the difficulty raised by the application of the rule in *Russell* v. *Russell*, which, as is well known, forbids evidence not merely as to the fact of such access, but also as to the opportunity therefor. Counsel for the respondent rightly objected to questions by the petitioner's counsel tending to show that the petitioner had been abroad, while his wife remained in this country, for a period prior to the birth of the child rendering it impossible for him to have been the father, which would have had the effect of bastardising a child born during wedlock. These objections I was bound to uphold ; but since there is no similar objection to evidence of non-access being given by witnesses other than the spouses themselves, I was equally bound to admit such evidence from third parties. The necessary testimony, showing that the petitioner continued on duty abroad from the end of January until late in November, has been given both by a number of superior officers and by the official records of the Air Ministry, which have been produced (with the consent of the Secretary of State) by two eminent civil servants.

"Mrs. Amphitryon, on the other hand, supported by the testimony of a number of servants in the house, has sworn positively that she was visited by the petitioner in July and August of that year. She alleges that on both occasions he made a descent by parachute from an aeroplane which circled over the house at such a height that its distinguishing marks were not visible. She declares, however, that she attached no importance to this fact, as the petitioner had been in the habit of paying 'flying visits' (as she aptly expressed it) to the matrimonial home whenever his duties permitted. She has testified further that he stayed two nights with her on each occasion, and the evidence of her maid went far to corroborate her statements.

"The child Hercules was born on the 29th April last, and the petitioner alleges that not he, but Mr. Jupiter, is the father of that child.

"Faced by a conflict of evidence of this character, in which the witnesses on both sides were unshaken by cross-examination, I freely confess that I should have found the utmost difficulty, but for one circumstance, in deciding this primary question of fact—Did or did not the respondent commit adultery? And if so, with whom? I am bound to say that the respondent gave her evidence in a sincere and straightforward manner, and I have no adverse comment to make on the evidence of her servants. Nor, on the other hand, had I any reason to distrust the testimony of the distinguished officers and officials who have testified on behalf of the petitioner.

"The one circumstance which has enabled me to decide

this difficult question of fact has been the public-spirited action of the last witness, Mr. Mercury, who, though a foreigner only recently arrived in this country, has hastened to give the Court the benefit of his assistance. Mr. Mercury has told, through an interpreter, a most extraordinary and well-nigh incredible story. His evidence amounts to this—that the co-respondent, who he alleges is the President of the independent State of Olympus, has for some years past made a habit of practising the art of impersonation, and that he has not only successfully deceived the relatives and intimate friends of those persons whose appearance and manners he cleverly imitates, but has even succeeded in assuming the guise of various animals—a guise so impenetrable that even zoological experts have been taken in thereby.

" Counsel for the petitioner raised an objection to the admission of this witness's evidence on the ground that he refused to take the oath in the ordinary way, but insisted, somewhat surprisingly, on swearing by the name of the co-respondent, a procedure which he stated was usual for persons of his country and religious beliefs. His taking of the oath in this manner was accompanied by the sacrifice of a bull and the catching of its blood in a saucer in open Court. Inconvenient and distressing as these proceedings were to the Court itself, as well as to the members of the Bar, solicitors, and the public present at the time, I was unable to uphold counsel's objections on the subject. At common law the form of the oath is immaterial, provided that it be binding upon the witness's conscience, and the Oaths Act, 1909, has made no difference in this respect, for it expressly provides that, where a witness is neither a Christian nor a Jew, the oath is to be administered in any manner which was lawful prior to the passing of the Act. Cases are not lacking where the oath has been taken in the appropriate fashion by a Mahomedan, a Chinaman and a native of the East Indies professing the Gentoo religion." His Lordship here dealt at length with the authorities, and continued: " In all these cases it was held that evidence given under an oath sworn according to the formalities and ceremonies of the religion professed by the witness is evidence properly to be admitted, and I am not prepared to hold that an oath sworn even in the unusual manner before the Court in this case is any less valid and binding than an oath sworn in the manner common among Christians.

" In support of Mr. Mercury's testimony, counsel for the respondent called and examined at considerable length two ladies whose evidence has placed the matter beyond the shadow of a doubt. Miss Leda, an eminent ornithologist, has deposed to her encounter with the co-respondent in the form of a swan; Miss Europa, who is well-known as a stockbreeder, has described how she found him masquerading as a bull. Of the details of their acquaintance with the co-respondent, the less said the better; it is no part of my duty to utter strictures upon the conduct of independent sovereigns, but I feel bound to say that such conduct constitutes a grave reflection not only upon the co-respondent's standard of morality, but also upon his mental condition.

" Mr. Mercury has further testified that, on or about the material date, the co-respondent left Olympus by air for an unknown destination in a disguise which, described by the witness with minute accuracy, is easily recognisable as representing the form and countenance of the petitioner. To give the deception a further verisimilitude it appears that the co-respondent had arrayed himself in a uniform of the appropriate rank in the Air Force of this country. It is worthy of note that the witness had no hesitation or difficulty in pointing out the petitioner, dressed though he is in civilian costume, in the body of the Court, merely from his recollection of the clever disguise assumed by Mr. Jupiter more than a year ago. This seems to me to be conclusive, and I have come to the conclusion that there is overwhelming evidence for the proposition that the man who in fact visited and stayed with the respondent at the material dates, whom both she and her servants implicitly believed to be her husband, was in fact Mr. Jupiter, the co-respondent in this suit.

"I therefore find, as a matter of fact, that acts of intimacy did take place between the respondent and the co-respondent on the material dates. This, however, is by no means the end of the matter. In order that such acts may constitute adultery it must be shown that they took place with the consent of the respondent, and it is clear law that submission on the part of the wife, owing to a mistake, either as to the nature of the act or the identity of the person doing the act, and induced by the fraud of that person, does not constitute consent. If there were any doubt on the matter, it would be set at rest by sect. 4 of the Criminal Law Amendment Act, 1885, which provides, in clear and unequivocal terms, that a person who induces a married woman to consent to acts of intimacy by impersonating her husband is guilty of rape.

"On this point, therefore, I propose to follow the comparatively recent decision in the case of *Clarkson* v. *Clarkson*, and to hold that the respondent was not guilty of adultery with the co-respondent. The case against her therefore falls to the ground, and the petition must be dismissed, with costs.

"The question of the paternity of the child, Hercules, has greatly exercised my mind from the very start of the case, and I have been unable to find any authority exactly pertinent to the point at issue. On the one hand, the evidence shows clearly that the petitioner is not the father of the child; on the other hand, in view of my finding that the wife has not been guilty of adultery, this child, born during the subsistence of the marriage, might appear to be legitimate. But this point does not arise directly in the present proceedings, and the interested parties may, if they think fit, formally petition the Court for a declaration of legitimacy, under sect. 188 of the Judicature Act, 1925, to which proceedings the Attorney-General must, of course, be made a respondent in the usual way.

"Against the co-respondent there is clear evidence of an adulterous association with Mrs. Amphitryon, and in ordinary circumstances the petitioner would have been entitled to heavy damages against him. The Court's jurisdiction over a co-respondent depends neither on domicil, allegiance nor residence, and, if he be once served, the Court's jurisdiction is established. The rank and fortune of the co-respondent, too, are relevant so far as they assist in valuing the wife and measuring the extent of the injury inflicted on the husband, the blow to whose marital pride is the greater in proportion to such rank and fortune.

"Unfortunately for the petitioner in this case, such considerations are stultified *ab initio*. The co-respondent has set up a plea to the jurisdiction of the Court on the ground that he is a foreign sovereign, and a letter from the Foreign Office has been put in certifying that Olympus is an independent State, that Mr. Jupiter is the President of that State, and that he owes no allegiance to, and is not under the control of, any other Government. In these circumstances, I have no option but to follow the decision in *Statham* v. *Statham*, and I am bound, though with considerable reluctance, to dismiss Mr. Jupiter from the suit, with costs against the petitioner."

Judgment was entered accordingly.

FORCED LANDING

KING'S BENCH DIVISION.
DAEDALUS (suing as Administrator of Icarus, deceased) v. DAEDALUS & SON, LTD.

Negligence—Breach of warranty—Type aircraft approved by Air Ministry—Fatal accident due to negligent use of wax in construction of glider—Loss of expectation of life—Law Reform (Miscellaneous Provisions) Act, 1934—Assessment of damages—Deceased transported to Elysian Fields—Elevation to rank of demi-god at moment of death—No proof of special damage.

IN this action, before Mr. Justice Poseidon, a number of important and difficult questions were raised on the assessment of damages for loss of expectation of life, under the provisions of the Law Reform (Miscellaneous Provisions) Act, 1934. The following is a report of his Lordship's judgment:

" In this case Mr. Daedalus, a well-known aeronautical engineer, brings an action in his representative capacity, as administrator for his late son, Icarus, against Daedalus & Son, Ltd., a company engaged in aircraft manufacture and design, against whom he claims damages for negligence and breach of warranty. No claim is made under the Fatal Accidents Acts, the action being brought only under the Law Reform (Miscellaneous Provisions) Act, 1934, as a claim on behalf of the deceased for damages for loss of expectation of life.

" The melancholy circumstances attending the accident from which the action arises are well-known. Both the plaintiff (who has a controlling interest in and is a life director of the defendant company) and his deceased son had for some time past been greatly interested in aviation, and in particular in that branch of the science known as 'gliding.' Some eighteen months ago Mr. Icarus ordered from the company a new and improved form of glider which they had advertised as being 'the lightest ever made.' According to the expert evidence of Mr. Hermes, an official of the Air Ministry, this somewhat simple contraption consisted of little more than a series of struts to be fitted to the body of the aviator, to which two planes or wings were attached, but containing no engine or other means of propulsion. The same witness gave evidence of the issue of a certificate of airworthiness, a fortnight or so before the accident, in respect of a 'type aircraft' of this pattern, and from what he has told the Court I am satisfied that, given proper construction, in accordance with the specification and the type submitted, such an aircraft is perfectly adapted for the purpose to which it is usually put. I say 'given proper construction' advisedly, and I will return to the point when I consider the evidence on which the charge of negligence is based.

"Shortly after the delivery of the glider which he had ordered, the late Mr. Icarus, accompanied by the plaintiff (who was flying a glider of a similar pattern), took off from a cliff on the coast of Crete. His intention, apparently, was to glide for a short distance over the sea, and finally to come to earth in a valley some few miles away, affording plenty of space for a suitable landing. According to the plaintiff's evidence it seems that all was apparently going well for the first twenty minutes of the flight, and the plaintiff attached some significance to the fact that the sun was during this period obscured by clouds. As soon, however, as the sun broke through, the plaintiff observed the deceased to be in difficulties; first one and then the other of the planes or wings attached to his shoulders became loose and broke away from the structure, and the plaintiff suffered the terrible experience of helplessly watching his son's body hurtling into the waves below from a height of several hundred feet.

"So soon as he was able to make a landing, the plaintiff did all that was humanly possible to organise a rescue party, which within an hour proceeded in boats to the scene of the accident. Unfortunately there was never more than a forlorn hope that Mr. Icarus, hampered as he was by the rest of the structure fastened to his body, would succeed in keeping afloat for more than a few minutes. So indeed it proved, and the bereaved father could do no more than recover his son's lifeless body. The detached planes or wings were found floating some little distance away, and were preserved for the purpose of the Air Ministry's inquiry into the cause of the disaster.

"That inquiry revealed an extraordinary state of affairs. The Court has heard from Mr. Hermes of the discovery, on the ends of the planes or wings, at the point where these were fastened (or should have been fastened) to the struts attached to the body of the deceased, of distinct traces of wax, but of little else in the nature of adequate wiring or securing together of the different parts of the apparatus. There can be no question but that this glider was put together in the most careless fashion; that the wax, which seems to have been intended to assist in binding the separate parts together, melted in the heat of the sun, and that the disintegration of the apparatus and the death of the deceased followed as a matter of course. Mr. Vulcan, the technical manager of the aircraft shops in the defendant company, has given evidence of the methods employed in testing these gliders before their delivery to customers, and, though he gave his testimony in a clear and straightforward manner, I was unable to avoid the conclusion that the company's methods of testing leave much to be desired. I therefore decide, as a matter of fact, that the deceased met his death through the negligence of the defendant company, its servants or agents, and that the defendants were liable to the deceased, at the moment of his death, in damages for that negligence. It is unnecessary for me to go into the further details which might have arisen under the conditions implied by the Sale of Goods Act, 1893.

"I now turn to the more difficult part of my task—one which has puzzled judges and juries alike ever since the Law Reform (Miscellaneous Provisions) Act, 1934, came into force—the question of the assessment of the damages. It is unnecessary for this Court to deal in detail with the controversies which arose when the Act first came into force; the principle that damages may be awarded for loss of expectation of life was settled, as every lawyer knows, by the highest tribunal in the land in *Rose* v. *Ford*, where Lord Atkin said :

"'I am of opinion, therefore, that a living person can claim damages for loss of expectation of life. If he can, I think that that right is vested in him in life and, on his death, under the Act of 1934, passes to his personal representative. I do not see any reason why the fact that the expectation is realised, that is, that death comes at the time anticipated, or sooner, should make any difference.'

"There, succinctly phrased, is the general principle. But, as frequently happens in such cases, it is in the application of that principle that the difficulties arise. That the noble and learned Lord, whose *dictum* I have quoted, himself foresaw some of the difficulties that might arise in this connection is clear from the following further passage in his judgment:

" ' A man is injured in the prime of life : evidence is given that he is not likely to live more than two or three years ; the tribunal estimating damages will take this fact into account, not only in estimating actual money loss, . . . but as an item of personal damage.'

" Since those words were uttered a great many cases have fallen to be decided—cases where the age of the deceased has ranged from that of an infant of three or four to the years of middle age. As another learned judge has put it, in *Turbyfield* v. *Great Western Railway Co.* :

" ' In the end it comes to this. If the directions which have been given must be followed, it means that one has to take into account, in arriving at some assessment of what his life is worth to a person with a normal expectation of life, what he may have to pass through— its normal vicissitudes, with all its joys, all its sorrows, with its hardships and its various burdens and duties.'

" With these broad principles to guide me, let me now look at the facts. The deceased was at the time of his death a young and vigorous man, in an established position in life, doing useful work, popular and beloved by his friends. With the normal expectation of life before him, he probably had fifty or more years to live. Of that period of life the wrongful act of the defendants has deprived him and, taking all the circumstances into account, I should normally, on the evidence which the plaintiff has adduced, have assessed the damages at a very considerable figure.

"Account must, however, be taken—as I have said advisedly—of *all* the circumstances; in endeavouring to arrive at the estimate of damage no item of evidence is to be excluded. Hence I am bound no less carefully to bear in mind the evidence for the defence—evidence which goes to the very root of this question of damages. This evidence is, to put it mildly, of an extraordinary character, amounting to nothing less than an attempt to show that the deceased, far from being the loser by the loss of expectation of the earthly life of which he has been deprived, has actually gained by being translated, a number of years earlier than would normally have been the case, into a new life elsewhere which is infinitely richer, more varied, more crowded with all joy and empty of all sorrow, than anything which he could have experienced in his normal mortal span.

"I am bound to say that the testimony of Mr. Pluto, to the effect that the deceased was at the moment of his earthly death elevated to the rank of a demi-god, at first left me profoundly unconvinced. The law of England does not recognise any such status, and I was unable to take judicial notice of the existence of such a rank as conferring any special rights upon or involving the holder in any particular disabilities. I cannot, however, ignore the very material testimony of this highly respectable witness and of his deputy, Mr. Rhadamanthus, who presides (as he told me) over the distant region known as the Elysian Fields. This name, though somehow associated in my mind with the capital of the French Republic, applies, it seems, to a delectable country in the Far West; its precise geographical situation is ill-defined, though I rather gathered that it was somewhere in the neighbourhood of the State of California. Be that as it may, these two unimpeachable witnesses for the defence were insistent that they were well acquainted with the late Mr. Icarus ; that at the day and hour of his alleged death he arrived in the best of health and spirits in the Elysian Fields ; that they had seen him only a few days ago, and that from a careful physical and psychological examination of his condition they are convinced that he is not only entirely immune from all human ailments and infirmities, but actually immortal. They add, moreover, that he and the persons with whom he associates are accustomed to spend their time reclining on soft beds of asphodel, feeding on ambrosia and quaffing goblets of nectar ; that that happy region enjoys a perpetual summer and that such institutions as war, disease, the income tax, newspapers and child film-prodigies are entirely unknown.

"I have been strongly urged by counsel for the plaintiff to disregard this evidence, which he not only described as irrelevant, but suggested was the outcome of a fevered and diseased imagination. I am bound, however, to say that both witnesses were quite unshaken by his cross-examination, and have produced, as samples of the staple articles of food and drink in the region in question, exhibits which I have personally subjected to the strictest possible tests of sight, touch, smell and taste, to my entire satisfaction." (His Lordship's face was at this point observed to beam with unaccustomed geniality.) "Such testimony, given upon oath, it is not for this Court to reject out of hand, however inherently improbable or even incredible it may appear ; it is on evidence, and evidence alone, that I am justified in basing my conclusions of fact.

"I hold, therefore, as a matter of fact, that any damages

to which the deceased was at the moment of his death entitled by reason of being deprived of his normal expectation of life on earth—damages which would, in accordance with the Act of 1934, have survived for the benefit of his estate—were more than counterbalanced by his translation, at that same moment, into a life of limitless extent, free from all the cares and burdens of this world. I cannot follow the somewhat ingenious argument of the plaintiff's counsel to the effect that, even though it be conceded that, by the wrongful act of the defendants, the deceased has achieved a happy immortality, nevertheless, without that wrongful act, he, would have enjoyed something more, *viz.*, his normal span of earthly life with immortality at the end of it. Not a shred of evidence has been adduced to support this startling proposition, and in any event (if the time of the Court is to be wasted in metaphysical disquisitions) I should have thought that, other things being equal, a period of fifty years' expectation of life on earth could scarcely equal in value a similar period spent in the blissful enjoyment of the products of the deceased's present domicil.

" In all the circumstances I can only assess the damages to the deceased's estate in terms of the smallest coin of the realm, and I give judgment for the plaintiff accordingly, for one farthing damages, without costs. The action was entirely misconceived."

Judgment being entered accordingly, his Lordship returned to a further prolonged investigation of the exhibits, from which he had not yet emerged at the time of this report going to press.

WEIGHTY EVIDENCE ON THREE HEADS

King's Bench Division.
EURYSTHEUS *v.* HERCULES (otherwise Heracles, otherwise Alcides).

Service Contract—Defendant to perform twelve works and labours specified in Schedule—Inclusion of task of taking Cerberus to upper world—Whether criminal offence rendering entire contract illegal—Larceny Act, 1916, s. 5—Whether three-headed animal included in term " dog " therein—Dogs Act, 1906, s. 2—Subject matter of taking not " thing capable of being stolen "—Task of cleansing stable—Diversion of rivers—Action by riparian owners—Whether reasonable and proper method of carrying out work—Quantum of damages.

THE following is an extract from the judgment of the Lord Chief Justice in this action for damages for breach of contract and an indemnity by Mr. Eurystheus, described as a contractor, against Mr. Hercules, described as a " professional strong man " :—

" By a service agreement, dated the 4th of Boedromion, in the Second Olympiad, the plaintiff agreed to employ the defendant and the defendant to serve the plaintiff for a period of twelve years from the date thereof, for the purpose of carrying out certain works and labours specified in the Schedule thereto at a remuneration of four talents of silver *per annum*. The agreement provides that the works are to be carried out diligently and expeditiously, in a proper and workmanlike manner, and that the defendant is to give his whole time and attention to the business of the plaintiff. There are also other clauses, not relevant to the present action, usual in agreements of this kind. The Schedule is divided into twelve parts, each of which describes the work to be undertaken in each respective year of the term, but does not specify in any great detail the manner in which the work is to be performed.

"Evidence has been given that the contract has been carried out by both parties in a satisfactory manner for the past four years. This dispute has arisen over the manner in which the defendant has performed, or purported to perform, the work specified in Part V of the Schedule. The plaintiff complains that this work has been negligently performed by the defendant, so as to render the plaintiff liable to third parties for such negligence, and the plaintiff claims damages for breach of contract, and an indemnity. The defendant pleads that the work has been carried out reasonably and in a proper and workmanlike manner ; alternatively, he pleads that the contract contains an illegal term which renders it unenforceable and void. I propose to deal with this alleged illegality as a preliminary point.

"The term as to which this illegality is alleged occurs in Part XII of the Schedule, and reads as follows :

"'Proceed to Hades ; take and carry away Cerberus and return with him to upper world ; consign to Eurystheus free on rail Thebes.'

"This Cerberus is stated on the pleadings to be the house-dog of a Mr. Pluto, the owner and occupier of Hades, and the defence sets forth that this part of the Schedule imposes on the defendant the duty of stealing a dog, which is a criminal offence, and thus renders the contract illegal and void.

"In this connection it must be borne in mind that, by the common law, a dog is not larcenable, so that if the defendant is to succeed on this point it must be under some statute. Such a statutory prohibition against the larceny of a dog is, indeed, to be found in sect. 5 of the Larceny Act, 1916, and I have now to see whether it can be applied in this case.

"The evidence for the plaintiff, however, has shown that this plea is by no means so simple as it looks. Dr. Chiron, the well-known veterinary surgeon, who has carefully examined the animal in question, has testified that in his opinion it is not a dog at all. His evidence, which was unshaken by cross-examination, disclosed the surprising fact that the creature has no fewer than three heads; he has also declared, on his oath, that it has the tail of a serpent, and that live snakes protrude from its necks. I freely confess that such a description would sound incredible in the mouths of most witnesses, but the standing of this eminent expert is such that I cannot take the responsibility of disbelieving his testimony. Moreover, he is corroborated in material particulars by the other biological and zoological experts who have seen the beast. To what *genus* of *fauna* the creature belongs they are reluctant to say, but they are unanimous that it represents no known *species* of dog. I ought also to observe that the evidence offered by the defence as to the habits of the creature was so exiguous as to be useless; no witness was even able to say whether it was carnivorous or herbivorous, though one of them volunteered the extraordinary piece of information that it had been known to swallow with avidity dog-biscuits, manufactured by a well-known firm, the chief constituents of which are poppy-seeds and honey. This, however, is by no means conclusive, any more than is the evidence on the other side that the animal wanders at large without a collar, contrary to sect. 2 of the Dogs Act, 1906, and the Orders made thereunder. As for the allegation of the defence that the alleged owner once exhibited the creature at Crufts, this has been categorically denied in the box both by Mr. Pluto and by an official of that organisation. In my opinion, taking the evidence all round, the defendant has not discharged the onus of proving that it is a dog—or indeed a domestic animal—of any kind.

" It is clear, then, that the Larceny Act is not applicable, and does not help the defendant's plea. I am bound to add (though this is not necessary to my decision) that such an animal is a dangerous thing, liable to do damage if it escapes, and, in my opinion, being on the land of Mr. Pluto, comes within the Rule in *Rylands* v. *Fletcher*. I am firmly of opinion that Mr. Pluto would be well advised to have it put under restraint or destroyed at once. However that may be, I have not the least doubt that this creature is an animal *ferae naturae*; and on the evidence I have heard I am not disposed to believe that it can have become the property of any person *per industriam;* still less, from its description, *propter impotentiam*. I am thus bound to conclude that this Cerberus is not a 'thing capable of being stolen' within the meaning of the Larceny Act, and that the task which the defendant, under this part of the Schedule, was bound to perform is no offence—either at common law or by statute. I therefore find nothing to preclude me from holding that this service agreement constitutes a perfectly valid contract, the alleged breach of which by the defendant it is now for me to investigate.

"The pleadings show that the alleged breach relates to Part V of the Schedule, reading as follows:

"'Proceed to Elis; report at Augeas Farm; thoroughly wash out, sweep, cleanse, scour and white-wash where necessary stables for 3,000 oxen; then paint and varnish where previously so treated with two coats of good oil colour.'

"It appears from the evidence that, so far as the matter of this part of the contract is concerned, the defendant has done what he contracted to do. The stables are, in fact, now thoroughly cleansed and decorated as required. It is the method by which the work has been executed that forms the subject of the plaintiff's complaint, and to investigate this it is necessary to examine the state and condition of the premises before the work was commenced.

"This part of the evidence discloses a state of affairs as lamentable as it is unusual. Mr. Augeas, who calls himself a gentleman farmer, and whose estate runs into several thousand acres, appears to be a person of the most casual and slovenly habits. Despite his 3,000 head of cattle, he admitted in the witness-box that the stalls had not been cleaned out for the past thirty years. It is not surprising that there have been several outbreaks of foot-and-mouth disease and other ailments among his cattle, and it is a matter of wonder that the consequences to human beings have not been serious. There is no record of an inspection of the cowsheds, dairies and milk-shops by the Medical Officer of the Rural District concerned, and one can only conclude that the local sanitary authorities must be singularly remiss in carrying out their duties under sect. 54 of the Public Health Acts Amendment Act, 1907. I shall see that the matter is brought to the notice of the proper authorities and that appropriate action is taken.

"I do not again propose, nor is it now necessary, to go into the somewhat offensive details of the evidence relating to the filthy and neglected condition of the stables at Augeas Farm. It is enough that on that evidence I am more than satisfied that the defendant, on his arrival to perform his work, was faced with a gigantic and almost superhuman task. It has, in fact, been estimated by expert witnesses that the stables were in a condition which would ordinarily require six or eight months' work by a gang of twenty men to put them to rights. Messrs. Harridges, who have given expert evidence upon the correct method of cleaning stables of this character, have deposed from their skilled knowledge that the only feasible method was to make use of 378 vacuum cleaners, all operating at the same time and, although the expense would have been considerable, it is their testimony, which I accept without hesitation, that (as their foreman picturesquely phrased it) 'a very good job could have been made of it.'

"Now, the defendant is a man of extraordinary physique and unusual bodily strength, and a perusal of the various parts of the Schedule makes it clear beyond all doubt that his physical abilities go to the very root of the contract and were, indeed, the main inducement to the plaintiff to hire him for the tasks therein described. No time limit is specified for the performance of the work, either in the body of the contract or in the Schedule ; beyond the general provision that the work must be carried out diligently and expeditiously, and in a proper and workmanlike manner, the method of performance is left entirely to him. There must, indeed, be implied a proviso that the method shall be a reasonable one, but whether from a too rigid adherence to the maxim *delegatus non potest delegare*, or from an over-literal interpretation of the word 'expeditiously' he did at all events decide that the work must be carried out by himself alone, and that within a single day.

"The method by which the defendant proceeded to carry out the cleansing of the stables is typical of his unusual physical powers and his impulsive character. This was nothing less than to divert the course of two rivers which flow—or, as I should rather say, formerly flowed—through the district, and thus, by partially flooding the entire area, to wash out the accumulated refuse, which was to be carried away by the stream. This ambitious project he proceeded to carry out without delay, and I should be doing less than justice to his abilities were I to deny that, so far as the cleansing was concerned, the effect was precisely that which he had intended. The stables, as the evidence shows, are to-day a model of cleanliness and in excellent decorative condition, and the health of the cattle which they house has never been better. Mr. Augeas has given evidence for the defence, and has deposed to his complete satisfaction with the work.

"Not so, however, the owners of the land through which the rivers formerly flowed. Dwellers on the banks of a stream have, as is well known, extensive riparian rights, and he who takes water from the stream for other than purely domestic purposes must return that water substantially unaltered in quality and undiminished in quantity. In the events which I have outlined, not only has no attempt been made to restore the water used, but the whole course of the stream remains diverted, so that the riparian owners have been permanently deprived of all the rights they formerly enjoyed. In these circumstances it is not surprising that these owners have taken action against the present plaintiff, and at the recent trial in this Court (*Kallikrates and Others* v. *Eurystheus*) recovered heavy damages. It is against these damages that the plaintiff seeks to be indemnified by the defendant. But since the basis of his action is the alleged breach of contract, the claim to an indemnity must stand or fall therewith.

" The effect of this extravagant piece of exhibitionism, quite apart from the invasion of the riparian owners' rights to which I have referred, was to let loose a torrential flood of water devastating the entire countryside. Many of the local inhabitants suffered substantial damage, but I shall take only one illustration.

" This has reference to the pitiful plight of a certain Mr. Leander, as disclosed in his evidence, which was never challenged by the defendant.

" It appears that, on the evening of this ablutionary feat, this gentleman (who is of independent means and occupies his time in historical research) was seated in the study of his charmingly appointed residence in the neighbourhood of the estate in question, when he was interrupted by his wife's enquiring, apprehensively, whether a tap had been left running in the bathroom above. Before Mr. Leander could make any reply, a veritable deluge descended upon the house and all its occupants, and, as we have heard from him in the witness-box, in terms whose vigour testified to the searing nature of his experience, before he knew where he was he had been swept out to sea. It was after three days of great hardship that he found himself washed up on the shores of Crete, where also, to his astonishment and, we must hope, to his delight, Mrs. Leander was similarly beached.

"The serious potentialities of such an invasion of private rights, and the lamentable experience which this unfortunate gentleman underwent, might very easily have led to the appearance of the defendant in some other place upon a charge of manslaughter, if not of murder. He may regard himself as exceptionally fortunate that the well-known prowess of Mr. Leander as a swimmer has enabled him (the defendant) to escape the danger of a criminal charge.

"Needless to say, immediately Mr. Leander was able to satisfy the inhabitants of Crete that he was a person of substance, notwithstanding his damp and impoverished appearance, he chartered a galley and sailed for the mainland with all speed, although he encountered many adventures *en route* upon which I do not intend to dilate. Suffice it to say that, after the expiration of five months, he found himself back among the ruins of his once peaceful home. He immediately instructed his solicitors to institute proceedings against everyone concerned in this major outrage, and he has recovered against the plaintiff in this action damages which another Court has thought adequate to compensate him for his manifold sufferings.

"Can it be said, then, that the defendant has committed a breach of his agreement? That the work has been carried out diligently and expeditiously there can be no doubt, but has it been carried out in a proper and workmanlike manner? The question that I must ask myself is, would this singular method of proceeding have entered the mind of any sane or rational person? A person who is employed to clean out stables is not ordinarily faced with a condition of neglect and uncleanliness such as the evidence has disclosed; but neither, on the other hand, is he in the normal way required or expected to divert the course of rivers for the performance of his task. Whatever the degree of difficulty involved in the performance of the work, the obligor must use such skill and strength as he possesses and must adopt such reasonable means as are adapted to the fulfilment of the task in hand. But in the case before me, while I have every sympathy with the defendant's difficulties and his anxiety to complete the work efficiently and in the shortest possible time, I cannot hold that the diverting of the course of two rivers was a reasonable means of carrying out even the gigantic task with which he was faced.

"I therefore decide that the plaintiff has made out his case, and there will be judgment for the plaintiff with costs, under both heads. The plaintiff is awarded five talents as an indemnity against the sum which he has had to pay the plaintiffs in the previous action to which I have alluded. As to the breach of contract itself, the plaintiff has suffered no damage other than that covered by the indemnity—in fact, he has benefited rather than lost through having had the work so rapidly and efficiently performed. He is entitled only to nominal damages for the breach, and these I assess at two obols."

A stay of execution was granted, on terms.

EXTRAORDINARY MEETING

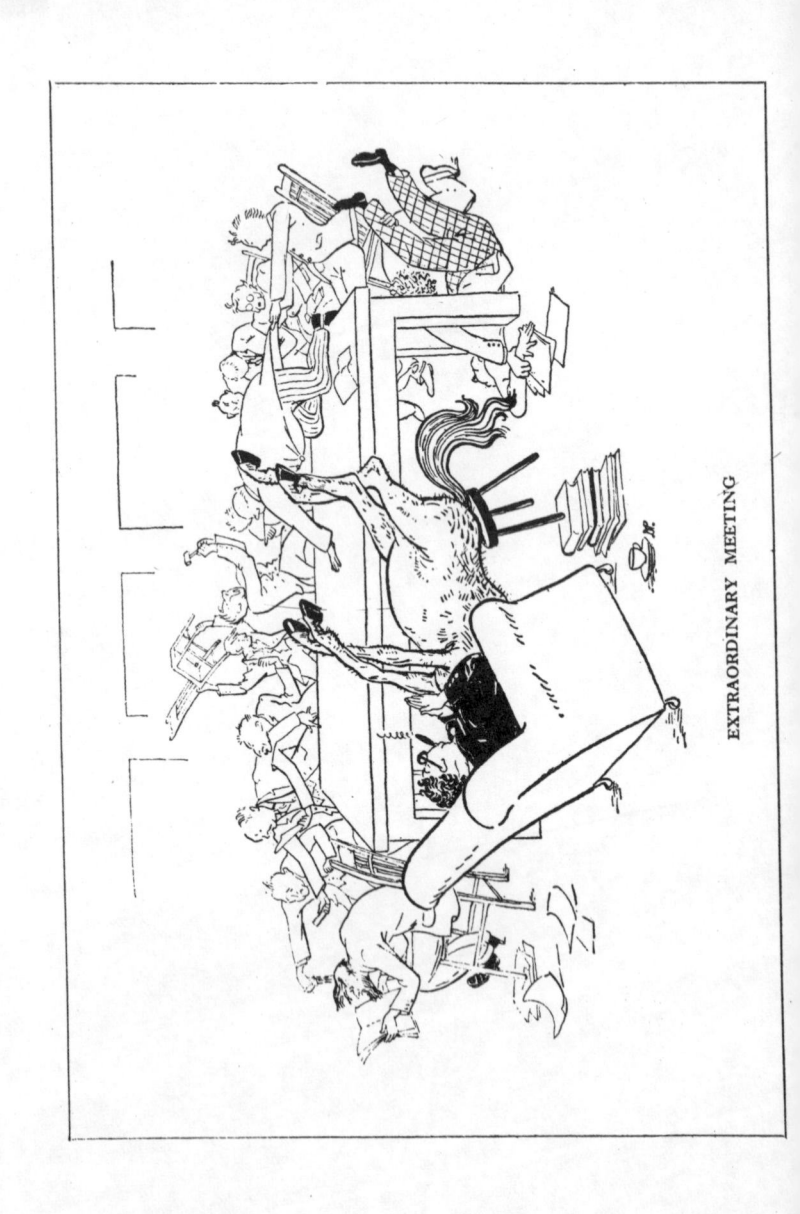

HOUSE OF LORDS.
Re GOLDEN FLEECE, LTD.

Private Company—Substratum or main object—" Winning and exploitation of Golden Fleece, gold and precious metals "—Company engaging in yoking of fire-breathing bulls and other agricultural pursuits—Ultra vires—Joint shareholding—Centaur voting by " show of hooves "—Companies Act, 1929, First Schedule, Art. 54—Contract to allot shares to respondent—Company already having fifty members—Companies Act, 1929, ss. 26, 27—Breach of Contract—Winding-up petition—Companies Act, 1929, s. 168—Application of assets.

THEIR Lordships dismissed this appeal from a judgment of the Court of Appeal, affirming a winding-up order made by Hermes, J., in the Companies Court. The Lord Chancellor delivered the following judgment:

" My Lords, the appeal now before your Lordships originally came on in the form of a petition presented in the Companies Court, before Mr. Justice Hermes, by Miss Medea, the present respondent, for the winding up of a company registered under the name of Golden Fleece, Ltd. The present appellants, who are all shareholders and directors of the company, were joined as defendants. A winding-up order having been made by the learned judge, the defendants appealed, but the judgment below was affirmed by the Court of Appeal some months ago. The defendants (the present appellants) thereupon asked and obtained leave to appeal to your Lordships'

House. The grounds will sufficiently appear from the judgment I am to deliver.

"My Lords, this company, Golden Fleece, Ltd., was incorporated under the Companies Act as a private company two years ago, with a capital of 100,000 drachmae, divided into 10,000 shares of 10 drachmae each. The principal objects of the company are described in the memorandum of association, as follows:

"'(1) To take over as a going concern the business of prospecting, exploration and shipping now carried on by Mr. Jason (hereinafter called the vendor) at Iolcus and elsewhere under the style or firm of Jason & Argo, and all or any of the assets and stock-in-trade in connection therewith, and for that purpose to adopt, with or without modification, an agreement already prepared and expressed to be made between the vendor of the one part and the company of the other part.

"'(2) To search for, win, purchase or otherwise acquire the material known as the Golden Fleece, now situate at Colchis, and the appurtenances and accessories thereof, and all other (if any) the gold, silver, bullion, jewels and articles of virtu therein, thereon or therewith.

"'(3) To purchase, take on lease or in exchange, or acquire by licence, concession, grant or otherwise any lands, mines, mineral rights, easements and privileges, machinery, plant and other effects whatsoever, which the company may from time to time think proper to be acquired for any of its purposes.

"'(4) To carry on the business of mining, smelting, refining and dealing in gold and precious metals of all kinds, and, as auxiliary thereto, to purchase or hire and work vessels, railways, tramways and other means of locomotion and transport of every kind.'

"The memorandum also contains a comprehensive clause enabling the company 'to carry on any other business of a description which may seem to the company capable of being advantageously carried on in connection with or in furtherance of the objects of the company,' and other clauses in the wide terms usual in such documents.

"These, my Lords, are the relevant clauses, and they are, in my opinion, sufficient to indicate that the *substratum* or main object of the company is the winning and exploitation of this so-called Golden Fleece and of gold and other precious metals in some form or other. It is important that this should be borne in mind, as it is a consideration to which I shall more than once have to advert during the course of this judgment.

"To the articles, which adopt Table 'A' with modifications, I need not refer in detail, except to remark in passing that they include the clause (essential in the articles of private companies) prohibiting any invitation to the public to subscribe, limiting the membership to fifty and restricting the transfer of shares to such persons as the directors may approve.

"In this connection it is worthy of note that, shortly after the company's incorporation, the greater part of the authorised capital was issued and the shares were allotted to the exact number of fifty members, all of whom proceeded to take an active part in the company's business. As might have been expected in the circumstances, the affairs of the company were, from the first, conducted in a somewhat unorganised and slovenly manner. That spirit of mutual trust and confidence, so essential to the success of an enterprise carried on by a corporate body, was decidedly lacking—to such an extent, in fact, that at the first meeting of shareholders no fewer than fifty nominations to the Board were submitted and all fifty were elected directors, with a quorum of the same number. This is, I am bound to say, most unusual, but it is not contrary to law, and I refer to it in passing merely as one indication of the unsatisfactory conduct of the company's affairs. The appellant, Mr. Jason, who is described as a shipowner and company promoter, was elected Chairman.

"My Lords, it is an unfortunate fact, which nevertheless I cannot afford to ignore, that the whole history of the company, from the date of its incorporation to the present time, comprises a series of incidents of the most turbulent and discordant nature. Trouble arose almost immediately, at the first meeting of shareholders, over the clause in the articles providing that:

"'Where two or more persons hold a share or shares jointly, they shall be treated as a single member.'

"Strong objection was taken by two of the members, Messrs. Castor and Pollux (who appear to form what is known in medical circles as a 'Siamese twin'), to a ruling of the Chairman that they were a 'single member' within the meaning of this clause. The Chairman was persuaded to alter his ruling only on their threatening, by withdrawing, to render the entire proceedings nugatory. Scarcely was this dispute composed when another arose, on an equally trifling matter of procedure. Among the shareholders is a Mr. Chiron, well-known in academic circles as a person of scholarship and culture. I should most profoundly regret it if any words of mine were to be construed as a reflection upon a gentleman of his charm and natural distinction, but I am bound to mention that he suffers (through no fault of his own) from the physical disability or abnormality of being a centaur—that is to say, he is a man down to the waist, while the rest of his body is that of a horse. Nothing but sympathy will be felt by all right-minded people with a gentleman who, owing to some undeserved congenital misfortune, is afflicted in this manner, but it is a regrettable fact that in a community comprising diverse elements there will always exist individuals ready to exploit such misfortunes for their own malicious ends. A number of such persons were included among the shareholders of this company and they, only too anxious to sow discord among their colleagues, and not content with seeing that Mr. Chiron had a seat (if that be the appropriate expression in his case) upon the Board, attempted to carry a special resolution which was to make a drastic change in Clause 54 of Table 'A,' relating to voting at meetings. This was to add, after the expression 'show of hands,' the words 'and show of hooves' and, though the amendment was defeated, the dispute waxed so hot that fisticuffs were freely exchanged before the Chairman was able to restore order.

"Up to this point, the conduct of the company's affairs, though leaving much to be desired from the standpoint of internal harmony and efficiency, had proceeded without coming into serious conflict with the outside commercial world. In accordance with the first of the objects clauses which I have read, the business of Jason & Argo was duly taken over, with all its assets. These included a vessel of 500 tons, which appears in the Register of Shipping as 'S.S. Argo,' in which the entire personnel of the company, comprising all the shareholders, set sail for Colchis in quest of the so-called Golden Fleece mentioned in Clause (2) of the objects in the memorandum.

"In due course the vessel arrived at Colchis, the voyage having occupied nearly a year, instead of the normal three months. They were well received by the ruling monarch, who granted them a concession over a considerable tract of land for the pursuit of their prospecting activities. As your Lordships will have noted, the acquisition of lands is permitted by Clause (3) of the objects in the memorandum, and the respondent does not dispute the company's power to take over this concession. She does, however, strongly deny the right, which the majority of the Board assumed, to submit to the following conditions laid down by the lessor in the lease which is before your Lordships:—

"'The lessee hereby covenants with the lessor as follows: To farm cultivate manure and manage the said piece or parcel of land hereby demised and (without prejudice to the generality of the foregoing):—

(a) To catch take and yoke two fire-breathing bulls now wandering at large on the said piece or parcel of land hereby demised;

(b) To plough in a good husbandlike manner the said piece or parcel of land according to the most approved methods of husbandry followed in the district;

(c) To keep the arable land clean and free from weeds and forthwith after such ploughing as aforesaid to sow the same with a full crop of dragon's teeth to be supplied by the lessor;

(d) Subject and without prejudice to the lessee's rights and duties under the Ground Game Act and the Agricultural Holdings Act or the custom of the district to kill and exterminate all ground game and vermin upon the said piece or parcel of land hereby demised.'

"Your Lordships will have observed that the covenants I have read, other than the first, are such as are normally inserted in an agricultural lease, and are inappropriate to a mineral concession of the kind which the company had been granted.

"It is at this point that the respondent comes upon the scene. As the lessor's daughter, apart from the liberal arts appropriate to her rank and station, she appears to have made a special study of agriculture and veterinary surgery, in both of which subjects she graduated at the local university. These facts need give your Lordships no cause for wonder; whatever the views which we as individuals may hold as to the propriety of permitting women to engage in such pursuits (and I freely confess myself to an old-fashioned prejudice against it), the fact remains that women, even of the highest station, have nowadays invaded this no less than other domains which men were formerly wont to consider peculiarly their own preserves.

"My Lords, it is clear on the evidence that the respondent early conceived a tender regard for the appellant Jason. Knowing the difficulties to which he was exposed under the onerous terms of the lease, owing to his abysmal ignorance of agricultural matters, she imparted to him a great deal of valuable information on the habits of fire-breathing bulls and the agricultural methods of dealing with dragon's teeth—information which enabled him to perform the first three of the covenants specified in the lease. But it is equally clear that her instruction was not given gratuitously. It is shown by the evidence (which was accepted in the Courts below) that the appellant Jason undertook, in return for such instruction, to pay the respondent the sum of 10,000 drachmae, to be satisfied by the allotment to her of 1,000 shares in the company, fully paid up. There is no doubt in my mind that he entered into this agreement on behalf of, and as agent for, the company, the beneficiary under the lease.

"Be that as it may, one point emerges clearly—that by some means or other the company was able to satisfy the onerous conditions on which this concession was granted, and finally to acquire the Golden Fleece which was the primary object of its existence.

"My Lords, the remaining facts may be disposed of very shortly. Accompanying the members on their homeward journey, the respondent attended the Annual General Meeting convoked at the company's registered office. At this meeting it was resolved, *nemine contradicente*, to frame the Golden Fleece (now the company's principal asset) and to suspend it in a conspicuous position in the registered office—in the words of the resolution, ' as a votive offering '—though what the significance of this apparently meaningless formality may have been, I do not pretend to understand. The company's insurers, at all events, very properly refused cover for so valuable an object in an unprotected position, and in the ensuing litigation a further 20,000 drachmae of the capital was recklessly wasted.

"The respondent now demanded that the terms of the agreement to allot her the 1,000 shares be implemented forthwith. The matter was fully and somewhat acrimoniously discussed at the subsequent directors' meeting, and produced a stormy scene ; it was left to Mr. Theseus, who spoke for a number of the directors, to point out that the allotment of shares to the respondent would increase the number of members above the maximum of fifty allowed to private companies, necessitating drastic revision of the articles, the filing of a statement in lieu of prospectus and a complete reconstitution of the company's organisation and status. (Companies Act, 1929, ss. 26, 27.) In the result, the motion to allot the shares to the respondent was heavily defeated. The respondent thereupon filed a petition, under sect. 168 of the Act, alleging that it was just and equitable that the company be wound up, on the ground that, the main object having been achieved, the *substratum* had gone, and that the directors had acted or were intending to act *ultra vires* in carrying on a course of dealing without authority either from the memorandum of association or under the general law. It was said that the company, having been formed for the main purpose of acquiring the Golden Fleece, and for the subsidiary objects of exploration, mining and the exploitation of minerals, had entered and was proposing to enter into agricultural and other pursuits which formed no part of its objects as set out in the memorandum.

"The appellants' answer to the petition was that the alleged agricultural and other pursuits were carried on in connection with or in furtherance of the company's main objects, and were authorised by the general clause in the memorandum to which I have referred. It further stated that the concession could not have been obtained if the company had not accepted the covenants in the lease.

"The learned judge below held, and held rightly, that he was bound by authority to hold that the contentions of the appellants were ill-founded, and made the winding-up order prayed for. His judgment was upheld on appeal, and it is for your Lordships' House to decide whether these judgments should be affirmed or no. I think the matter may be disposed of in very brief terms.

"My Lords, I have had no hesitation in coming to the conclusion that this appeal ought to be dismissed. I am not unmindful of the fact that it is not necessarily a ground for winding up that the *substratum* of the company is gone, if all that remains to be done is to distribute the surplus assets. In the case before your Lordships, the articles contain a clause empowering the liquidator, on a winding up, to distribute the assets among the members *in specie*, and that, as has been rightly said, is a matter for the domestic forum. But the case is otherwise if the directors have carried on, or are proposing to carry on, a business which is *ultra vires* the company. Where the primary objects enumerated in the memorandum are followed by general words in very wide terms, such general words must be read as incidental to those primary objects, and where the directors have wrongfully engaged, or are proposing to engage, in general business of a character not expressly authorised by the objects clause, a shareholder or creditor is entitled to a winding-up order to prevent misapplication of the assets.

"The appeal will, therefore, be dismissed and the judgment of the Court of Appeal and of the Court below affirmed. The respondent will have her costs here and in the Courts below."

The other noble and learned Lords concurred.

CUTTING IT FINE

PALATINATE COURT OF CHANCERY AT TUNIS.
In Re IARBAS' AND DIDO'S CONTRACT.
Vendor and Purchaser—Description of property—Identification by admeasurement—" Such part thereof as may be enclosed by hide of bull"—Latent ambiguity—Severance of bull's hide at completion—Law of Property Act, 1925, s. 49—Vendor's duty as trustee—Vendor tenant for life—Gift of immortality—Whether interest thereby converted into fee simple—Status of immortality not recognised by courts—Settled Land Act, 1925, Second Schedule.

Judgment of Mr. Justice Apollo:

"This application, made under sect. 49 of the Law of Property Act, 1925, raises two questions between vendor and purchaser which are of considerable importance to conveyancers, namely (a) as to the meaning and effect of the words describing the property in the contract of sale, and (b) whether the vendor is entitled to rescind the contract on the grounds that he is unable or unwilling to comply with a requisition as to the proper payment of the purchase money.

"The contract in question was made between the Vendor, Mr. Iarbas, of Gaetulia, Tunisia, described as a local chieftain, and the Purchaser, Mrs. Elissa Dido, of Tyre, Syria, widow. The contract incorporates by reference the form of conditions known as the 'National Conditions of Sale.'

"As to the former point, relating to identity, I find that,

while a plan is annexed to the contract and the sale property is described with reference thereto, the particulars of the property to be sold relate only to part of the property shown on the plan and are described in somewhat unusual terms. It is to decide the proper construction of these particulars that the first part of this application is made. The sale property is therein described as follows:

'All That piece or parcel of land (now in the occupation of the vendor) on the north-eastern portion of the coast of Tunisia the dimensions and extent whereof are delineated on the plan annexed hereto and thereon coloured pink or such part thereof (whichever shall be the lesser parcel) as may be enclosed by the hide of the black bull known as " Nigger " (now in the custody of the Vendor's solicitor) which for the purpose of identification only and not by way of limitation has been branded with the seals of the parties hereto prior to the date hereof.'

"Clause 3 of the contract fixes the date and place of completion of the purchase, and goes on to provide that:

'On the said completion date the said bull shall be slaughtered and delivered to the Purchaser as her absolute property. The Purchaser, before payment of the purchase price, shall in the presence of the Vendor ascertain the dimensions and extent of the property hereby agreed to be sold in the manner provided by the particulars of sale hereinbefore set forth, and the Vendor shall thereupon forthwith execute a conveyance to the Purchaser of the said property delimited thereby.'

"Pausing there for a moment, it is clear that, unusual

In re IARBAS' AND DIDO'S CONTRACT 59

and over-ingenious as may be the wording of these two clauses, there is no such patent ambiguity on the face of the document as would debar me from hearing parol evidence in regard to its construction. The parties have taken considerable pains to set out, in clear and unmistakable language, the method by which the sale property is to be ascertained, and if they have chosen to introduce terms which render such ascertainment a complicated or difficult matter, the law will not prevent their doing so.

" It was not until the completion date arrived that the latent ambiguity in the particulars became apparent. The Purchaser duly presented herself on that date at the place named with a bank draft for the purchase money ; the bull was duly killed, delivered to the Purchaser and stripped of its hide, and all was ready for the admeasurement of the land. Evidence has been given that, at that point of time, the dimensions of the hide were approximately seven feet by four feet on the body, and that, allowing for the extensions formed by the head, legs and tail of the animal, the entire hide outspread covered an area of thirty-five square feet or thereabouts. The Purchaser, however, had other intentions. Using a sharp pair of garden shears, she cut up the entire hide into a large number of very narrow strips, each no wider than a piece of thin string, and by laying these end to end was able to enclose an area approaching fifty acres of the Vendor's land. She then tendered the agreed purchase price to the Vendor's solicitor, who not unnaturally refused to complete and sought to rescind the contract. The Purchaser took out this summons to have decided the question of construction of the particulars and other matters.

" The first question I have to decide is whether, on the

true construction of the particulars of sale, the words used can reasonably bear the meaning ascribed to them by the Purchaser, or whether they are to be limited, as the Vendor contends, to such part of the land as could have been enclosed by the hide in its original state. With all respect I venture to assert that Counsels' arguments on both sides have been distinguished rather by their ingenuity than by their helpfulness. On the one hand I was treated to a learned, but misplaced, dissertation on tenancies by entireties and undivided shares ; on the other hand I was invited to consider a number of completely irrelevant cases on words of severance. None of these matters is, in my opinion, germane to the real issue, which is the applicability or otherwise of the maxim *id certum est quod certum reddi potest*.

" In my opinion this maxim applies to the words used in the particulars of sale—'enclosed by the hide of the black bull.' There is no word here to suggest that the hide must be retained in its pristine form, and it is not for the Court to insert an implied term in a contract unless such term is made requisite by necessary implication either from the context or the surrounding circumstances. It is impossible not to give full force to the words 'for the purpose of identification only and not by way of limitation' in their application to the bull's hide. It is impossible, too, to ignore the very pertinent term that 'before payment of the purchase price' the bull was to become the absolute property of the Purchaser, and that only after the completion of that transaction was the admeasurement of the land to take place. Now, it is well-established that a person may do as he wishes in respect of his own property, subject only to the proviso that he do not violate the general law of the land, commit any breach of contract or injure any other person thereby. The bull's hide having once become the property of the Purchaser, it was open to her to treat it as she thought fit in the interim between that point of time when the ownership therein was transferred to her and the time when the admeasurement began. If the Vendor desired to ensure that the hide should remain in its former entire condition when used for the purpose of delimitation, it was open to him to insert a stipulation in the contract to that effect.

"The Vendor asks the Court for relief on the grounds of mistake. This is an equitable remedy, and relief may be granted if the mistake was induced by the other party to the contract, or if it involves serious hardship and was not due to mere carelessness. There is no evidence before me that the mistake in this case, if such it be, is of such nature that equity could properly grant relief. But it is unnecessary for me to go deeply into the matter, owing to the application of the maxim that 'he who comes to equity must come with clean hands.' Evidence, to which I am disposed to give full credence, has been given that there was a deliberate attempt on the part of the Vendor to reduce the value both of the personal property and of the realty which he had contracted to sell, by lopping the animal's tail, cropping its ears, and above all, by keeping it on so restricted a diet, while it remained in his constructive possession, that from being a healthy, spirited animal of some six hundred pounds weight at the signing of the contract, it had shrunk to less than three hundred pounds at the date of completion, and its dimensions were correspondingly reduced. And since a Vendor, on the signing of the contract of sale, becomes a trustee of the sale property for the Purchaser, it is his duty to take reasonable care of it, and he becomes liable to the Purchaser for loss or deterioration which the Vendor ought to have prevented. He certainly did not take such reasonable care of the personal property represented by this bull, and his treatment of the animal's diet, carried out (as he frankly admitted) with a view to its ultimate employment as a kind of yardstick, amounts to a species of equitable fraud so far as the real property is concerned. That being the case, the Vendor cannot come to this Court asking for relief in equity when his own conduct has been such as equity would censure. I therefore decide the first question unhesitatingly in favour of the Purchaser.

" The second question for decision is equally curious. The first document of title submitted is a strict settlement thirty-five years old made by Mr. Ammon, the Vendor's father, described therein as a 'tribal deity,' and settling the property on the Vendor for life with the usual subsequent life interest for the wife and remainder to the children of the Vendor. There is the usual vesting deed under the Transitional Provisions of the Settled Land Act, 1925, vesting the fee simple of the property in the Vendor, but he has stated that he is unwilling or unable to comply with the following requisition by the Purchaser's solicitor :

'There must be at least two trustees, being individuals, or a trust corporation, to give a receipt for the purchase money on completion.'

" The Vendor's reply to this requisition is, first, that the sole trustee, the said Mr. Ammon (the vendor's father), though still living, is outside the jurisdiction, in a place vaguely described as 'the abode of the gods,' and before his departure omitted to execute any deed of

In re IARBAS' AND DIDO'S CONTRACT 63

appointment of a new trustee in his place, and that the Settlement gives no power to any other person to appoint a new trustee for this or any other purpose. Secondly, the Vendor alleges that it is unnecessary to make any application to the Court to appoint new trustees for the purpose of receiving the purchase money, since he (the Vendor) is capable of conveying the fee simple in the property and of receiving the purchase money as if the land were not settled land. He contends that, in the events which have happened, he is now solely and beneficially entitled to the fee simple and that his interest is no longer subject to any other interest or charge subsisting or capable of being exercised under the settlement.

"The reasons given by the Vendor for this alleged state of affairs are that, on his attaining his majority some sixteen years ago, his father Mr. Ammon, the settlor, conferred upon him the gift of immortality. And the Vendor contends that, his span of life having thus been perpetually extended, his life interest in the property has *ipso facto* been notionally converted into a fee simple absolute in possession, with the result that the life interest to his wife and the remainder to his children (and, indeed, all interests subsequent to his prior life interest) must automatically fail.

"I have carefully considered the evidence given in support of these extraordinary statements, and I am bound to admit that it is uncontroverted. Counsel has attempted to demonstrate, in a long and able argument, that the terms of the settlement violate the rule against perpetuities and are therefore void in any event. I am unable to follow him in his contentions, for the simple and sufficient reason that, when the dispositions thereunder took effect, the interests in the property must necessarily vest within the period of a life in being, namely, the life of the Vendor, and I fail to see how the matter can be affected by the subsequent prolongation of that life to an indefinite extent. I was more impressed with the argument that immortality is a question of status and that, whatever be the legal position in the place where the Vendor is domiciled, immortality is not such a status as can be recognised, as a matter of law, by the English Courts. With this point of view I express my concurrence, and hold that the trusts of the settlement remain valid and subsisting, and that the Vendor must make the appropriate application to the Court for the appointment of two trustees, or a trust corporation, to receive the purchase money. There will be a declaration in favour of the Purchaser to that effect, and to the effect that the Purchaser is entitled to specific performance of the contract for sale of the property as admeasured by her at the date fixed for completion. The costs of this summons will be payable by the Vendor."

"WAS THIS THE FACE WHICH LAUNCHED A THOUSAND SHIPS?"

Probate, Divorce and Admiralty Division (Divorce).
MENELAUS v. HELEN AND PARIS.
Husband and wife—Wife's withdrawal from cohabitation—Evidence of adultery—Ten years' efforts by petitioner to induce respondent to return—Whether delay unreasonable—Assessment of damages—Wife ten years older at date of presentation of petition—Effect on quantum *of damages*.

JUDGMENT was given last week by Mr. Justice Apollo in this suit brought by Mr. Menelaus, of The Castle, Sparta, against his wife, Helen, and the co-respondent, Mr. Paris, of The Towers, Troy. The facts appear sufficiently from the judgment, extracts from which are reproduced below:

"This is a suit for dissolution of marriage brought by Mr. Menelaus against his wife, Helen, on the grounds of her adultery with Mr. Paris. The misconduct is alleged to have taken place on board a liner in the Aegean Sea, on several occasions at the Towers, Troy, and elsewhere, and the petitioner claims 60,000 drachmae damages. The respondent and the co-respondent have appeared and by their answers denied the alleged adultery.

"It appears that the petitioner and respondent married some twelve years ago and cohabited at Sparta and other places. Both were at that time domiciled in Greece. There are no children of the marriage.

"The petitioner has thought fit to emphasise that his wife was, at the time of the marriage, a lady of surpassing beauty; she is indeed described in the petition as ‘the most beautiful woman in the world'. An application before the Registrar to strike out this part of the plea on the ground of irrelevance, as being couched in the language of hyperbole common, I am informed, among those who have but recently entered upon the state of matrimony, failed, the Registrar holding that it might be material to the assessment of damages, as affecting the value of the wife and the magnitude of the blow to the husband's marital pride. On this matter I shall have more to say later on.

"It was not until the appearance of the co-respondent on the scene that unhappy differences between the spouses arose. I have observed Mr. Paris' demeanour in the witness-box, and I have come to the conclusion that he is the sort of man who would make a strong appeal to a married woman of a certain type. He made no secret of the fact that he is at present residing on Mount Ida with a shepherdess to whom he is not married, and I have no hesitation in stigmatising him as a man of promiscuous habits and unscrupulous character.

"The co-respondent resided for some months with the married pair in Sparta shortly after their marriage. Though a guest in their home, he had no hesitation in paying his attentions to the wife, and she, apparently, was not averse from accepting them. The petitioner says that at that time he saw nothing to arouse his suspicions, and his subsequent conduct, when the catastrophe took place, is sufficient indication, if any were needed, to rebut any suspicion of connivance.

"The complacency of the petitioner received a rude shock when, returning home one day from his work, some ten months after the marriage, he found his guest gone, without an explanation, without even a word of thanks for the hospitality he had enjoyed. His suspicions were deepened when the respondent, who had been out shopping during the afternoon, failed to return that night. An examination of her room showed that she had taken away all her clothes and a number of wedding presents given by gods and goddesses in the highest ranks of society. His worst fears were realised when he learned, on enquiry at the offices of the Asia Minor Lines, Ltd., that a man and woman answering the description of the runaway pair had embarked the same evening in a liner bound for Troy.

"I have heard the evidence of the steward and stewardess and of other members of the crew who observed the pair. It is unfortunate for the petitioner, in more ways than one, that more than eleven years have elapsed since the elopement. Witnesses cannot be expected to observe complete accuracy in carrying the details in their minds over so long a period, but I am satisfied on the evidence available that misconduct took place on the voyage.

"The petitioner spared no efforts to induce his wife to return to him. He sent her cables and affectionate letters ; he offered to forgive all if she would only come back. I pass over the details in silence. Suffice it to say that the petitioner did all, and more than all, that could be reasonably expected of an injured husband in the circumstances—except in one respect, which I shall deal with in a moment. His sincerity is beyond question.

"It is at this point that the principal difficulty in the petitioner's case arises. From the events I have described to the date of the presentation of the petition more than ten years have elapsed. It is established law that the Court is not bound to pronounce a decree of divorce if the petitioner, in its opinion, has been guilty of unreasonable delay in presenting the petition. But what is unreasonable delay?"

His Lordship here dealt with the authorities, and continued:—

"The circumstances of this case are unprecedented, and I have had the greatest difficulty in applying to them the principles laid down in the cases to which I have referred. For the petitioner, finding persuasion useless, resorted to direct action. Collecting a number of his friends and relatives, he set sail for Troy, determined to try force where persuasion had failed.

"For ten long years this injured husband essayed in vain to regain possession of his erring spouse. For ten long years he was unsuccessful. She remained shut up in the co-respondent's house, and the petitioner's attempts even to have speech with her were in vain.

"These circumstances, I repeat, are unprecedented, and I should be failing in my duty if I allowed either sympathy with his wrongs and admiration at his pertinacity, on the one hand, or disapproval of his indiscretion, on the other, to influence me unduly in deciding this part of the case. The matter is further complicated by the evidence I have heard that, according to the family law of the then domicil of the parties, a wife is considered as the chattel of her husband."

His Lordship here referred to his notes, and, having read extracts from the evidence of Dr. Homer, Mr. Euripides and other foreign experts, continued:—

"The notion that the owner of a chattel, who is wrongfully deprived thereof, may retake it if he can, is well established in that part of the world, and a similar principle is not unknown to our law. True, we insist upon the proviso that no breach of the peace shall be occasioned by such retaking. But even on this point the petitioner has a good answer, for it was by a stratagem, and not by force, that he at last succeeded in accomplishing his design.

"The respondent, apart from her susceptibility to the attentions of the opposite sex, has one great weakness —almost, one might say, a passion—for those large and strident automobiles, of offensive odour and repellent aspect, known (for some reason which I am unable to fathom) as 'sports cars.' She awoke one morning to find a luxurious and well-appointed automobile of this type outside the front door, driven by a chauffeur in livery. She naturally concluded that it was a new present from the co-respondent, who was that day absent in the country. Thrilled with excitement, she ordered the chauffeur to drive it into the garage (connected with the house by a covered way, and hitherto bolted and barred against all comers), where she proceeded at her leisure to examine the glistening object. Scarcely had she entered it when the petitioner, who had (with some difficulty) concealed himself in the tool-box, emerged and, despite her cries, drove off to the jetty, where he embarked with her on a ship which was just leaving for Greece.

"The petitioner has been very frank with the Court in disclosing his feelings on being thus reunited with his long-lost wife. His first impulse was one of jubilation, but he was careful to explain that in the confusion of capture and flight he had only a fleeting glimpse of her features. It was not until they were safely on the ship that he was able (as he cryptically expressed it) 'to take a good look at her.' What revulsion his feelings underwent in that moment it would be indelicate, even in a matrimonial Court, to enquire. At all events it is clear that he occupied a separate cabin on board, and that this petition was presented within a few hours of his return. Something of the matter may be understood when it is remembered that ten years had elapsed since her departure. 'Was this,' he exclaimed, 'the face that launched a thousand ships?' He might well ask.

"I have dealt in somewhat greater detail than is customary with these events, because I feel strongly that they are more than usually relevant to the questions of law which I have to decide, and in order that there may be no doubt of the considerations by which I have been actuated if the proceedings should come before a higher Court. On the facts before me I decide, first, that the petitioner was justified in doing what he did to recover his wife, and secondly, and as a necessary consequence of that decision, that he has not been guilty of such unreasonable delay in presenting the petition as to justify me in dismissing it out of hand.

"I have still to deal with two matters in issue—the question of adultery and the question of damages. As to the former, the respondent and co-respondent have denied on oath that any misconduct took place. Evidence —which on this point is not contradicted—has been given that the co-respondent's father, Mr. Priam (whose family life, unlike that of his son, appears to have been unimpeachable) was the parent of no less than fifty sons, and the suggestion is, as most of them were living at home at the time (under, I fear, somewhat overcrowded conditions) that the respondent and the co-respondent were adequately chaperoned. Be that as it may, it is in my opinion too much to ask the Court to believe that these two young people, who had fled together from the matrimonial home and who were residing for not less than ten years in the same house, preserved throughout that period the innocent relationship which they allege. I find as a fact that adultery was committed, and I pronounce in favour of the petitioner a decree *nisi* with costs.

"There remains the question of damages. I have already animadverted to this matter, and to the peculiar circumstances giving rise to the magnitude of the petitioner's claim. Here, however, he is in a difficulty. Although, as I have said, his delay in presenting the petition should not, in my judgment, deprive him of the relief of dissolution, it must inevitably affect the *quantum* of damages. The delay, reasonable as it was, was nevertheless of his own making. If a man in the petitioner's position, with the best of motives, chooses to take matters into his own hands and to wait ten years before seeking from the Court the relief to which he is entitled, he must take the consequences. For the wife, exceptional as may have been her beauty when she married him at the age of twenty-two, at the date when this petition was presented was almost thirty-four years of age. She has appeared before me in this Court, and I have, with regard to all the circumstances, to assess the value of what the petitioner has lost through the wrongful act of the co-respondent. In short, the damage the petitioner claims has, by this inordinate lapse of time, become too remote. In all the circumstances, I cannot assess the damages higher than the purely nominal sum of ten drachmae, and I give judgment accordingly for that amount."

A DANGEROUS THING

King's Bench Division.
MINOS *v.* THESEUS.

Trespass—Conversion—Personal injuries to defendant—"Fabulous monster"—Animal ferae naturae—*Whether qualified right of property therein—Defendant on plaintiff's premises for purpose of being devoured—Invitee—Unusual danger—Duty of plaintiff to warn—Negligence of plaintiff's daughter—Agency.*

Judgment of Mr. Justice Apollo:

"This is an action by Mr. Minos, of Knossos, Crete, against Mr. Theseus, of Athens, for damages for trespass on the plaintiff's land and for conversion of a chattel, the property of the plaintiff, thereon. By his particulars of claim the plaintiff alleges that the defendant wrongfully entered a part of the plaintiff's land, known as 'The Labyrinth,' and used the plaintiff's path thereon: and, further, that the defendant wrongfully deprived the plaintiff of a Minotaur, an animal belonging to the plaintiff, by wilfully destroying the same. The defendant counterclaims for damages against the plaintiff for injury by the said Minotaur, owing to the negligence of the plaintiff, his servant or agent, and the particulars allege that the defendant, being an invitee on the plaintiff's land, was attacked and injured by the said animal, which the plaintiff failed to keep under proper control; that the presence of the said animal on the plaintiff's premises was a hidden danger of which the plaintiff knew or ought to have known and of which he failed to warn the defendant ; and the defence alleges that the defendant, in destroying the said animal, acted reasonably in defence of his person.

" The full facts at issue have been difficult to elucidate, and the conflict of evidence on certain points is, to say the least, remarkable. It is common ground that the plaintiff has constructed on his freehold property at Knossos an enclosure in the form generally known as a ' maze,' known locally as ' The Labyrinth,' of which plans have been produced, and which has been fully described by the architect who was called as an expert witness. It is also agreed that the plaintiff kept within the confines of ' The Labyrinth ' the creature described in the pleadings as a Minotaur. I confess that I have been at some pains to ascertain further details of the nature and habits of this creature, which appeared to be unknown to any of the distinguished anthropologists and zoologists who have given evidence during the trial. Some desired to classify it as an animal of the bovine species, but I was impressed and, I may add, shocked by the description ' half-man, half-bull,' given by a learned Fellow of the Royal Society, which led to my hearing (*in camerâ*) a good deal of evidence of a distinctly unsavoury character regarding the creature's parentage and birth—evidence which I am bound to say reflects no credit on the plaintiff and his family. There was at one stage a lengthy argument by the defendant's counsel for the proposition that this Minotaur was human or, at any rate, capable of being considered in law as a natural person, and that consequently the plaintiff's claim for deprivation thereof disclosed no cause of action. It was admitted that, if that proposition were accepted, difficult questions would arise as to the plaintiff's vicarious liability to the defendant for personal injuries inflicted by the Minotaur. It was by no means clear to me whether Counsel was to be taken as arguing that the Minotaur, when it attempted to devour the defendant, was in the position of an agent or servant of the plaintiff, and whether and to what extent it was acting within the scope of its employment when it scorched the defendant's face with its fiery breath, or whether it was accepted that in performing these functions it was merely on a frolic of its own. I do not consider it necessary to enter in detail into these recondite questions, as I was regretfully unable to accept the proposition that the Minotaur was a natural person ; nor did the alternative argument appeal to me that it might be considered as a 'legal' (that is, an artificial or fictitious) person, such as a corporation sole. The points were put with clarity and with considerable ability. But there was no attempt to produce evidence that this Minotaur owed its creation to a charter or to any statutory provision, or that it was in the habit of employing a common seal, and I could not but feel that counsel was a little unhappy in this branch of his argument. Be that as it may, I have come to the conclusion that the creature must be considered as an animal, the term 'fabulous monster,' which recurred with monotonous frequency during the trial, constituting a classification not recognised by the common law.

"Having then established this preliminary point, the next question, which is germane to the issues both of wrongful deprivation of the plaintiff's property and of personal injury to the defendant, is this—into which legal classification of animals does the creature fall? I am constrained by the evidence, notwithstanding the somewhat peculiar circumstances of its birth, to hold that it was *ferae naturae*; it was certainly a carnivore and, if the defendant's further evidence is to be believed, an anthropophagous creature. I am, at any rate, satisfied that it was of a savage nature and liable to attack mankind; *à fortiori*, it cannot be said that by habit and training it was accustomed to live in association with man. Now, generally, as is well known, an animal *ferae naturae* is not a chattel, and cannot be the subject of ownership. But the plaintiff asserts that he was in law capable of acquiring that kind of qualified property in this Minotaur which the law recognises as arising, either *per industriam*, by taking, training or reclaiming animals *ferae naturae*, or *ratione impotentiae et loci*, where such animals are born on the land and while young cannot escape, or *ratione soli*, where the plaintiff is the person owning the land on which the animal is for the time being to be found. On the evidence before me—the degree of control exercised by the plaintiff over this Minotaur, the pains which he took to provide an enclosure for its comfort, and food for its maintenance, and (I venture to add) the evidence of some *cognatio* (happily in a somewhat remote degree) between the creature and the plaintiff himself—I have no hesitation in finding as a fact that the plaintiff was capable in law of having such a qualified property therein as will support an action for trover against a defendant who wilfully destroys such an animal.

"Here, however, I must turn again to the facts of the case, for the law which I am to apply depends upon the fundamental question—in what capacity did the defendant enter upon the plaintiff's premises? A man who chooses to keep animals of a savage and irreclaimable character, though there is nothing unlawful in his doing so, keeps them at his peril and, under the well-known rule in *Rylands* v. *Fletcher*, is liable for injuries committed by them, irrespective of negligence or knowledge. But the rule does not extend to protect a mere trespasser, who by reason of his trespass brings the injury upon himself. If the defendant was a trespasser, the plaintiff's sole liability towards him was that he must not deliberately set a trap, and there has been no suggestion in this case that the Minotaur was planted (if that be the appropriate expression) in 'The Labyrinth' expressly for the purpose of trapping the defendant. It is not denied that the creature was, and had at all material times been, living therein. If, on the other hand, the defendant was, on the facts, an invitee, or even a mere licensee, on the premises, it was the duty of the plaintiff to warn him of any hidden danger of which the plaintiff knew or ought to have known.

"What, then, are the facts? It is common ground that the defendant came to Knossos by the plaintiff's invitation, as one of a party of young people whom the plaintiff was entertaining. But from that point the evidence is in conflict. The plaintiff alleges that the purpose of the visit was to enable the defendant and his friends to enjoy a conducted tour through the plaintiff's domains, where they could refresh their bodies and improve their minds by fresh air, exercise and a study at close quarters (under careful safeguards) of the many and varied animals in the plaintiff's private collection. The plaintiff insists that it was made clear to all visitors that it was dangerous for them to venture into or near 'The Labyrinth' in the absence of the plaintiff's expert guide and animal-trainer, his daughter, Ariadne. And the plaintiff goes on to allege that the defendant, disregarding all warnings, ventured alone into 'The Labyrinth,' without the plaintiff's knowledge or consent, having fraudulently induced the said daughter, by a promise of marriage, to give him admission; that the said daughter, in admitting the defendant, acted without the plaintiff's authority; that the defendant was a trespasser, and that the plaintiff had no duty of care towards him other than the duty not to set a trap.

"The defendant, on the other hand, tells a very different story. While admitting that the purpose of the visit to Knossos was represented by the plaintiff to be that alleged by him, he contends that the true purpose of the plaintiff was to induce the defendant and his friends to come to Knossos in order that they might be used as food for the Minotaur, which it is alleged had a predilection for a diet of human flesh. It was therefore argued that the defendant, having gone on to the plaintiff's premises in what my Scottish brothers might term an 'alimentary' capacity, so far as the Minotaur was concerned, or, in other words, on business which concerned and was for the benefit of the plaintiff, and on his express invitation, was there in the capacity of an invitee, and that therefore it was the duty of the plaintiff to take reasonable care that the premises were safe, and to prevent injury to the defendant from unusual dangers which were more or less hidden, and of the existence of which the plaintiff was or ought to have been aware.

"I am driven to the conclusion, after hearing all the evidence, that the contention of the defendant is correct. I find as a fact that the presence of the defendant on the plaintiff's premises was due primarily to the plaintiff's intention to cause him to be devoured by the Minotaur; that such intention formed a purpose which was for the benefit of the plaintiff, and that the defendant was therefore an invitee. I find that the plaintiff's daughter, Ariadne, was at all material times the servant of the plaintiff; that when she admitted the defendant to 'The Labyrinth' she was doing an act within the general scope of her employment, which was to show visitors over and guide them through the premises in question. Whether she acted at that particular moment without the authority of the plaintiff *ad hoc* is immaterial, for the act was clearly within the scope of her general authority. Through her negligence the defendant was injured, and her negligence, on the facts which I have found, renders the plaintiff liable. I therefore find for the defendant on both the claim and counterclaim, and award him damages in the sum of 50,000 drachmae.

"It only remains for me to add that this is emphatically a case where I conceive it my duty to send the papers to the Public Prosecutor. More than that it would not be proper for me to say."

WINDING UP A SUIT

COURT OF APPEAL.
PHEMIUS *v.* ULYSSES.
Breach of promise of marriage—Husband absent on service—Appellant's offer of marriage accepted by wife subject to condition—Marriage to be postponed till completion of weaving task by wife—Wife deliberately delaying completion—Anticipatory breach—Husband not heard of for over 10 years—Matrimonial Causes Act, 1937, s. 8—Public Policy—Unexpected return of husband—Order for fresh trial on new evidence.

THEIR Lordships allowed this appeal by Dame Penelope Ulysses, of the Manor House, Ithaca, against Mr. Phemius, a composer, who had been awarded 2,000*l.* damages for breach of promise of marriage against her in an action before the Lord Chief Justice and a special jury in the King's Bench Division. The Court ordered a new trial on the ground that fresh evidence had come to light which could not with reasonable diligence have been discovered before the trial.

The Master of the Rolls, who read the judgment of the Court, made the following observations:

"In this appeal by Dame Penelope Ulysses against the judgment of the Court below there are a number of unusual and surprising features; I might, indeed, go so far as to say that the facts of the case are almost unprecedented in the annals of this or any other Court. The original action belongs to a type which is unfortunately not in itself of extreme rarity—an action for breach of a contract to marry. It is in the sequence of facts giving rise to the action that the unusual nature of the case manifests itself, and this Court has had imposed upon it a threefold task—first, to seek to apply the principles to be found in the authorities to those most unusual facts; secondly, to consider the effect upon that application of recent reforms in the matrimonial law; and, thirdly, to consider how far, if at all, the new evidence which has come to light since the original trial, if it had been before the jury at the time, might have modified their verdict.

"The appellant (the defendant in the original action) is a married woman, the wife of Brigadier-General Ulysses, a famous soldier who served his country gallantly in the recent war against Troy. The respondent (the original plaintiff) is well known as a composer of dance lyrics and as a jazz-band leader.

"The matters of which the respondent complained are of very long standing, having extended over a period of nearly five years. It is necessary, however, in order that the reasons for the decision of the Court may be clear, to go back still further and to recapitulate facts which are now over twenty years old.

"Shortly after the declaration of war against Troy, now more than twenty years ago, General Ulysses, then a comparatively young man, was called to take an important post on the Intelligence Staff of the Expeditionary Force. Hoping fondly, like so many other young husbands, that the war would be over in a few months, he bade farewell to his wife and embarked for Asia Minor with many protestations of love and fidelity on both sides.

"During the entire ten years of the war, General

Ulysses, whose services, owing to his unusual command of foreign languages and high aptitude as a strategist, were too valuable to be spared, remained at the front or as near thereto as his exalted rank and duties permitted ; he was never once granted leave. During the same period, the appellant threw herself with enthusiasm into war work at home. She took a prominent part in organising canteens and other entertainment for the troops on leave, but she will be chiefly remembered as the inventor of the famous 'Penelope Pullovers,' in the weaving of which she excelled and for the mass production of which, by her Corps of Women Weavers, she was responsible. The work of the 'C.W.W.,' as it was affectionately termed by the troops, in providing warm comforters for the soldiers in the rigours of the Trojan winter, will long be gratefully remembered, and it is not surprising that her work was recognised by the Government at the end of the war by the award of the Grand Cross of the Order of the Grecian Empire.

"The war having terminated, some ten years since, demobilisation was gradually carried out and a number of famous commanders returned to a well-deserved ovation from the populace of their respective states. For some unaccountable reason, however, General Ulysses did not return. His brother-officers—colleagues on the Staff, who had been closely associated with him throughout the period of hostilities—were able to assure his wife from personal knowledge that he had never been in the slightest danger and that he had, in fact, come through the war without a scratch ; but when five years had elapsed and nothing more was heard of him, his friends began to fear that his vessel had struck a mine on the voyage home. Not so, however, the appellant, who, it is only fair to say, despite the hard things said about her during the trial here and in the Court below, has proved herself a faithful and devoted wife.

"In that period of relaxation of public morals, such as invariably follows after a great war, it was not long before the possibilities of the situation began to dawn on a number of young members of the local county families near the General's home. The appellant (who had married at an extremely early age) was still young and very attractive, and her fame and brilliance had travelled far and wide. Reports were not lacking, either, of the wealth she had deservedly acquired (as frequently happens in such cases) as the indirect result of her patriotic and public-spirited activities during the war. Whatever the reason, she was eagerly sought in marriage by a number of eligible young men, among whom the most favoured was the respondent in the present appeal.

"The respondent, despite his exotic and somewhat effeminate appearance (which seems to be typical of his profession), is nothing if not tenacious, and seems to have pressed his suit with as much energy as was possible to a person of his lethargic temperament. It is admitted by the appellant that he proposed marriage to her a number of times over a period of no less than four years, and he claims that on the last occasion, two years ago, the appellant accepted his offer.

"There seems to be no doubt, however, and the point is not disputed by the respondent, that the appellant's acceptance was conditional. In her loneliness she had returned to her old activity of weaving, and it is admitted by both parties that the promise to marry the respondent was conditional upon the termination of the task upon which she was then engaged—the weaving of a particularly warm 'pullover' for Mr. Laertes, her aged father-in-law.

"So much is common ground, but the respondent alleges that, in breach of her contract, the appellant deliberately failed to complete her task. The particulars of claim allege in some detail that the appellant, for a period of some months, went so far as to unravel each night the parts of the garment which she had woven during the day. The respondent's remonstrances, at first playful, became more serious; disputes culminated at last in a bitter quarrel in the course of which the appellant was unwise enought to admit the truth of these allegations. Thereupon the writ in the original action was issued.

"Pausing there for a moment, it is, of course, clear law that breach of a contract may take place before the time fixed for its performance has arrived. If the promisor, by his own act, disables himself from performing his promise, the other party is entitled to treat the contract as at an end, and to sue for damages without waiting until the time fixed for performance. The point is well covered by the authorities and is not in issue in this appeal.

"Nor was any difficulty caused to the respondent's case by the fact that he, the original plaintiff, was a man and the defendant a woman. It is clear law that the remedy is mutual, and that either a man or a woman may sue for breach of promise of marriage. No issue has been raised by the appellant hereon.

"By her defence in the original action the appellant, while making no attempt to traverse the above allegations, pleaded simply a point of law. She said that, at the time when the contract to marry was made, she was, to the knowledge of the other party to that contract, already married, and she pleaded that the contract was void as being contrary to public policy and would not support an action for damages at the suit of the then plaintiff.

"The plaintiff, by his reply, did not traverse the defendant's allegations, but pleaded that for a period of seven years and upwards the other party to the marriage had been continuously absent from the defendant, that neither he nor the defendant had any reason to believe that the other party had been living within that time, and that in these circumstances there could be nothing contrary to public policy in holding that the defendant's acceptance of his offer of marriage constituted a valid and enforceable contract. In his argument in the Court below the plaintiff's Counsel supported this plea by pointing out that, under the provisions of sect. 8 of the Matrimonial Causes Act, 1937, these facts would constitute evidence that the defendant's husband was dead until the contrary should be proved. He also cited the decision of the House of Lords in *Fender* v. *Mildmay*, and submitted that the principle therein established might well be extended from the case of a promise by one spouse, after decree *nisi* but before decree absolute, to marry another person, to cover the case of a similar promise by a wife whose husband has been continuously absent from her for seven years and upwards and whom she has no reason to believe to have been living within that time.

"The learned judge in the Court below, on the analogy of the decision of the House of Lords in *Fender* v.

Mildmay, held that he was bound to apply the principle enunciated in the judgment of the majority in their Lordships' House, and to hold that, in the particular circumstances of this case, the defendant's promise to marry the plaintiff was binding and that the contract was not against public policy. On this the jury found for the plaintiff and awarded him heavy damages.

"Against this statement of the law the defendant appealed, and she now reinforces her case by adducing the surprising piece of additional evidence, which has been discovered only since the original trial, that her husband is still alive and has actually returned to her.

"Whether the learned Lord Chief Justice was right in holding as he did it is now for this Court to consider. It is a unique point on which, so far as I have been able to ascertain, no direct authority exists. All that this Court can do, therefore, is to seek the principle involved in the statutes and the decided cases and, with due circumspection, to find such analogy as it can.

"In the first place it is to be noted that the section of the new Matrimonial Causes Act to which reference has been made does not go so far as to say that seven years' absence on the part of one spouse shall entitle the other to presume the death of the absent spouse, but merely that, on a petition to the Court for a declaration of presumption of death and dissolution of the marriage (whatever that may mean), the fact of the seven years' absence shall be evidence that the absent spouse is dead until the contrary is proved. No such petition to the Court has been made in this case, and the value (if any) of the section to the respondent's case is, in my opinion, merely evidentiary. The section cannot be applied at all, except by analogy, to the facts before us.

" So far as its evidentiary value is concerned, it appears to this Court that such notional evidence is rebuttable and, in fact, the section itself contains the words ' until the contrary is proved.' In the case before us the contrary has been proved, and that in a very definite manner, by the discovery that the appellant's husband is alive and has returned to his wife.

" It is impossible to contend that this fresh evidence, if it had been before the jury in the trial below, could not have affected their verdict. On this ground alone this Court feels itself bound to order a new trial.

" It thus becomes unnecessary for me to deal in detail with the difficult question of public policy, as modified by the recent decision in *Fender* v. *Mildmay*, but as so much has been heard of this question in argument, the Court feels that a few observations on the point, even though merely *obiter*, may not be inappropriate. The dangers of permitting an extension of the varying and arbitrary standards of what constitutes public policy are too well known to need elaboration on my part. ' To avow or insinuate,' said a famous Lord Chancellor in one case, ' that it might be proper for a judge to prevent a party from availing himself of an indisputable principle of law, in a Court of justice, upon the ground of some notion of fancied policy or expedience . . . has a direct tendency to render all law vague and uncertain.' 'Public policy,' said another noble and learned lord in the same case, 'is always an unsafe and treacherous ground for legal decision, and in the present case it would not be easy to see on which side the balance of convenience would incline.'

"That is an observation which, as it appears to this Court, applies precisely in the appeal under consideration. On the one hand, there is the principle, considered until recently to be unassailable, that a contract to marry where, to the knowledge of the parties, the other party is already married, tends to produce conduct which violates the solemn obligations of married life, and is therefore contrary to public policy and void. On the other hand, we have had recently the highest judicial authority in the land for the proposition that, notwithstanding the undoubted existence of the above principle, it has no application when the normal obligations and conditions of marriage have been discontinued, as they have after the pronouncement of a decree *nisi*. 'Not only,' said one noble and learned lord in the recent case, 'are the parties not living together, but they are not entitled to require that conjugal rights should be restored. The *consortium* is broken.' If that represents the considered opinion of their Lordships' House in a case where a decree *nisi* had been granted (although, as was fully admitted, until decree absolute the marriage was still subsisting), it appears to follow that similar considerations should apply to a case like the present where, under the provisions of the recent Act, the appellant, had she wished, could have petitioned the Court for a decree of presumption of death and of dissolution of the marriage, and must, on the evidence then available, have succeeded in her petition. Whether or not this view is correct it is fortunately unnecessary for this Court now to determine. On the new evidence which has been discovered since the jury's verdict was given, the case must be remitted to the Court below for retrial."

Judgment was entered accordingly.

SHADY PROCEEDINGS

CHANCERY DIVISION.
PLUTO v. CHARON.

Franchise of ferry over River Styx—Prohibited Area—Defence (General) Regulations, 1939—Carriage beyond ferry limits—Ultra vires—Carriage of mortals—Interference with rights of " shades " entitled to be carried—Persons not contemplated by grant—Injunction.

Judgment delivered by Mr. Justice Phaethon :

"This is a motion for an injunction brought by Mr. Pluto, of Hades, against Mr. Charon, of Tartarus. The defendant is the grantee of a right of ferry across the River Styx, and the plaintiff is a resident in, and a ratepayer of, the harbour on the Hades side of the ferry. A plan of the disputed locality is before the Court, and the area in which the ferry operates is a prohibited area under the Defence Regulations.

"The plaintiff's Statement of Claim, while admitting the prescriptive right of the defendant (under a presumed grant dating from time immemorial) to ferry across the river, between the points shown on the plan, all peaceable wayfarers willing to pay the toll, alleges that the defendant has from time to time (a) carried persons of a class not contemplated by the presumed grant or permitted by the prescriptive right, (b) carried persons having no legitimate business in the said prohibited area, and (c) carried such persons on excursion trips beyond the ferry limits to different parts of the Rivers Acheron and Styx, bordering on the plaintiff's property. The plaintiff alleges that these acts on the part of the defendant are *ultra vires*, and asks for an injunction to restrain the defendant from so using his ferryboat.

"The evidence by or on behalf of the plaintiff shows that, from time immemorial, the defendant has possessed a franchise conferring an exclusive right of ferry across the River Styx between the points shown on the plan, in respect of persons of the class referred to as 'shades,' at a toll of twopence for each of such persons. So much is clear and uncontroverted. It is on the distinguishing characteristics of these so-called 'shades,' as contrasted with persons of other classes, that the evidence is ambiguous and conflicting. The difference is clearly not one of age or sex; nor have I received any assistance from the distinction drawn in the books between 'natural' and 'legal' persons, which does not here appear relevant. Several witnesses have bandied about such terms as 'shadowy,' 'insubstantial' and even 'incorporeal.' Acquainted though I am with the difficult and sometimes indeterminate conceptions known to all equity lawyers, I confess that the term 'incorporeal' as applied to a person is new to me. The surprising and extremely inconvenient fact remains that no such type of person has been produced before the Court, the explanation being that they are all beyond the jurisdiction and cannot be subpœnæd. In the absence of the *corpora* I can only form my own conclusion from the evidence given, which is that the distinguishing mark of the normal passenger in this ferry is his abnormally light weight—so light that it is alleged that a hundred or more may be, and frequently are, crowded into this flimsy and shallow craft without any danger of capsizing it. There, I fear, this difficult preliminary question must

PLUTO v. CHARON

for the moment be allowed to rest, except that I desire to place on record, as a finding of fact, that I am satisfied that from time immemorial transit across this ferry has been confined to persons of an unusually light weight and of slight physique.

"The plaintiff has, however, produced satisfactory evidence to show that, on more than one occasion, the defendant has conveyed in his ferryboat persons outside this usual class of passenger. Three cases in particular have been brought to the Court's notice of the use of this craft for the conveyance of persons of a substantial size and weight, two of them being General Odysseus, a distinguished leader in the Army of our Hellenic Allies, and Major-General Aeneas, of the Army of Troy. Each of these officers is said to weigh considerably over 200 pounds, and having had the advantage of observing them in this Court in full uniform and warlike accoutrements, I have no doubt that the estimate is sound. The third person of whom complaint is made is a Mr. Hercules, described as a 'professional strong man,' and he is said to be 280 pounds in weight. He also has appeared before me, and I am satisfied, from the collapse of the substantial oak seat which he occupied, and the condition of the witness-box after he had left it, that his weight has been understated rather than exaggerated. I am therefore driven to the conclusion that the plaintiff has successfully established the facts relating to the first part of his claim.

"It is incumbent upon me at this stage to deal in part with the law bearing upon the matter in dispute. A public ferry is a highway of a special kind for all the King's subjects paying toll. (*North and South Shields Ferry Co. v. Barker.*) It is a toll franchise, and can be acquired by prescription at common law. (*Hammerton v. Earl of*

Dysart.) The grant, whether actual or presumed, may be in more or less extensive terms. (*Matthews* v. *Peache*). The ferry-owner's rights are commensurate with his obligations, and he cannot maintain an action for disturbance, or maintain his exclusive rights, if the convenience of the public requires a new passage for a new and different kind of traffic from that which he has been in the habit of carrying. The ferry-owner must carry all peaceable wayfarers who are willing to pay his toll (*Hammerton* v. *Earl of Dysart, supra*), subject, of course, to what has been said above as to the terms of the grant. And it must necessarily follow from these principles that the ferry-owner is liable to lose his rights if, by his breaking the conditions of the grant and engaging in a new and different kind of traffic, peaceable wayfarers, of the class originally intended to be conveyed, have been excluded from, or delayed unreasonably in, their transit across what is, by definition, a public highway of a special kind.

" Evidence has been given that, owing to the use of the ferry for the conveyance of the three persons to whom I have referred, a number of these so-called ' shades ' have been delayed in, if not actually excluded from, going about their lawful occasions, a number of them having been marooned for hours on the bank of the river while the ferry-owner was engaged in conveying the two Generals and Mr. Hercules, respectively.

" It has been argued on behalf of the defendant that there is no evidence of the limitation of the original grant to persons exclusively of the class described as ' shades,' and that there was no reason for the defendant to refuse transit to the three persons of whom complaint is made. It therefore becomes relevant to consider whether these last-named persons come under the description of 'peaceable wayfarers,' or otherwise.

"The Defence Regulations, 1939, have made of this part of the River Styx a prohibited area, access to which is forbidden to all but a very limited number of persons of a few specific descriptions. The two Generals have admitted in the witness-box that they did not require transit in connection with their military duties (which in any event are carried out in a part of the country remote from this area) but each of them alleges, with a strange unanimity, that he wished to cross to the Hades bank for the purpose of visiting his father. Visits by children to parents are excepted from the general prohibition under the Defence Regulations, but I am bound to say that this fact appears to be the sole justification for their statements of the alleged purpose of their visits. For when each was asked in cross-examination to give the present address of his father, the answer was in each case the same—'He is dead.' It is not for me to animadvert on the possible true purpose for which these two officers desired transit across the ferry, and they have been so insistent throughout their evidence on the alleged truth of the two contradictory propositions—that their respective fathers are dead and that they came to visit them—that I am forced to conclude, either that they are committing deliberate perjury, or that the interpreter is failing in efficiency. Be that as it may, I am unable to accept the argument that they can, in the circumstances, be considered as peaceable wayfarers, anxious to cross for a *bonâ fide* and lawful purpose.

"As to Mr. Hercules, it is to his credit at least that he has made no attempt at a pretence that his desire to employ the ferry was on a lawful occasion at all. With singular and engaging frankness he has admitted that he wished to pass across to Hades for the purpose of taking the plaintiff's watchdog, a purpose which he fulfilled, though the fact that he afterwards returned the animal to its lawful owner has, as he told me, led to his acquittal on a charge of larceny in another Court. The taking itself, however, constitutes a tortious act, and is sufficient to justify me in holding that Mr. Hercules was not a peaceable wayfarer entitled to transit across the defendant's ferry.

"These considerations would justify me in finding for the plaintiff on the issues which I am here to try, but, lest this case should go before a higher Court on the questions of law involved, I am constrained to deal with the third of the plaintiff's allegations. This is that the defendant has used his craft on more than one occasion for purposes other than ferrying. Evidence has been given to show that both General Odysseus and Major-General Aeneas, as well as a certain Mr. Dante (described as a poet, of Italian nationality) have at different times been conveyed by the defendant in his ferry-boat on sightseeing tours, up and down the course of the Rivers Acheron and Styx, on three separate bank holidays. And it is alleged, and not denied, that in the course of their peregrinations these persons visited the underground caverns, forming part of the plaintiff's private property, but recently requisitioned by the War Department for purposes to which the Official Secrets Acts, 1911 to 1920, apply.

"I cannot too strongly condemn the conduct of the defendant, in thus violating, not merely his civil liabilities, but the security regulations of a Government Department in time of war. I am told that proceedings are being taken elsewhere on behalf of the Secretary of State for

War against both the present defendant and the passengers concerned, though this matter is beyond my present purview.

" What concerns my present purpose is the law relating to the unauthorised use of a ferry-boat for purposes other than ferrying. There is direct authority of the very highest kind for the proposition that such acts are *ultra vires* and can be restrained by any person having a good title and interest to sue. In *Dundee Harbour Trustees* v. *Nicol*, certain harbour trustees, who had a franchise of ferry within certain defined limits, maintained a service of steamers for ferry traffic. When the steamers were not required for such traffic, the trustees let them out on hire for excursion trips beyond the ferry limits. It was decided by the House of Lords that the acts complained of were *ultra vires* the grant, and that the plaintiffs in that case, who were harbour ratepayers, had a good title and interest to bring an action of interdict. The only distinction in the present case—a distinction which is in the plaintiff's favour—is that the defendant Charon has used his craft for *ultra vires* purposes at times when it *was* required for ferry purposes, to the great inconvenience and hardship of members of the very class of persons by whom it was contemplated the ferry should be used. It is of no use for the defendant to contend that he had always understood the rivers in question to form part of the Underground Transport system of the local statutory Board—a contention which is unsupported by any evidence whatsoever—and that the Board's system is a public one, for the use of all members of the public. The acts of the defendant are clearly *ultra vires*, and, when considered in conjunction with the other allegations in the Statement of Claim, justify me in granting to the plaintiff the injunction prayed, with costs in his favour. There will be judgment for the plaintiff to that effect, and I desire to add that I shall esteem it my duty to send the papers in the case to the Director of Public Prosecutions."

LARCENY WITH AGGRAVATION

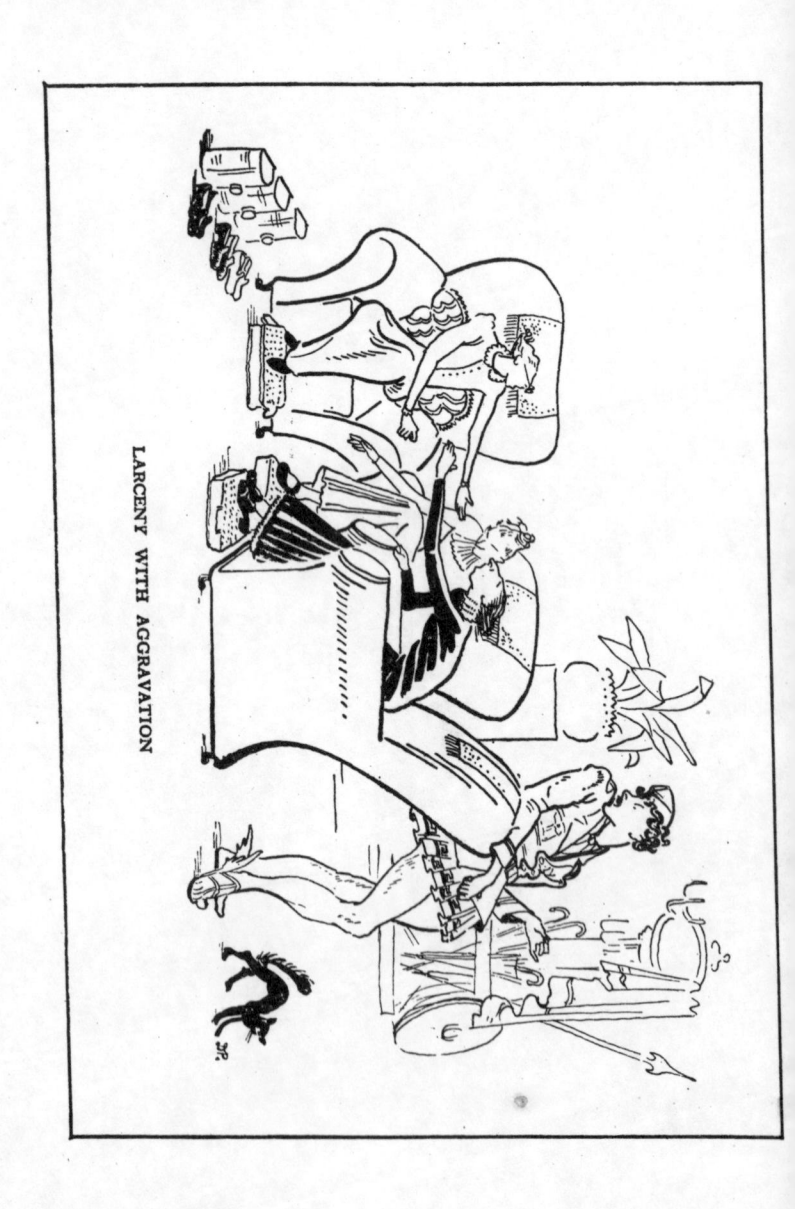

COURT OF CRIMINAL APPEAL.
REX v. PERSEUS.

Larceny of eye and tooth—Larceny Act, 1916, s. 1(3)—Whether " things capable of being stolen "—Whether " property of some person "—Analogy of severance from realty—Larceny Act, 1916, s. 1(2) (ii)—Whether owner's consent given—Ibid. s. 1 (iii)—Part owner—Permanent deprivation—Felonious intent.

The judgment of the Court was delivered by Lord Chief Justice Hermes, who made the following observations:—

"This is an appeal by Flight-Lieutenant Perseus, an officer of the Royal Air Force, against a conviction for larceny at Quarter Sessions, where he was sentenced by the learned Recorder to eighteen months' imprisonment in the second division. The grounds of the appeal are, first, that the subject-matter of the alleged larceny is not ' anything capable of being stolen ' at common law or within the meaning of the Larceny Act, 1916 ; secondly, that there was no taking ' without the consent of the owner,' and, thirdly, that there was no intent, at the time of the taking, ' to deprive the owner permanently thereof.'

"The appellant appears to be a young man of high technical ability, both in the science of aeronautics and in the art of camouflage. The evidence before Quarter Sessions shows that he has perfected an invention (the details of which have, at the request of the Secretary of State for Air, been withheld from disclosure) known popularly as 'the winged sandals,' which, it is said, permit the wearer to practise aerial navigation without the aid of any aircraft; he is also said to have devised a camouflaging apparatus, cryptically referred to at the trial as 'a helmet of darkness,' which renders the user practically invisible even to persons at a few yards distance. The relevance of these matters will appear in due course.

"The informant, who was one of the victims of the larceny of which the appellant has been convicted is a Miss Euphemia Graea, who resides with her two sisters in a small bungalow near the appellant's station. The evidence given at Quarter Sessions, and there accepted by the jury, is that these ladies are all three of such advanced age, and suffering from so extreme a form of senility, that they have but one tooth and one eye in common, which they pass from one to another, from time to time, as occasion arises. I will freely admit that I have found some difficulty in giving ready credence to this piece of evidence, but it has been accepted by the jury (after hearing a number of medical witnesses) as a question of fact; no issue has been raised thereon, and this Court is in no position to say that there was no evidence on which the jury could properly come to its conclusion on this point.

"The further facts found by the jury are that the appellant, during the course of one of his flights in the vicinity, made a forced landing in the neighbourhood of the informant's bungalow and, wearing the camouflage apparatus to which reference has been made, surprised the three sisters at the moment when the informant had detached the common eye and tooth from her own head and was about to pass them to one of her sisters. It is stated that the appellant, coming close to where they stood, so successfully imitated the voice of the second sister that the informant delivered the eye and tooth into his outstretched hand, under the mistaken belief that it was the hand of her sister. The appellant, removing himself to a safe distance from their groping, thereupon informed them in his proper voice of what he had done, and expressed his intention of detaining the eye and tooth unless and until they would give him directions to enable him to find the neighbouring aerodrome. Having no means of identifying him, they not unnaturally refused, in the interests of national security, to do so, and it was not until the female domestic, who was in the house at the time and had observed what passed (so far as it was visible), had summoned the police, that the *corpus delicti* was taken from the appellant and impounded for the purposes of evidence, to the great inconvenience of the informant and her sisters.

"The first ground of this appeal is that the subject-matter of the larceny charged is not 'anything capable of being stolen,' either at common law or by statute. So far as common law is concerned, it is well established that a human body is not capable of being stolen, and counsel has argued that what applies to the whole must apply equally to any of its parts. It is not, however, necessary for the Court to express an opinion on this question, since the Larceny Act, 1916, now provides a very full and clear definition. Sub-sect. (3) of sect. 1 of that Act provides as follows:

"'Everything which has value and is the property of any person, and if adhering to the realty then after severance therefrom, shall be capable of being stolen.' (The provisos to the sub-section are not material to the point under discussion.) It is established by the authorities that, while the thing must be of some appreciable value, it need not be of intrinsic value, nor of the value of any known coin, and that it is sufficient if it be of value to none but the prosecutor. Had the tooth contained a gold filling, or had it been part of an artificial denture, it is clear that the first test would have been adequately fulfilled; but it is equally true that, had it possessed merely a sentimental value for its owner, by reason of association of events, the identity of the dentist who extracted it, or otherwise, it could still have been said to have value within the meaning of the sub-section. Similar considerations might apply to an artificial eye, of glass or other material. It follows, then, *a fortiori*, that the test of value must be fulfilled in a case where three elderly persons are relying upon one effective eye and one working tooth between them. I have no hesitation, therefore, in deciding that the first part of the statutory definition applies.

"But the thing alleged to be stolen must also be the property of some person, and here we are on more difficult ground. The three divisions of property are realty, chattels real, and chattels personal. If the *corpus delicti* in this case is property at all, it must fall under the third head. Chattels personal, again, fall into the two subdivisions of choses in action and choses in possession, sometimes described respectively as 'incorporeal' and 'corporeal' chattels. The definition of the latter by Blackstone (2 Com., p. 387) is as follows:

"'All things which are at once tangible, movable and visible, of which possession can be taken, . . . that can properly be put in motion and transferred from place to place.'

"Now there can be no question that it might be

difficult to apply this definition to the ordinary human eye or tooth, constituting a portion of the living body, implanted by nature in its proper place and naturally connected by nerve and muscle with the complex cerebral system. It is otherwise, however, with an object like a tooth which, in common experience, may have become detached, by natural or artificial means, from the socket which formerly held it in position. Is not such a tooth at once tangible, movable and visible, transferable and capable of becoming the subject of possession? Is it not *primâ facie* the property of the person from whose jaw it has come? May it not be said to have either an intrinsic value of its own, or a sentimental value in the eyes of that person, as I have suggested above, sufficient to justify him in an action of conversion against one who has wrongfully deprived him thereof? I apprehend that it may well be so; that such a tooth meets every part of the definition which I have quoted, and is therefore a corporeal thing, in the class of chattels personal. Why, then, should a movable, transferable and detachable eye, of the description which the jury have accepted, be differently treated? I can see no reason for any such distinction. For these reasons it is unnecessary for this Court to deal with the ingenious argument of counsel for the Crown, seeking to apply by analogy the words 'and if adhering to the realty then after severance therefrom' to the eye and tooth in question after severance from the human head. Had any such further argument been necessary, it would have sufficed to point to the definition in sect. 1(2) (ii) of the Larceny Act, 1916, of the expression 'carries away,' which is as follows:

"'The expression "carries away" includes any removal of anything from the place which it occupies, but in the case of a thing attached, only if it has been completely detached.'

"I will not go so far as to say that, in passing this piece of legislation, Parliament may have had in mind circumstances similar to those of this case, but it is clear that the statutory words apply precisely, and without any violence to their literal meaning, to the circumstances before us. I apprehend that if A, without authority and with felonious intent, extracts a tooth from B's mouth, while B is under an anaesthetic or otherwise unconscious, and commits a conversion of the tooth, whether *lucri causa* or not, A will be guilty of larceny; *à fortiori* if he takes and carries it away and commits such conversion after the tooth has been extracted, as in the case before us. It is clear from what I have said that the Court has come to the conclusion that the things in question are things capable of being stolen within the meaning of the Act, and that this part of the appeal therefore fails.

"The remaining grounds of the appeal may be shortly disposed of. The second ground is that there was no taking 'without the consent of the owner,' and the appellant argues that the subject-matter of the alleged larceny was placed in his hand by the informant herself, voluntarily, and without force on his part. It is clear, however, from the evidence which the jury have accepted, that the appellant obtained possession by means of a trick, namely, by personating the informant's sister, standing close beside her and imitating her voice, while keeping himself concealed. It is equally clear that the consent of the informant was apparent only, and not real, and that her mind did not go consensually with her action. 'Larceny by a trick' is a common enough ground for prosecution in cases of this kind, and the Court has not thought it necessary to hear Counsel for the Crown on this part of the appeal, on which the appellant likewise fails.

"The third and final ground is that the prosecution has not proved, and that there was no evidence on which the jury could properly find, an intent on the part of the appellant, at the time of the taking, permanently to deprive the owner of the chattels in question. We have heard argument on the word 'owner' as employed in the Act, and it will suffice (for the purpose of rebutting the appellant's arguments) to quote the definition in para. (iii) of sub-sect. (1) of the first section, which reads as follows:

"'The expression "owner" includes any part owner, or person having possession or control of, or a special property in, anything capable of being stolen.'

Whether it be contended that the 'owner' was the informant, both or either of her sisters, or all three together, is therefore immaterial.

"But the further argument on behalf of the appellant is that his intention at the time of the taking, as evidenced by the words he used to the informant and her sisters, was not to deprive the owner permanently, but merely to detain the chattels until such time as they might give him the information which he was demanding, holding them, as it were, to ransom. This argument was ably put forward on behalf of the appellant at Quarter Sessions, and no fault can be found with the learned Recorder's summing-up, when he gave a very lucid exposition to the jury of the law applicable to this point. The jury have found as a fact that the intention of permanent deprivation was present, at the time of the taking, in the appellant's mind. The only ground on which this Court could interfere with such finding would be that there was no evidence on which the jury could properly come to such a conclusion.

"It appears to me that there was ample evidence for the jury to find a felonious intent. The question of intent is a question of fact, and can be inferred only from the overt acts and words of the accused. The original taking was unlawful, fraudulent and without any claim of right whatsoever. The appellant had no reason to believe that his unlawful action and the threats which he had made would succeed in their object and force the disclosure of the information which he required. Had these courageous old ladies persisted in their refusal (of which, up to the time when the police intervened, there appeared to be a strong probability), is there anything in the evidence to indicate that the property would have been restored to them? The evidence is all the other way. The appellant threatened to detain the chattels until disclosure was made, and they were still in his possession when he was arrested. If the appellant's contention were accepted, it would become a matter of common form, in all prosecutions for larceny, for the thief to allege that he always intended to restore the goods. It is impossible for this Court to interfere with the finding of the jury, and the appeal must be dismissed."

TABLE OF CASES CITED

	Page
Clarkson v. Clarkson, (1930) 46 T.L.R. 623	18
Dundee Harbour Trustees v. Nicol, [1915] A.C. 550	105
Fender v. St. John Mildmay, [1938] A.C. 1	92, 94
Hammerton v. Earl of Dysart, [1916] 1 A.C. 57	101, 102
Kallikrates & Others v. Eurystheus (unreported)	40
Matthews v. Peache, (1855) 5 E. & B. 546	102
North & South Shields Ferry Co. v. Barker, (1848) 2 Exch. 136	101
Rose v. Ford, [1937] A.C. 826	26
Russell v. Russell, [1924] A.C. 687	14
Rylands v. Fletcher, (1868) L.R. 3 H.L. 330	36, 80
Statham v. Statham, [1912] P. 92	20
Turbyfield v. Great Western Rly. Co., [1937] 4 All E.R. 614	27

TABLE OF STATUTES

	Page
Ground Game Act, 1880	50
Criminal Law Amendment Act, 1885, s. 4	18
Sale of Goods Act, 1893, s. 14	26
Dogs Act, 1906, s. 2	36
Public Health Acts (Amendment) Act, 1907, s. 54	37
Oaths Act, 1909, s. 2	16
Official Secrets Act, 1911, ss. 1, 3	104
Larceny Act, 1916, s. 1	111, 113
s. 5	35
Official Secrets Act, 1920, ss. 9, 10	104
Agricultural Holdings Act, 1923	50
Settled Land Act, 1925, Second Schedule	62
Law of Property Act, 1925, s. 49	57
Supreme Court of Judicature Act, 1925, s. 188	19
Companies Act, 1929, s. 26	53
s. 27	53
s. 168	53
First Schedule	49
Law Reform (Misc. Provisions) Act, 1934, s. 1	23, 26, 30
Matrimonial Causes Act, 1937, s. 8	92, 93
Defence (General) Regulations, 1939, Regs. 12, 13	103

INDEX

Page

ACCESS
   evidence as to husband's, by wife . . . 14, 15

ACCIDENT
   fatal, beneficial results of 30
   no proof of special damage in . . . 30

AGE
   beautiful wife's, effect of, on husband's damages   73

AGRICULTURE
   pursuit of, *ultra vires* 53

AIR MINISTRY
   certification of glider by 24

AMPHITRYON
   absence of, on service 14
   flying visits to wife by 15
   impersonation of, by Jupiter 18
   non-access by, evidence as to 15
   paternity disputed by 14

BREACH
   anticipatory, by Penelope 91
   negligence by aircraft manufacturer constituting   26
        of employee constituting . . 42

                                                            Page

BULL

    fire-breathing, yoking of, *ultra vires* . . . 53
    hide of, admeasurement of land by . . . 58, 59
    improper behaviour of 17
    paternity of, scandalous allegations as to . . 78
    sacrifice of, under Oaths Act, 1909 . . . 16

CASTOR

    Pollux, joint shareholding with 48

CERBERUS

    application of Dogs Act, 1906, to . . . 36
                  of Larceny Act, 1916, to . . 35, 36
    diet of, particulars as to 35
    taking and carrying away of . . . 34, 104
    whether domestic chattel 36

CHARON

    franchise of ferry, grant of, to . . . 99, 100
    ultra vires acts by . . . 99, 101, 105

CHIRON

    disability of 49
    medical capacity of 35
    voting rights of 49

COMPANY

    affairs of, unsatisfactorily conducted . . . 48
    agricultural pursuits of 50, 53
    breach of contract by 53
    Castor and Pollux, joint membership of, in . 48
    dragon's teeth, sowing of, by . . . 50, 51
    extraordinary meeting of, disorderly proceedings
        at 49

COMPANY—*contd.*
  fire-breathing bulls, yoking of, by . . . 50
  Golden Fleece an asset of 52
  hooves, show of, voting by, at meetings of . 49
  Medea, allotment contract with, by . . . 52
  private, maximum membership of . . . 53
  Siamese twin, joint voting rights of, in . . 48
  ultra vires acts by 53, 54
  winding-up of 54

CONTRACT
  allotment, breach of 53
  breach of, by company 53
         by Hercules 42
         by Penelope 91
  marriage, whether contrary to public policy 92, 93, 94
  service, terms of 33

CRUFT'S
  exhibition of Cerberus at, denied . . . 36

DAEDALUS & SON, LTD.
  aircraft manufacture by 24
  negligence of 25, 26

DAMAGES
  against co-respondent, awarded to Menelaus . 73
  loss of expectation of life, assessment of . 26, 27, 30

DANGER
  concealed, Minotaur constituting - . . 77
         duty of occupier in respect of . . 81
  Theseus, position of as invitee, in respect of . 82

DELAY
  husband's, effect on value of wife . . . 73

DEMIGOD
  elevation of deceased to, effect on damages . 28

	Page
DIDO	
purchase of land by	59
severance of bull's hide by	59
DOG	
meaning of, in Dogs Act, 1906	36
in Larceny Act, 1916	35, 36
whether term applicable to Cerberus	35, 36
EURIPIDES	
expert evidence by	70
EUROPA	
(see BULL, improper behaviour of)	
EURYSTHEUS	
action by riparian owners against	40
FABULOUS MONSTER	
classification of	79
constituting concealed danger	77, 81
right of property in	80
whether animal *ferae naturae*	80
FEE SIMPLE	
conversion of life interest into	63, 64
(see also IMMORTALITY, gift of)	
FIELDS, ELYSIAN	
conditions in, evidence as to	28, 29
domicil of Icarus in	29
exhibits from, satisfactory nature of	29, 30
FLEECE, GOLDEN	
exploitation by company of	46, 47
refusal by underwriters to insure	52
suspension of, in company's registered office	52
HADES	
carrying away of Cerberus from	34, 104
prohibited area, under Defence Regulations	103
sight-seeing tours in	104

	Page
HELEN	
adultery of, evidence as to	69, 73
beauty of, effect of delay on	71, 73
decree *nisi* against	73
face of, ship-launching propensity of	72
HERCULES	
bodily strength of	38, 39
contract of service, breach of, by	42
diversion of rivers by	39
impulsive behaviour of	39
parentage of, disputed	14, 15
stables, unusual method of cleansing, by	39
HOMER	
expert evidence by	70
HOOVES	
amendment in articles as to	49
show of, at company meeting	49
Table 'A,' effect of, on	49
HUSBAND	
absence on service of	14, 88
access by, evidence as to	14, 15
delay of ten years by, whether unreasonable	73
impersonation of, by co-respondent	15
paternity, denial of, by	15
revulsion in feelings of	71
unexpected return of	94
ICARUS	
apotheosis of, effect on damages	28
fatal accident to	25
ILLEGALITY	
effect of, on service contract	34
IMMORTALITY	
gift of, effect of, on life interest	63
status of, not recognised by Court	64

Page

IMMUNITY
   claim of Jupiter to, from jurisdiction . . 13, 19

INVITEE
   devouree held to be 82
   duty of occupier to 81

JASON
   election of, to chairmanship of board . . 48
   sale of business by, to company . . . 46

JUPITER
   impersonation of husband by 18
   scandalous conduct of 17
   status of, as foreign sovereign . . . 16, 19

LEANDER
   action as riparian owner by . . . 40, 41
   special damage suffered by 41
   swimming exploit by 41

LEDA
   shocking nature of evidence by . . . 17
   (see also SWAN, inexcusable conduct of)

MEDEA
   allotment contract of, with company . . 52
   liberal education of 51
   winding-up petition by 45, 53

MENELAUS
   decree *nisi* in favour of 73
   delay of, effect on damages 73

MERCURY
   extraordinary evidence of 16
   unusual manner of taking oath by . . . 16

MINOS
   liability of, as occupier 78, 82
   Minotaur, equivocal affinity of, with . . 80

	Page
MINOTAUR	
duty of occupier to keep under control	80
right of property in	80
whether animal *ferae naturae*	80
MONSTER, FABULOUS	
(see FABULOUS MONSTER)	
MORTALS	
right of ferry over Styx, exclusion of, from	99, 101
visit to prohibited area of	104
NEGLIGENCE	
by aircraft manufacturers	26
diversion of rivers constituting	42
stables, cleansing of, in	42
NON-ACCESS	
husband's, evidence of	14, 15
OATH	
taking of, litigant's name employed in	16
sacrifice of bull in	16
statutory provisions as to	16
OLYMPUS	
independent status of, Foreign Office certificate as to	19
PARACHUTE	
descent by, of husband	15
of divine co-respondent	15
PARIS	
liability of, as co-respondent	73
low moral standard of	68
PATERNITY	
bull's, effect on Minotaur of	78
in issue in matrimonial suit	14, 19

	Page
PENELOPE	
anticipatory breach by	91
marriage contract of	90
war activities of	89
PERSEUS	
Air Force, service in, by	109
conviction of	109
PLUTO	
franchise of ferry, grant of, by	99
injunction granted to	106
ownership in domestic animal of	36
POLLUX	
(see CASTOR)	
PULLOVER	
delayed completion of, breach of contract by	91
SHADES	
interference with transit of	102, 105
rights of, to ferry over Styx	100
status of	100
STABLES, AUGEAN	
cleansing of, unreasonable method in	39
duty of Medical Officer of Health as to	37
STYX	
franchise of ferry over	99
sight-seeing tours on	104
prohibited area, under Defence Regulations	103
SWAN	
inexcusable conduct of	17
TEETH	
detachable, whether larcenable	114
dragon's, sowing of, *ultra vires*	50, 53

	Page
TENANT FOR LIFE	
interest of, effect of immortality on	63
powers of, under Settled Land Act, 1925	62
THESEUS	
whether invitee or trespasser	81
VENDOR	
divine parentage of	62
gift of immortality to	63
trustee capacity of	61
whether life interest extended	64
WIFE	
access by husband to, evidence of	14
adultery with co-respondent, not guilty of	18
beauty of, vitiated by husband's delay	73
promise to marry by, when actionable	92, 95
pursuit of, by composer	90
sports-cars, excessive attraction of, for	71

WINDING-UP
   (see COMPANY, winding-up of
       MEDEA, winding-up petition by)

II
MORE LEGAL FICTIONS

A CONSTRUCTIVE DEFECT

See Page 81

MORE LEGAL FICTIONS
A Series of Cases from Shakespeare

**TO MY NIECE
HELEN**

ACKNOWLEDGMENTS

The reception by the public of *Legal Fictions*, the first book of this series, has encouraged me to prepare, and my Publishers to print, this second volume. These cases, like those contained in the previous book, first saw the light in *Law Notes*, to the learned Editors of which I once again make grateful acknowledgment for help and advice so kindly rendered to me as a tiro in the law.

My best thanks are due to my Publishers, who have by their courtesy and helpfulness rendered my task so easy and pleasant at all times. I desire also to express my appreciation of the interest shown by the many readers, lay and legal, who have been good enough to send me encouraging comments, and by the critics who have reviewed the earlier book in kindly terms.

A.L.P.

St. John's Wood,
September, 1946.

CONTENTS

Acknowledgments	*page*	7
Rex v. The Author : ex parte *Shakespeare*		11
Attorney-General *v.* Albany	(K.B.D.)	17
Bottom *v.* Goodfellow	(K.B.D.)	27
Caliban *v.* Prospero	(Ch.D.)	39
Capulet *v.* Montague	(P.D.A.)	49
The King *v.* Claudius	(C.C.C.)	61
Leonato *v.* Borachio	(K.B.D.)	69
Pyramus *v.* Bank of Babylon	(K.B.D.)	79
Sebastian *v.* Sebastian	(P.D.A.)	89
Shipton *v.* The King	(C.C.A)	101
Shylock *v.* Antonio	(C.A.)	113
Table of Cases Cited		121
Table of Statutes		123
Index		124

The first thing we do, let's kill all the lawyers.

> SHAKESPEARE, *King Henry VI*, Part 2,
> Act IV, Scene 2.

REX v. THE AUTHOR
Ex parte SHAKESPEARE

There is a tradition, familiar to all readers of detection literature, that the criminal will sooner or later re-visit the scene of his crime. Though this principle has not so far been accorded judicial recognition, there is an analogous rule in the law of evidence, relating to criminal cases, which is well established. To prove guilty knowledge or intention, where these are the essence of the offence, evidence is admissible to show that the accused has in the past committed acts of a similar nature connected with those with which he now stands charged, and that the past and present offences constitute one entire criminal system or course of conduct.

The present author, who in *Legal Fictions* has already trifled with the law, is well aware of the risks involved in committing this new outrage. Contempt of Court is not the only offence in the indictment. It has been strongly argued that to bring the great name of Shakespeare into ridicule or contempt amounts to criminal libel.

The only defence open to the present author—and that not a recognised legal defence—is to reply *Tu quoque*.

It is clearly arguable, from both extrinsic and intrinsic evidence, that Shakespeare had neither respect nor affection for lawyers or the law. From 1578, when William was fourteen years of age, his father's fortunes began to decline; his property was sold or mortgaged;

he was involved in costly litigation, and even imprisoned for debt. In 1586, when a distress was levied upon his goods, it was found that there were no goods upon which to distrain. The legal persecution of the poet himself by Sir Thomas Lucy, following a poaching adventure in Charlecote Park, Worcestershire, embittered him considerably and, according to some biographers, led to his leaving his native county for a time. There is little cause for wonder, after these experiences, that Shakespeare's references to the law should exhibit hatred, ridicule or contempt.

Thus Hamlet, listing " the ills that flesh is heir to," links together

" The pangs of misprised love, the law's delays,
 The insolence of office, and the spurns
 That patient merit of the unworthy takes."

Later on, in the churchyard scene (Act V, Scene 1), Hamlet reflects with grim bitterness on the skull dug up by the Sexton:

" There's another ; why may not that be the skull of a lawyer ? Where be his quiddities now, his quillets, his cases, his tenures, and his tricks ? Why does he suffer this rude knave now to knock him about the sconce with a dirty shovel, and will not tell him of his action of battery ? This fellow might be in's time a great buyer of land, with his statutes, his recognizances, his fines, his double vouchers, his recoveries ; is this the fine of his fines, and the recovery of his recoveries, to have his fine pate full of fine dirt ? Will his vouchers vouch him no more of his purchases, and double ones too, than the length and breadth of a pair of indentures ? The very conveyance of his lands will hardly lie in this box ; and must the inheritor himself have no more ? "

In *Measure for Measure* Isabella bitterly attacks the legalistic hypocrisy of tyrants like Angelo—

"Bidding the law make courtesy to their will."

Of the same nature are the specious legal arguments put into the mouths of the prelates in Act I of *King Henry V*, by which, for their own selfish ends, they seek to justify a declaration of war on France. The events dealt with in *King Henry VIII* were recent in Shakespeare's day: yet in the great trial scene in Act II he contrives it so that all our sympathy is with the condemned Queen Katherine, while her judges' attitude calls for nothing but contempt.

The trial in Act IV of *The Merchant of Venice* is such a patent travesty of justice that the scene is invariably played so as to portray Shylock as a victim of persecution. In *King Henry IV, Part 2*, the smug self-righteousness of the newly-crowned Henry V and his Lord Chief Justice render the blatant roguery of Falstaff and his friends quite lovable by contrast.

More playful, though equally contemptuous, is Mercutio's subtle dig in *Romeo and Juliet* (Act I, Scene 5):

"O, then, I see, Queen Mab hath been with you . . .
Her chariot is an empty hazel-nut,
Made by the joiner squirrel or old grub,
Time out of mind the fairies' coachmakers.
And in this state she gallops night by night
Through lovers' brains, and then they dream of love;
On courtiers' knees, that dream on court'sies straight;
O'er lawyers' fingers, who straight dream on fees;
O'er ladies' lips, who straight on kisses dream. . . ."

As for ridicule, Shakespeare was a master of the art. Dogberry and Verges, in *Much Ado about Nothing*, taking down the depositions against the prisoners : Shallow and Silent, the decrepit country justices, in *King Henry IV, Part 2*, exchanging reminiscences of their legal education and selecting recruits for Falstaff's draft ; Shallow again, in *The Merry Wives of Windsor*, " Esquire, in the County of Gloucester, Justice of the Peace and Coram," behaving in a manner quite unworthy of the dignity of the Bench— all these are excellent fooling. And then, to sum up the evidence, comes the picture in *As You Like It* of the successful man in his maturity—the fifth of the Seven Ages—

" And then the justice,
In fair round belly, with good capon lined,
With eyes severe and beard of formal cut,
Full of wise saws and modern instances ;
And so he plays his part."

What, then, was the lawyer in Shakespeare's eyes ? An image of dignity, a repository of learning, a fountain of justice ? Not at all. To England's greatest poet the salient characteristics of the English lawyer are a well-filled paunch, a solemn pose, a fund of trite remarks. What complaint, then, has Shakespeare of the *riposte* contained in these pages ? The biter's bit, " and thus," in the words of the Clown in *Twelfth Night*, " the whirligig of time brings in his revenges ! "

On this reasoned defence the Author rests his case. If he should, nevertheless, be convicted and sentenced on the evidence of these pages, he will ask for his previous offences to be taken into consideration.

TESTAMENTARY INCAPACITY

King's Bench Division.
ATTORNEY-GENERAL v. ALBANY.

Estate Duty—Finance Act, 1894, s. 2 (1) (c)—" Bona fide possession not . . . retained to entire exclusion of donor "—Gift inter vivos—Whether conditional—Benefits accruing to donor under bond—Penalty clause—" Forbearance to curse " by obligee—Whether good consideration—Donor not entirely excluded from benefit.

JUDGMENT of Mr. Justice Shakespeare:

"This action arises out of an information by the Attorney-General, on behalf of the Crown, claiming estate duty upon the death of the donor, Mr. Lear, in respect of certain property comprised in two deeds of gift dated 3rd November, 1937, in favour of his daughters, Goneril and Regan, respectively. The donor died in April, 1943, intestate, and Mrs. Goneril Albany is sued as administrator of the estate.

"By the combined operation of the two deeds, which are practically identical in form, the donor, in consideration of his natural love and affection for his said daughters, purported to convey to them the whole of his real and personal estate (other than chattels and effects passing by delivery), as to his real estate in fee simple and as to his personal estate absolutely, in equal moieties. It was further declared in the said deeds that all the live and dead stock, furniture, plate, goods and chattels formerly in the possession of the donor were the sole property of the said daughters, in equal shares, having previously passed by delivery to them, and by way of confirmation the donor assigned them to his daughters absolutely. At the time when the deed was executed the donor was nearly ninety years of age and had long since ceased to take any active part in the management of his property. He is described as a man of domineering temperament and, when thwarted, was apt to break out into ungovernable fury, using profane language and freely scattering curses and imprecations on all around him.

"The Crown claims estate duty upon the death of the donor, in respect of the property comprised in these deeds of gift, by virtue of sect. 2 (1) (c) of the Finance Act, 1894, as being 'property taken under any gift, whenever made, of which property *bonâ fide* possession and enjoyment shall not have been assumed by the donee immediately upon the gift, and thenceforward retained to the entire exclusion of the donor or of any benefit to him, by contract or otherwise.'

"Frequent suggestions were made during the course of the trial that the motives of the donor and the donees alike, in carrying out this transaction, were to escape death duties. I feel constrained to dispose once and for all of these suggestions by the short answer that the existence or otherwise of such motives is irrelevant, except as evidence for or against the *bonâ fides* of the transaction. There is the highest authority for the proposition that, if a man can lawfully so order his affairs that the payment of revenue duties of any kind is reduced or avoided altogether, there is no legal objection to his doing so. Whatever may be thought as to the morality of such transactions in these times from the point of view of patriotism and public spirit, there is no ground for ignoring their legal effect unless such transactions be proved to be a mere sham, such as those falling within the words 'not *bonâ fide*' in the Act of 1894, or the phrase 'artificial transaction' in the Finance Acts of more recent years.

"But the Crown relies in this case on something more than mere motive ; it asserts that this transaction falls within the latter words of the section to which I have referred—'not . . . retained to the entire exclusion of the donor or of any benefit to him, by contract or otherwise.' It is suggested that the gifts in question were not unconditional, but were subject to an undertaking, express or implied, on the part of the daughters that they would jointly maintain the donor during the remainder of his life and afford accommodation and entertainment, each in alternate months, not only to him but to his servants and staff, numbering one hundred persons. The defendant denies the existence of any such undertaking and says that the donor was content to rely upon the filial affection and gratitude of the defendant and her sister to afford him shelter, maintenance and comfort in his old age.

"The first argument of the Crown is that, whatever be the true version of the facts relating to such undertaking, there was not an entire exclusion of the donor within the meaning of the section if he had *in fact* access to properties which were included in the gift and enjoyed an advantage by being there. The Crown further contends that there was not an entire exclusion of any benefit to him, by contract or otherwise ; since there is uncontested evidence that the arrangement for monthly sojourns with each of the daughters in turn by the donor and his very considerable staff of servants was in fact carried out, for however short a time. The learned Attorney-General cited (*inter alia*) the provisions of the Food (Rationing) Order, 1939, the Food (Restriction on Dealings) Order, 1941, the Acquisition of Food (Excessive Quantities) Order, 1939, and the Meals in Establishments Order, 1942, in support of his contention that very considerable benefits accrued to the donor (and correspondingly great inconveniences to the donees) by reason of the arrangement in question, having regard to the well-known difficulties in times like these of boarding and catering for large numbers of persons. I cannot but give great weight to this argument, nor am I prepared to assert that the word ' benefit ' in the section is confined to a benefit conferred by the deeds of gift or issuing out of the property thereby conveyed. But I have come to the conclusion that the words ' or otherwise ' must be read as *ejusdem generis* with the word ' contract,' and that, if such a benefit were enjoyed by the donor gratuitously, by leave and licence of the donees, it would not fall within the section. As to the donor's access to the properties which formed the subject-matter of the gifts, similar considerations apply. I understand the Act to mean that the ' possession, enjoyment and benefit ' from which the donor must be entirely excluded must be derived from some enforceable right—not from a claim based upon so nebulous a consideration as filial love or duty (*A.-G.* v. *Seccombe*). And in construing a revenue statute there is no presumption in favour of extending its scope.

" The claim of the Crown therefore turns upon the question—was there or was there not an enforceable contract between the parties whereby these two daughters were bound to maintain their father and his servants ? I have come to the conclusion that there was such a contract, in the form of a promise by the daughters, which is enforceable at law. True, the consideration for such promise does not appear to have been constituted by the deeds of gift or by the promise of the donor to execute those deeds. But two documents have been produced—described in the pleadings as bonds—bearing the same date as the deeds of gift and apparently executed contemporaneously with them. So far as form goes, they are in the nature of bonds, but their provisions are so unusual that I feel it right to read the documents in full. In the first, the daughter Goneril appears as principal and her sister Regan as surety; in the second, these *rôles* are reversed. Otherwise they are in identical terms. I will read the first document:—

Know all men by these presents that we Goneril Albany of *etc.* (hereinafter called " The Principal ") and Regan Cornwall of *etc.* (hereinafter called " the Surety ") are jointly and severally bound and firmly obliged to the Foul Fiend Flibbertigibbet and the Prince of Darkness Mahu (hereinafter together referred to as " the Evil Ones ") in the sum of Ten Thousand Paternal Curses and all the liabilities thereof including (but without prejudice to the generality of the foregoing) the liability or liabilities of blasting withering and bursting and of conversion into all or any of the following namely a screech-owl a serpent and a toad as the Evil Ones shall in their full and unfettered discretion think fit To which liabilities well and truly to be borne we for ourselves and our successors do bind ourselves jointly and severally by these presents.

Sealed with our seals the 3rd day of November 1937.

" Then follows a recital of the deed of gift to which I have referred, and the document continues:—

The Condition of the above-written obligation is that if the Principal when lawfully called on in that behalf shall duly and faithfully maintain and keep the Donor and his one hundred servants during the residue of his life in the same state style and condition as heretofore and shall permit the donor and his said servants to reside at all times hereafter upon the said premises so long as the donor shall think fit so to do then this obligation to be void and of none effect or else to remain in full force and virtue.

"I have been at some pains to ascertain the circumstances in which these peculiar documents were executed, and it seems that considerable misplaced ingenuity has been employed by the solicitor who was responsible for the drafting. I understand that the form of a bond rather than of an out-and-out contract was thought to be preferable, owing to the advanced age of the donor and of certain eccentricities in his behaviour which must have raised serious doubts in the minds of the other parties as to his mental condition and capacity to contract. It is no part of my duty in this case to consider whether, and if so to what extent, the deeds of gift themselves were vitiated by mental infirmity on the part of the donor, and no proceedings appear to have been commenced by any interested party to set them aside on that account. But the little evidence I have heard on the subject discloses a shocking state of affairs, and suggests that the family and legal adviser of the deceased might well have invoked the jurisdiction of the Chancery Division, and applied for the appointment of a Receiver of his property and a Committee of his person. What are we to think of daughters who allow a man of his years to roam about in all weathers in the heart of the country, in the hours of black-out, consorting with tramps and persons of no fixed abode? And how are we to regard a solicitor who takes instructions from a client in the donor's condition, and draws and attests that client's execution of a document, purporting to be a settlement, upon a person described as 'Tom o'Bedlam,' to hold certain property, as the donor phrased it, 'Upon Trust for my little dogs Tray Blanch and Sweetheart in equal shares as tenants in common and to the survivors or survivor of them during their respective lives AND after the death of the last survivor in trust for my grey cat Grimalkin absolutely'? It is fortunate indeed that, in the events which have happened, the property in question has reverted to the deceased's estate, the tenants for life having met untimely ends in the lethal chamber, following a severe attack of distemper, and the remainderman having been destroyed by the local veterinary surgeon as a result of incurable mange. There is little I can do to remedy the situation at this late hour, but I conceive it my duty to bring the facts to the notice of the Law Society.

"But I am unduly digressing from the main tenor of my judgment, which is to consider the form of these so-called bonds and to decide whether they constitute a legally enforceable obligation upon the defendant and her sister. It has been explained that the somewhat unusual form of obligation was characteristically chosen by the donor in lieu of a money obligation, and that, had it been expressed in the form of a penalty, it might have been a penalty from which the obligor would have been relieved by a Court of Equity. As to that, I need notice only in passing the argument that the obligees are 'non-existent or fictitious persons' within the meaning of sect. 7 of the Bills of Exchange Act, 1882, an enactment whose interpretation clause counsel somewhat over-elaborately strove to import into the construction of these documents.

It is fortunately not necessary for me to express an opinion on these contentions, or on the laborious arguments that a paternal curse is not legal tender or good and lawful money of Great Britain, or that the liability on the obligors of being changed into toads, serpents or what not cannot be said to fall within the equitable doctrine of conversion. It is sufficient for me to point to two main facts —first, that these documents (be they properly described as bonds or not) were executed under seal, and, secondly (lest the circumstances of the sealing should be questioned in another place), that the unpleasant and inconvenient consequences which were intended thereby to follow any breach of the condition to maintain the donor and his followers, and to afford them shelter, constituted a sufficient ' detriment, loss or responsibility suffered or undertaken ' by the obligors (*Currie* v. *Misa*). Or, putting the matter in another way, since it is well-established that forbearance to sue (*Alliance Bank* v. *Broom*), or even a promise to cease molestation, may be a good consideration for a promise (provided the promisee has reasonable ground for believing he has a good cause of action), I see no difficulty in holding that forbearance to curse, where (as in this case) the promisee reasonably believes he has just cause to do so, constitutes equally valid consideration in the eyes of the law.

" I therefore uphold the contention of the Crown upon this matter. There was not such an ' entire exclusion of the donor, or of any benefit to him, by contract or otherwise,' as the section requires, and estate duty is therefore payable on the whole of the gifts the subject-matter of the two deeds of 1937. The costs must come out of the deceased's estate."

DEFAMATION BY INNUENDO

King's Bench Division.
BOTTOM v. GOODFELLOW.

Defamation—Ass's head placed by defendant on plaintiff's shoulders—Whether reasonably capable of bearing innuendo alleged—Whether libel or slander—Whether fair comment without malice—Damages.

INTERESTING questions in connection with the law of defamation were argued in this case, which was recently concluded after a trial lasting six days before Mr. Justice Theseus and a special jury. His Lordship, during the course of his summing-up, made the following observations:—

"In this case Mr. Nicholas Bottom, of 'The Weavers' Arms,' St. John's Wood, a repertory actor, claims damages from Mr. Robin Goodfellow (better known in certain circles as 'Puck'), of no fixed abode, whose occupation is stated to be that of a 'world-flyer.' From the defendant's replies to questions asked in cross-examination, it appears that he is one of those restless individuals who spend the greater part of their time in flitting from one hemisphere to another, in sometimes flimsy and often inadequately-equipped aircraft, at considerable risk to their own lives and those of the unfortunate persons who are subsequently required to go out in search of the wreckage. I have frequently been at pains to understand what possible result, for themselves or for humanity generally, is to be expected from these temerarious and ill-advised excursions into the void, other than a great deal of undesirable publicity, but I am informed by the defendant that his aim in life is to set up a 'record.' He explained this somewhat loose and nebulous term by giving as an example his present ambition (I quote the picturesque metaphor which, I presume, is common in aviation circles) to 'put a girdle round about the earth in forty minutes.' Allowing for the airy self-confidence and natural hyperbole which is a characteristic of those who follow such adventurous occupations, you will have to consider in due course whether the defendant is the sort of young man who might be led by mere youthful exuberance to indulge in the kind of prank complained of, or whether his action is to be attributed to some less creditable motive.

"I have judged it well to start my summing-up with an appraisal of the defendant's character, because you will, in the course of your deliberations, be brought up against the question of malice. With that question itself I shall deal at the proper time, but it is well at the outset to carry in your minds a clear picture of the mentality of the defendant whose motives you are to analyse.

"The plaintiff, Mr. Bottom, is a man of a very different character. Serving, as he told us, his apprenticeship among the looms of Lancashire, he rose eventually to the position of managing-director in the very mills where he once worked as a boy. Retiring five years ago from his arduous duties, he set himself to take an active interest in the repertory drama, of which he had long been a generous patron and, as the evidence of Mr. Peter Quince and other producers has shown, he has met with a certain success in that no less than in his previous profession.

"I now turn to the Statement of Claim, which alleges that the defendant, on the night of the 24th June last, published of and concerning the plaintiff a defamatory libel. The Particulars of Claim set out that 'on the date aforesaid the defendant did, at the Open Air Theatre in Regent's Park, in the County of London, at the conclusion of the play in which the plaintiff had performed, place and/or exhibit upon the head and shoulders of the plaintiff the representation of an ass's head, meaning thereby that the plaintiff was a stupid and obstinate person, unamenable to reason; that his acting and diction were defective and/or unintelligible; that his voice was displeasing and/or cacophonous; and that he was unfit to take part in dramatic representations and/or to associate with actors and/or to have any connection with the stage or the theatrical profession generally,' whereby it is alleged that the plaintiff has suffered serious damage in his professional career.

"The defendant by his reply admits the act complained of, but denies its defamatory nature and pleads that it is incapable of bearing the innuendo alleged. In the alternative he pleads that the act complained of, if defamatory at all, is not actionable without proof of special damage, and he denies that the defendant has suffered the damage alleged or any damage whatsoever. In the further alternative he says that 'in so far as the innuendo consists of statements of fact, it is true in substance and fact, and that in so far as it consists of expressions of opinion it constitutes fair comment made in good faith and without malice upon the said facts, which are matters of public interest.'

"Before I go on to direct you further on the points at issue, it may be well to recapitulate the happenings on the night of the 24th June, which were brought out in the evidence for the plaintiff, and not denied by the defendant.

"It seems that on the evening in question, Mr. Bottom was taking the principal part in a performance of the well-known tragedy *Pyramus and Thisbe* in the Open Air Theatre. It being midsummer, the weather was very hot, and it was inclined to be thundery. Mr. Bottom had been exerting himself rather more than usual in the last scene of the play, and it is not surprising that, after divesting himself of his make-up and putting on his ordinary clothes, a certain lassitude overcame him. He remembers awakening at about 11 o'clock in his dressing tent and seeing the defendant bending over him, with what he has described as 'an elfish grin' on his face. As he rose to his feet, the defendant ran off, and Mr. Bottom, imagining that he was one of the attendants who had thought fit to rouse him before shutting the enclosure, thought no more of it. He still felt weary, and experienced, as he told us, some slight difficulty in breathing, but this he attributed to the excessively sultry atmosphere.

"By this time the audience had dispersed, and most of the other actors had gone. Mr. Bottom walked, as was his custom, away from the theatre and along the Inner Circle of the Park towards Baker Street. He noted that those of his fellow-actors whom he met regarded him, at first with consternation, and then with repressed laughter, but could not understand what was arousing their mirth. He passed his hand once or twice over his head, remarked only that he was (as he expressed it in the witness-box) 'marvellous hairy about the face,' and made a mental note to go to his barber's early on the following morning. By the time he reached Baker Street he found himself followed by a crowd of ragged urchins who, for some reason which he was unable to appreciate, requested him, in shrill and raucous voices, alternately to 'Gee-up!' and 'Whoa!' Two of these young persons have given evidence before you. One of them, by the name of Mustardseed, even had the effrontery to offer a bundle of hay, while another, whose name was given as Cobweb, requested him to partake of a handful of dried peas. It was not until he reached the omnibus stop at the corner of Marylebone Road, where (as ill-luck would have it) a group of his fellow-actors was standing, that the full significance of his appearance dawned upon him. Reflected in a mirror in a neighbouring shop window he saw his body surmounted by a mask in the shape of an ass's head, which entirely concealed his own impressive features. Hastily wrenching it off—a task of some difficulty in his exhausted and embarrassed condition—he found himself the centre of a crowd of onlookers (including several of his colleagues), convulsed with laughter. Standing close by him in the centre of the crowd, to add to his embarrassment, were two constables, who advised him with some asperity to 'move on,' as he was causing an obstruction.

"There was no difficulty in identifying the author of this extraordinary outrage, who was pointed out by the urchins afore-mentioned as having followed the plaintiff from the borders of the Park, mimicking his movements and emitting what were apparently intended to be asinine noises. The defendant made no attempt to deny his responsibility and gave his name and address without demur. No apology being forthcoming, the writ in the present action was issued early in July.

"Whether the act complained of is, in its implications, defamatory it is for you, members of the jury, to decide. The defendant has denied its defamatory nature, and you must ask yourselves what is likely to be the effect, on the minds of onlookers, of the sight of a well-known and respectable actor walking along Baker Street displaying a head and features reminiscent of some of the denizens of the neighbouring Zoological Gardens. The first question to which you must give an answer is this: 'Was the act complained of, in its necessary implications, calculated to lower the plaintiff in the estimation of right-thinking members of the community generally?' (*Sim* v. *Stretch*.)

"Whether the act complained of is reasonably capable of bearing the meaning alleged in the innuendo is for the Court to decide, and in this case I have had no hesitation in answering this question in the affirmative. Here is a perfectly respectable gentleman, a successful repertory actor, who has recently completed a performance calling for lucid diction and histrionic talent of a high order. Taking advantage of him at a moment when he is off his guard, the defendant places him in the ridiculous position of having to go about surmounted by the head and features of an ass. The obstinacy and stupidity of this animal are proverbial; his voice is raucous and displeasing, and I have little doubt that the defendant's action can reasonably bear the implications which the plaintiff has set upon it in his Statement of Claim. Whether the act complained of in fact conveyed the various meanings imputed to it I must leave you, members of the jury, to decide. In this connection it is my duty to recall to your minds the evidence of Mr. Peter Quince, of Mr. Snug and Mr. Flute, all colleagues and fellow-actors of the plaintiff's, whose testimony has strongly supported his case." His Lordship here read from his notes, and resumed:—

"I now turn to the first of the alternative pleas put forward by the defendant, where he denies that the act complained of, even though it be defamatory of the plaintiff, constitutes a libel, and suggests that it is not actionable without proof of special damage, the existence of which he denies. As to this it is true that libels generally consist in written or printed words, but this is not invariably necessary; the defamatory matter may be conveyed in some other permanent form. A statute, a caricature, an effigy, a sign or a picture may constitute a libel, and all these have, at different times, been held actionable without proof of special damage." His Lordship here dealt at length with *Monson* v. *Tussaud's* and other authorities, and continued: "On the decided cases, and the principles enunciated therein, I can see no difference between making an effigy of the plaintiff and placing it in a waxworks among the effigies of murderers and other criminals, and placing upon the living body of the plaintiff, and leaving for all to see, the representation of the head of an animal whose name is a byword of reproach for blind perversity, crass stupidity and sonorous vacuity. In short, I have no doubt that the action of the defendant, if it was defamatory, constituted a libel and not a mere slander, and that no proof of special damage is required.

"Lastly, I come to the defendant's third line of defence—the 'rolled-up plea,' as it has been termed. I am under no compulsion, members of the jury, to waste your time and that of learned counsel in detailing the long discussions which have taken place, right up to the House of Lords itself, as to the character and implication of that defence. True, the defendant made a half-hearted attempt, during his evidence, to justify his action on the grounds of the plaintiff's allegedly pompous and over-rhetorical manner, and suggested that the plaintiff's reputation was already lost before he (the defendant) appeared on the scene. 'Mr. Bottom'— he said in the box—' true to his name, is trying to argue *à posteriori.*' Vulgar witticisms of this kind carry no weight with me, and you may feel inclined to stigmatise this kind of coarse humour in no uncertain manner when you deliver your verdict.

"But I digress from the point I am considering at the moment—the rolled-up plea. It is established law that the defence thus put forward amounts to a defence of fair comment only (*Sutherland* v. *Stopes*), and it is for you to decide whether the comment was in fact fair and whether it was made without malice. It is for me to determine whether the matter in respect of which the comment was made was in fact a matter of public interest, as the defendant alleges. On this last point I shall be following the authorities in holding that a play which has been performed, like a picture which has been exhibited, is a matter of public interest (*Merivale* v. *Carson*).

"As to the fairness of the comment, it is not for you to substitute your own opinion as to the dramatic value of the plaintiff's acting for that of the defendant, who purports to be a critic of the drama. You may, however, go on to consider whether the action of the defendant, in its necessary implications, goes beyond the confines of honest criticism and amounts to a personal attack upon the plaintiff (*McQuire* v. *Western Morning News*). You should also consider whether the defendant's action, in its necessary implications, represented the honest and *bonâ fide* opinion even of the defendant himself.

"Closely allied to these matters is the question of malice. No comment can be fair which is made by a critic who, in making it, is actuated by personal spite or ill-will towards the plaintiff. That is malice in its popular sense. But the term has another and a wider meaning, which you must now consider, and which includes every unjustifiable intention to inflict injury on the person defamed or, more simply, in the words of a famous judge, ' any wrongful motive in a man's mind' (*Clark* v. *Molyneux*).

"Was the defendant, in doing the action complained of, actuated by this kind of malice ? You are not called upon to say what the wrong motive was, if you can say that there was a wrong motive. If you find that the defendant was actuated by some motive other than that which alone would excuse him, your verdict on this point must be for the plaintiff.

"To assist you in deciding this point you may look at both the intrinsic evidence—the act itself—and the extrinsic evidence—the relations between the parties and the state of the defendant's mind.

"With the former I have already dealt sufficiently. As to the latter, it is my duty to recall to your minds the evidence adduced by the plaintiff on the defendant's propensity towards practical joking of the more boisterous kind and the admissions by the defendant in cross-examination. The defendant has clearly admitted that he has been in the habit of playing frequent tricks on young betrothed couples and elderly women alike; you have heard the description of how he offered himself as guide to Mr. Demetrius and his *fiancée* on a country walk and left them hopelessly lost at midnight in the middle of a forest; how he is in the habit of frequenting country inns and splashing beer over the faces of quiet and well-behaved customers or pulling their chairs from under them at the most unexpected moments. You may feel that this and other evidence of a like nature will weigh with you in determining this important question—Was the defendant, in doing what he did, actuated by malice?"

The jury then retired, and after an absence of forty minutes returned the following replies to the questions left to them:—

1. Did the act complained of in fact convey the meanings imputed to it in the Statement of Claim?—Yes.

2. If so, was it defamatory of the plaintiff?—Yes.

3. Did the act complained of, in its necessary implications, constitute fair comment by the defendant upon the plaintiff's acting?—No.

4. Was the defendant, in doing the act complained of, actuated by malice in the sense of wrongful motive?—Yes.

5. Damages, if any?—Five thousand pounds.

Judgment was entered accordingly, with costs.

A CONTINUING NUISANCE

CHANCERY DIVISION.
CALIBAN *v.* PROSPERO.

Nuisance—Noises, stenches and vibrations—Responsibility of defendant—Method of production immaterial—Plaintiff a feeble-minded person—Injunction.

AFTER a hearing lasting several days, Mr. Justice Gonzalo delivered the following judgment in this action:—

" In this case Mr. Caliban sues *in formâ pauperis* by his next friend, Mr. Trinculo, for an injunction to restrain the defendant from continuing and apprehended acts of trespass and nuisance. The facts are somewhat unusual and the issues involve difficult questions of law.

" The defendant, who is described as an author and explorer, is a native of the city of Milan, but is now resident in this country. The plaintiff, who is described as a domestic servant, has been certified under s.5 of the Mental Deficiency Act, 1913, as a feeble-minded person. He is clearly *inops consilii*—a person of arrested mental development, requiring care, supervision and control, and a reception order will, in due course, doubtless be made. Mr. Trinculo is a music-hall artist of modest means who has, nevertheless, out of very commendable feelings of compassion, befriended the plaintiff and now brings this action on his behalf.

" The matters set forth in the pleadings originally included certain issues which the Court has no jurisdiction to decide, involving as they did certain questions of title to land abroad. The matter is now simplified by the defendant's abandonment of his defence on these issues.

"It appears that the plaintiff's mother, Mrs. Sycorax, died a widow about thirteen years ago, leaving the plaintiff, her only child, but no other known relatives, her surviving. She died intestate, possessed of no movable property other than a heterogeneous collection of objects, comprising a tall hat, a broomstick, a cauldron and a number of toads, bats and beetles. She was, however, the owner (apparently in fee simple) of a small island in the Mediterranean Sea, which seems to have escaped the imperialist ambitions of the neighbouring powers. This island, as the defendant now admits, became on her decease the property of the plaintiff.

"It is therefore unnecessary for me to express an opinion on the difficult and doubtful question of title, for the defendant now admits that he was himself a mere trespasser on the plaintiff's land. He pleads, however, that the acts alleged against him fall into no known category of nuisance and disclose no cause of action; he also says that the plaintiff is not entitled to an injunction, but that his proper remedy, if any, is in damages. This, then, is the issue which it is now incumbent upon the Court to decide.

"It may assist in clarifying the reasons for my conclusions if I first briefly sum up my observations on the character and mental calibre of the defendant. The evidence and his general demeanour in the witness box have left me in no doubt that he is a man of great mental capacity, enormous learning and of the strongest personality. Witness after witness has testified to his authoritative manner and his power of overawing even normally courageous persons. It is clear on the evidence that, when he first came to the island, he set himself to win the confidence of the plaintiff—a confidence which he soon abused—and it is not surprising that the plaintiff was rapidly terrorised and reduced to a state bordering on abject servitude.

"The main part of the defence relates to the nature of the acts alleged to constitute the nuisance of which the plaintiff complains, and I cannot leave this part of the evidence without some reference to the repeated allegations that the defendant's researches into the occult have endowed him with supernatural powers. Three witnesses, who were shipwrecked on the island, have declared on their oath that, while they were wandering about this apparently desolate spot, their footsteps were dogged by strange and unaccountable noises—sometimes soft and melodious music, and sometimes in the form of the harshest and most hideous cacophony imaginable. These witnesses were quick to attribute these phenomena to supernatural causes, but no one who has followed with intelligent appreciation the development of the science of wireless telephony during the past two decades will find it necessary to resort to so unlikely an explanation of an all too common form of nuisance in modern every-day life. Other witnesses have asserted, with every semblance of sincerity, that a variety of strange creatures unknown to the biological world—harpies and what-not—infested the island, and that the defendant by his magic art caused them to appear and vanish in the most alarming manner. But here again the facts to which they testify are susceptible of the simplest explanation. I have observed with regret that the sobriety of several of these witnesses at the time of the alleged occurrences is subject to the gravest doubt, and even those of them whose character and reputation place them above suspicion in this respect were (as they then believed) survivors from a disastrous shipwreck, and in their dazed condition may well have failed to recognise the (to them) strange *fauna* of this semi-tropical place. If this had been all, I should have been disposed to hold that the alleged acts were nuisances of the commonest variety, and I should have considered the question of an injunction on this simple basis. But I am bound to say that there certainly seems, running through (if I may be permitted the metaphor) the woolly and impalpable mass of their exaggerations, one single thread of the same texture—a unanimous belief in the defendant's magical powers. All these witnesses exhibited a common insistence which compels respect and cannot be lightly dismissed as frivolous and, speaking with all the natural scepticism of the lawyer, I cannot deny that there are matters in the evidence which appear to be incapable of a rational explanation.

" I do not propose to decide in general terms whether the law of England recognises or takes cognisance of acts and causes alleged to be of a supernatural kind, nor is it necessary that I should do so. The effects of those causes—the phenomena themselves—constitute evidence to be given, received and weighed like any other evidence. And if the general nature of that evidence is such as to show that the plaintiff was injured in the rightful enjoyment of his land, so that his bodily health has suffered or his comfort been disturbed, and if, in addition, that evidence leads to the conclusion that the defendant (it matters not how or by what means) has been responsible for causing such injury, I apprehend that there is immediately constituted a cause of action by the plaintiff against him. To put the matter in technical form, where there is both *damnum* and *injuria*, indirectly caused by the defendant's act, an action on the case will lie (*Day v. Brownrigg*).

"The plaintiff, despite his mental disabilities, gave his evidence in a clear and graphic manner, illustrated by a wealth of gesture which told eloquently of the hardships he had suffered at the defendant's hands. His evidence has been corroborated in material particulars by other witnesses, and I have no reason to disbelieve him. He has related how, when he had committed some real or fancied *peccadillo*, the defendant awed him by terrifying threats of physical torment —'pinches, side-stitches and cramps,' as his poor vocabulary briefly but vividly phrased it—and how at the precise moment specified by the defendant in those threats he was tormented, as he alleges, by 'urchins and invisible spirits.' At other times, as he says, he was 'pitched in the mire' and led out of his way by 'will-o'-the wisps'; creatures like apes 'mowed and chattered' at him or bit him; hedgehogs inexplicably thrust themselves into the way of his bare feet, or adders entwined themselves hissing round his body. It is of no avail for the defendant to assert, as he did under cross-examination that the plaintiff suffers from insane delusions or a species of *delirium tremens*, for the evidence of two eminent specialists who have examined him not only disproved this allegation, but spoke eloquently of the scars on his body, which they agreed were caused by precisely the type of treatment which he describes. Moreover the plaintiff's evidence, corroborated by that of Mr. Stephano and Mr. Trinculo, has left me in no doubt that whenever such threats were made, some kind of misfortune, in the precise form which the defendant foretold, befell the plaintiff. Innumerable instances have been given, and while I am not unmindful of the fact that on some of these occasions the defendant was at a distance somewhat remote from the scene of the plaintiff's sufferings, it is too much to ask the Court to believe that the identity of each threat and of each ' accident ' (I use the word in the sense in which it is employed in the Workmen's Compensation Act, 1925) —an identity of time, of place and of nature—was due solely to coincidence. There is no doubt of the defendant's responsibility, and I will go so far as to say that he seems on the evidence to be suffering from that form of psychological abnormality or perversion known as sadism—a delight in inflicting suffering—and I would advise him to consult a psychotherapist without delay.

" Since, then, and as I have held, the plaintiff has suffered damage in the enjoyment of his property through the acts of the defendant, I have now to see whether those acts were justified or not. It is well established that a person cannot, by applying his property to special or extraordinary uses or purposes, restrict the rights of his neighbour in the ordinary and legitimate enjoyment of his land, or impose upon his neighbour burdens which, in the ordinary course of things, he is not called upon to bear (*Robinson* v. *Kilvert*). Such extraordinary user may consist of interference with the course of natural agencies, the use of premises for unusual, non-natural or noxious purposes, the bringing on to premises of matter which is likely to do damage if it escapes (*Rylands* v. *Fletcher*), and the user of property for dangerous purposes. The principle has been applied in innumerable cases to poisonous substances, electrical discharge, the pollution or vitiation of the atmosphere by noxious fumes, steam, smoke, smells and even the germs of disease, while other well-known instances (relating to material interference with ordinary comfort) are those of noises and vibrations. These instances are not exhaustive, and I have no hesitation in adapting the well-known and succinct phrasing of a very great judge and stating that the categories of nuisance (like those of negligence) are never closed. The principles which I have enunciated are wide enough to cover the putting by the defendant of the property in his occupation to non-natural or extraordinary user for the purpose of chemical, physical, biological or psychical research, the practice of occult arts or so-called magic—name it what you will—which has surrounded the plaintiff with creatures (corporeal or incorporeal) of a noxious and malignant nature, displeasing noises, unwholesome stenches, offensive sights and disturbances of the aether occasioning violent bodily and mental pangs. I hold, therefore, that the defendant has committed a number of nuisances calculated to injure the plaintiff in the enjoyment of his property. I have now to consider the remedy to which he is entitled.

" The jurisdiction of the Court to grant an injunction in nuisance cases is in aid of the legal right. At common law the plaintiff's remedy is in damages, but a Court of Equity has always power to prevent by injunction that sort of injury for which damages would not be an adequate or sufficient remedy. (*Imperial Gas Light and Coke Co.* v. *Broadbent.*) A special case for the exercise of the equitable jurisdiction arises where the injury is of a continuing or recurring nature, and this is particularly so where the defendant has acted in a high-handed or oppressive manner. I am emphatically of opinion that the present case is one in which the legal remedy of damages is utterly inadequate, both from the nature of the acts complained of, their continuance over a long period of years, and in particular the unconscionable conduct of the defendant and the plaintiff's incapacity. Having regard to all these matters, I cannot imagine a case in which the intervention of equity could be more appropriately invoked, or its jurisdiction more usefully exercised.

"Similar considerations apply to the trespass of which the plaintiff complains and to which the defendant has now abandoned his defence. Any threatened or apprehended trespass will be restrained, if the Court thinks fit, whether the defendant is or is not in possession under any claim of title or otherwise, and this is undoubtedly a case for the exercise of the Court's discretion in the plaintiff's favour.

"A suggestion has been made by counsel during the course of this trial that the two forms of injunction which I propose to grant—for trespass and for nuisance—are mutually incompatible, or, to put it differently, that an effective restraint on the defendant from trespassing on the plaintiff's island would render any further restraint in respect of the nuisance superfluous. But such a contention would be ill-conceived. In these days of rapid scientific progress considerations of space and remoteness are of ever-decreasing significance, and mere distance from the scene of danger no longer affords that protection on which reliance could formerly be placed. For the same reason such phrases, in the law of nuisance, as 'neighbour' and 'neighbouring property' are susceptible of a wide and extended meaning. In this case, particularly, the plaintiff is not unnaturally apprehensive that even without trespassing on his property, without ever setting foot again on the island which is the plaintiff's by right—nay, without even quitting the shores of England—the defendant might engage in practices or machinations which could, by some means or other, bring about a repetition of the injuries of which he complains. It would be intolerable that a remedy so hardly won should prove nugatory, and I therefore propose to make assurance doubly sure by restraining the defendant from committing nuisance as well as trespass against the plaintiff's enjoyment of his land.

"I therefore give judgment in favour of the plaintiff, and there will be a perpetual injunction to restrain the defendant from trespassing on the plaintiff's property, and from using or permitting any premises of the defendant's to be used, or for carrying on his work or researches, in any manner whereby a nuisance may be occasioned to the annoyance or injury of the plaintiff or his property."

A CLOSE FINISH

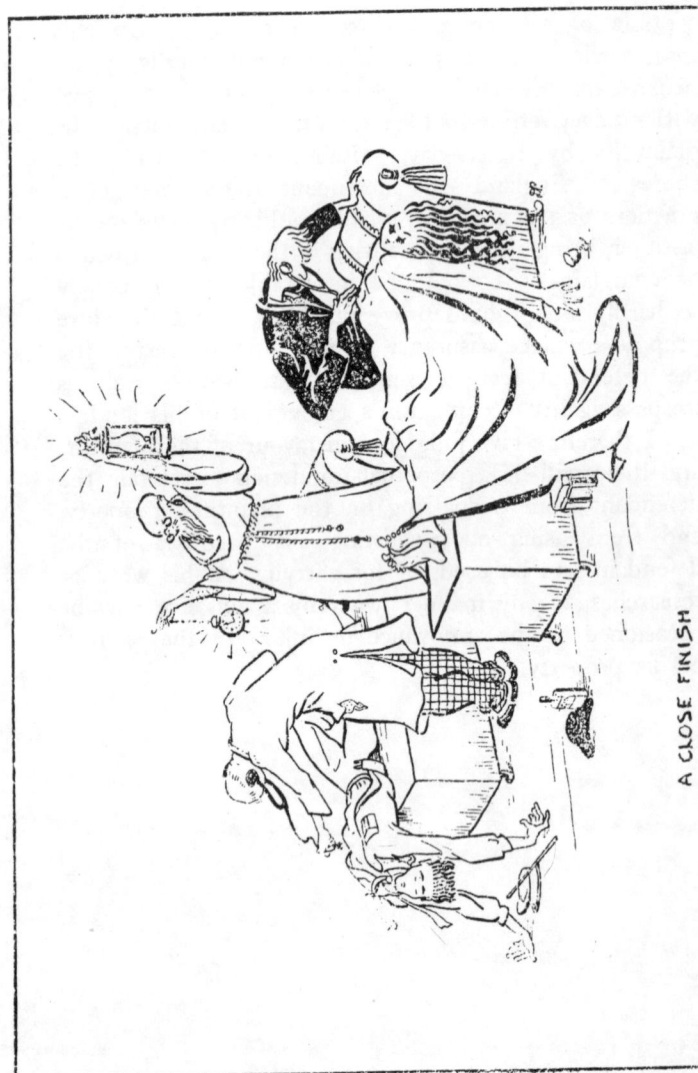

Probate, Divorce and Admiralty Division
(Probate).

IN THE ESTATE OF ROMEO MONTAGUE, CAPULET v. MONTAGUE.

Nuncupative will—Infant testator—Wills Act, 1837, s. 7—"Actual military service"—Wills (Soldiers and Sailors) Act, 1918, s. 1—Whether valid appointment of executrix—Whether revocation by marriage—Wills Act, 1837, s. 18—No consent by parents—Marriage Act, 1836, s. 10—"Wife" under sixteen years of age—Age of Marriage Act, 1929, s. 1—"Marriage" void—Survivorship—Law of Property Act, 1925, s. 184—Grant de bonis non.

THE President delivered a reserved judgment in this probate action, in which Mr. Capulet claimed that the Court should pronounce for the validity of a nuncupative will made by the deceased, Mr. Romeo Montague, three months before his death, and for a grant of administration *de bonis non* to his estate. The defendant, Mr. Montague (Senior) asked for a declaration that the deceased died intestate and for a grant of simple administration to himself as father of the deceased.

His Lordship, after stating the substance of the pleadings, continued as follows:—

' "The legal issues involved in this case are of a complicated kind, and the facts which it has been incumbent upon me to investigate are distressing in the extreme.

It can indeed, have been but seldom that a judge of this Division has had to deal with a series of events of so melancholy a nature, or calling for so much human sympathy with all concerned. *Sunt lacrimae rerum et mentem mortalia tangunt* is not a legal maxim, but I am tempted to apply it to the affecting details of this case.

"The form of the purported will is unusual, and I propose to defer consideration of that point until I have dealt with the question of capacity.

"The first point alleged by the defendant is that the deceased was at the time of his death only nineteen years of age, and thus obviously an infant at the date when the purported will was made. The deceased's birth certificate has been produced and corroborates this allegation, and the other evidence which I have heard leaves no doubt in my mind that the infancy of the deceased at the material date is beyond dispute. *Primâ facie*, therefore, it would seem from this part of the evidence that the deceased had no testamentary capacity and that the purported will is, under the terms of s. 7 of the Wills Act, 1837, invalid.

"Further extrinsic evidence, however, has been put forward to rebut this *primâ facie* presumption, on the ground that the deceased was a soldier in actual military service at the material date. It is not disputed that the deceased had, for about a year preceding his death, held the rank of Second-Lieutenant in his local regiment, and that, together with other members of that regiment, he was ordered to mobilise for active service during the serious civil disturbances which were, unfortunately, of frequent occurrence in his native city in that year. There is sufficient evidence that special powers were by statute conferred upon the Government to deal with the situation, including the right to make, by Order in Council, such military dispositions as might be necessary to cope therewith. There is also satisfactory evidence that the deceased took part, with his regiment, on several occasions in active operations in connection with these disturbances. It was strongly urged upon me, by counsel for the defendant, that most of the decided cases on the meaning of the term 'in actual military service' (the equivalent of the Roman phrase *in expeditione*) use the expression 'a state of war,' and refer to the existence of hostilities abroad." His Lordship here dealt in detail with *Re Yates* and other authorities, and proceeded:—

"However, learned counsel could refer me to no positive rule of law that foreign hostilities are essential to constitute a 'state of war' in this sense, and I am not prepared to hold that an officer who takes part with his regiment, under the orders of the Government of the day, in operations in connection with civil disturbances is any less in actual military service for the purposes of s. 1 of the Wills (Soldiers and Sailors) Act, 1918, than one who is on duty with an expeditionary force which has proceeded, or is about to proceed, abroad. On this part of the case, therefore, I decide as a matter of law that the deceased, though an infant at the material date, was a soldier in actual military service, and thus possessed the necessary testamentary capacity to validate the purported will, assuming that in other respects it is a proper testamentary document.

"I now turn to the question of form. The document in question is of a highly informal nature; it is unattested, and, if it is to be admitted as a will at all, it must be under the terms of the statute to which I have referred, regarding soldiers (including infant soldiers) in actual military service. It consists of a letter addressed to Miss Juliet Capulet, the daughter of the plaintiff, and is couched in the most extravagant terms. After making a number of effusive protestations of undying affection for the addressee, of no particular relevance to the present issue, the deceased proceeds, in a passage of extreme ambiguity, to refer to the probability of his continued absence from her side bringing about his imminent demise ; and he thereupon expresses a desire to give her the sun, the moon and the stars, followed, in successive paragraphs, by a purported dedication to her of his heart, his life and his soul. In none of these cases is it possible to construe the subject-matter of these purported gifts as falling under the head of a specific, demonstrative or residuary devise or bequest—still less of a pecuniary legacy ; it is impossible even to hold that any of the celestial bodies mentioned formed part of his real estate, or that a testator's heart, life or soul constitute personal property of which he is competent to dispose. These, however, are essentially questions of construction which fall within the purview of another Court ; here they are relevant only to the question of form. It must be admitted, however, that the writer in one place uses the phrase, 'All I possess shall be yours,' and the same expression is repeated, with variations, no less than six times in the course of the letter. Having regard to the references to his approaching death, and to the desire, clearly enough expressed, that the addressee shall take his entire estate ; having regard also to the very definite rule that it is not necessary (in order to validate as a will an informal document made by a soldier in actual military service) to show that he knew he was making a will, or had power to do so informally, I have come, with some hesitation, to the conclusion that this letter, as regards form, constitutes a valid testamentary document in the peculiar circumstances of the case.

"The question of executorship presents less difficulty. There is a clear indication on the part of the testator that Miss Capulet was not only to take the whole of his estate, but also to provide for his funeral and testamentary expenses. In no other sense can I construe the direction in the letter, 'Bury me in the garden of your heart!'; stripped of its poetic imagery the intention is beyond dispute. I have accordingly no hesitation in holding that Miss Juliet Capulet was by the deceased's will appointed sole executrix according to the tenor, as well as sole beneficiary of his estate. (See *In the Goods of Brown*.)

"This, however, is by no means the end of the matter. The defendant alleges that the document in question, even though held to be a valid will, was revoked under s. 18 of the Wills Act, 1837, by the marriage of the testator to Miss Juliet Capulet some two months after its execution. In support of this contention, he produces a certificate from the Registrar-General relating to the said marriage, corroborated by the evidence of the Rev. John Lawrence, by whom he alleges it was duly solemnised.

"The testimony of the Rev. John Lawrence amounts to this—that the testator, whom he had known for some time, produced to him a certificate of the Superintendent Registrar (granted with licence), together with the purported consent in writing of the bride's parents, the testator having admitted to him that she was under full age. I am loth to animadvert unfavourably on the conduct of a clerk in holy orders, but I am bound to say that his conduct throughout appears to have been negligent in the extreme ; some might be tempted to describe it in stronger terms. This reverend gentleman admits that, while the parents' consent was a consent to the marriage of their daughter, the name of the bridegroom was not mentioned therein ; the parents agree that they consented to her marrying, but that the prospective bridegroom was a Mr. Paris, a long-standing friend of the family, and that they would never have consented to the marriage to the deceased testator had they known it was in contemplation. This may perhaps explain the secrecy on which the witness says the bride and bridegroom insisted—a secrecy which he, strangely enough, did not conceive it his duty to dispel.

"Be that as it may, I am constrained to accept the combined effect of the evidence before me that the parties did actually go through a form of marriage before the Rev. John Lawrence, in respect of which a registrar's certificate was duly issued. It is clear law that the lack of proper consent by the parents does not invalidate such a marriage, since the consent required by s. 10 of the Marriage Act, 1836, is only directory. But for the further evidence submitted by the plaintiff I should have been bound to hold the marriage good and the will duly revoked thereby.

"It is alleged, however, by Mr. and Mrs. Capulet, supported by a birth certificate and by the testimony of their family nurse, that the bride was, at the time of the purported marriage, only fourteen years of age. This shocking state of affairs was fully investigated before me in this Court, and all three witnesses were subjected to the most searching cross-examination for several hours each. I cannot conceive how any self-respecting parents can have been so ignorant of the law as to consent to the marriage of their daughter, whether to Mr. Paris or anybody else, at an age prohibited by Act of Parliament; their excuse that they were unaware of the change in the law effected by s. 1 of the Age of Marriage Act, 1929, appears to me to be inadequate. I found the nurse a particularly unsatisfactory witness; her garrulity was especially irritating; and I would advise her to indulge her taste for ribald and rambling anecdote on the childhood idiosyncrasies of her charges elsewhere than in a Court of law. It is with deep feelings of repugnance that I must come to the conclusion that this purported marriage was null and void *ab initio* for want of age. The nurse's further evidence that this so-called marriage was actually consummated shocks me more deeply still.

"Since then this 'marriage' is no marriage at all, the will is not revoked thereby, and it must be admitted to probate as it stands. The only remaining question is to whom probate is to be granted, and to give my reasons for my decision on this question I must recapitulate the events leading up to the death of the testator and his reputed 'wife.'

"It appears from the evidence that these unfortunate young people found the burden of their secret more than they were able to bear. Their lot was rendered harder by the fact that, in the continued absence of the testator with his regiment, the plaintiff and his wife, ignorant of what had happened, pestered their unhappy child, with cajolements and even threats, to marry Mr. Paris, whose wealth and station in life rendered the match a suitable one in their not entirely disinterested eyes. Juliet's actual motive is obscure, but there is little doubt in my mind that the combination of circumstances —her ' husband's ' absence, her own equivocal position and the solicitations of her parents—reduced the poor child to a state of mind in which she contemplated taking her own life. I am further of opinion that the testator was not only privy to this design, but that he, himself, had a similar intention ; in other words, this desperate couple had decided upon what is popularly known as a ' suicide pact.'

" The detailed happenings of the tragic night are veiled in the obscurity of death. The plaintiff and the defendant have each described, in moving terms, the discovery of the bodies of their respective children, still locked in each other's arms. The deceased had both met their deaths by stabbing, self-inflicted. The medical evidence, which has been called to prove the probable times of the respective deaths, was inconclusive ; all that these eminent pathologists could tell me was that the deaths took place at approximately the same time. The other evidence of what took place on the fatal night is most conflicting. On the one hand, Mr. Balthasar, who acted as servant and orderly to Mr. Romeo Montague, told of accompanying him to the place where the bodies were subsequently found, and of leaving him in a very distressed condition, but certainly still living, alone with the dead body of Miss Capulet. I found Mr. Balthasar a very credible witness, but, on the other hand, there is the evidence (for what it is worth) of the Rev. John Lawrence, who swore positively that Miss Capulet was not dead at that time, but merely unconscious, having taken a large (but not fatal) overdose of aspirin in order to terrify her parents and force them to give up their design to marry her against her will. In view of the unreliable character of this witness, I cannot wholly accept his evidence; yet he was unshaken on this point in cross-examination, and his testimony is sufficient to raise a doubt in my mind as to whether Miss Capulet was actually dead when Mr. Balthasar saw her.

"In all the circumstances, I have no alternative but to have recourse to the Rule enacted by sect. 184 of the Law of Property Act, 1925, which provides that, in circumstances such as the present, the deaths shall be presumed to have occurred in order of seniority, and accordingly the younger shall be deemed to have survived the elder. I hold that Miss Capulet survived the testator, and there will, therefore, be a grant of administration *de bonis non* of his estate to the plaintiff, her father, to whom letters of administration in respect of her estate have already been granted. The costs will be paid out of the estate."

AN IMMATERIAL WITNESS

CENTRAL CRIMINAL COURT.

THE KING v. CLAUDIUS AND GERTRUDE

Criminal Law—Alleged Murder—Conflicting evidence as to cause of death—Ghost subpœnaed as prosecution witness—Non-appearance—Contempt—Whether alleged statement of ghost admissible as dying declaration—Hearsay—Purchase of poison by prisoner—Dangerous Drugs Act, 1920—Evidence insufficient—Acquittal.

THE trial was concluded yesterday, at the Central Criminal Court, Elsinore, before Mr. Justice Fortinbras, of Claudius, described as of no occupation, and Gertrude, his wife. The male prisoner was charged with the wilful murder of the late Mr. Hamlet, and the wife with being an accessory before the fact.

The Judge, in summing up the case to the jury, made the following observations:—

"It is admitted that the late Mr. Hamlet met his death last year in mysterious circumstances, while sleeping in his orchard, where it was his custom in the afternoon to rest from his daily labours. It is also common ground that the cause of death was at the time officially stated to be the bite of a serpent.

"Your task, and mine, is no light one, for we are at the outset brought face to face with a conflict of medical evidence on a vital issue—namely, the cause of death. On the one hand you have heard the evidence of Dr. Rosencrantz, a distinguished pathologist of foreign extraction, who was called by the prosecution to prove that, in the autopsy which he carried out some two weeks after the death, he discovered distinct traces of the poison known as hebona, which he is of opinion was introduced into the ear of the sleeping victim. I need not go again into the details of his evidence, which explained with admirable lucidity the effect of the drug on the blood stream of a human being.

"On the other side, Dr. Guildenstern, a rising young practitioner, who examined the body within a few moments of the tragedy, is equally positive that death resulted from the bite of a serpent. I was unable to take judicial notice of the existence of these *fauna* in a place of so temperate a climate as Elsinore, but evidence has been given by Professor Polonius that such creatures *feræ naturæ* have from time to time been observed in these parts. You may have found Professor Polonius at times an over-discursive witness; I myself had to rebuke him several times for rambling in his replies to counsel's questions; but it is your duty to see that natural irritation on that account does not lead you to treat his evidence as unreliable on a matter of which he has made a special study.

"Between the evidence of these two medical experts it is your difficult duty to choose, and on your choice will in great measure depend the verdict you are to give. But it is my duty to warn you that unless you are convinced beyond all reasonable doubt that Dr. Rosencrantz is right and that the dead man met his end by the effect of poison, it is your duty to acquit the accused. And even if you come to the conclusion that the death was caused by poison, extraneously injected, you will even then not be entitled to convict the male prisoner unless you are certain that it was his hand that injected the deadly fluid.

"It is now my duty to draw your attention to what is perhaps the least satisfactory part of the case for the prosecution—namely, the witness (unhappily now absent) who is alleged by three persons to have made his appearance on the castle walls shortly after the date of the tragedy. Counsel for the prosecution made much of this in his opening speech, and was emphatic that this so-called ghost would be called to give evidence in support of his case. Had this witness appeared, not merely on the castle ramparts, but in this Court, I will not say that the sequence of events in this trial might not have taken a different turn, but the fact remains that this witness has not taken the stand. Counsel for the prosecution has assured you that a *subpoena* was duly served—in itself a matter of some considerable difficulty, and, I may say, delicacy, and the diligence of the solicitor concerned is to be commended. But the writ has been disregarded, and I should have had no hesitation in ordering an attachment for contempt forthwith, were I not only too well convinced that this contumelious witness is beyond the jurisdiction of this Court."

His Lordship here pointed significantly downwards, and continued:—

"For the actual appearance of the ghost we have the evidence of three witnesses—Hamlet, the dead man's son, Horatio, described as a graduate of Wittenburg University, and Marcellus, who holds the rank of Captain in His Majesty's Army. Their evidence exhibited a marked inconsistency, and you may come to the conclusion that some or all of them are persons who are not to be believed on their oaths. Alternatively, you may more charitably conclude that, in plain language, they had been drinking.

Evidence has been elicited by the defence, in cross-examination, that it is customary, among the class to which these young men belong, to indulge in excessive potations of alcoholic liquor, even though it be a custom, as one of them picturesquely phrased it, 'more honoured in the breach than in the observance.'

"These witnesses were closely questioned by the defence on the appearance, movements and gestures of this alleged ghost. It is my duty to recall to your minds the varying answers they gave." His Lordship here read from his notes and continued: "I myself was most careful to seek corroboration on one point which is vital to identity, when I enquired whether the figure's beard was grizzled. The answer I got" (his Lordship again referred to his notes) "was this—'Oh, yes, my Lord, he had his beaver up.'

"You may consider that that answer, in its incoherence, its inconclusiveness—I might almost say, its levity—is typical of the evidence of these witnesses. It is for you to say whether they are to be believed or not.

"But the witness Hamlet goes further still. Not content with all this, he has sworn that the ghost actually spoke to him and gave him a highly circumstantial account of the manner of the victim's death. Counsel for the defence was quick to argue that such evidence was inadmissible as hearsay. Counsel for the prosecution was inclined to think that it might be receivable as a dying declaration. He pursued somewhat elaborately a theory that a ghost might be considered as a species of incorporeal interest such as is commonly met with in the more metaphysical discussions in the Chancery Division. However that may be, it is not for you to concern yourselves with their legal arguments, nor should you be led irrelevantly to speculate upon what this alleged ghost, if indeed it ever existed, might or might not have have told the witness. For I hold, and shall continue to hold, until I am constrained by higher authority to hold otherwise, that matters which a witness alleges he was told by a notional ghost are not admissible evidence in a Court of criminal law.

"Apart from all this there is little evidence against the accused. True, there was some talk of a purchase by the male prisoner of a vial of hebona for the purpose, as he says, of killing slugs. This poison does not appear in the regulations made under the Dangerous Drugs Act, 1920, and you must not dismiss from your minds the possibility that it may have been purchased for this or some other equally innocuous purpose. You must ask yourselves whether, indeed, there is any real evidence tending to connect him with the crime, if crime it was.

"In conclusion, it is my duty to direct your attention to the case of the female prisoner. The prosecution have contented themselves with dwelling on the indecent haste with which she married the male prisoner within two months after the death of her former husband. The period is short; the proceedings, I admit, were somewhat unusual. The explanation given by the wife, that her motive was economy, that (as she expressed it) ' the funeral baked meats did coldly furnish forth the marriage tables,' may not conform to your ideas of the mourning duties owed to her late husband by a spouse newly bereaved. But these are merely matters of tact and good taste with which we in this Court have nothing to do. The sole question before you is whether or not, without actually participating, she was accessory to the alleged murder—whether she in fact counselled or procured its committal. It is my duty as a matter of law to direct you that no evidence has been produced on which you could so find, and I direct you to return a verdict of acquittal."

The jury, without leaving the box, found both prisoners *not guilty*.

In discharging the prisoners the judge said:—

"It only remains for me to say that I am in entire agreement with the verdict given and that, in my opinion, this prosecution ought never to have been instituted."

HOLDING OUT

KING'S BENCH DIVISION.

LEONATO v. BORACHIO AND ANOTHER.

Defamation—Entry by first defendant into plaintiff's bedroom—Words and gestures of first defendant—Whether reasonably capable of bearing innuendo alleged—Slander of Women Act, 1891—Personation of plaintiff by second defendant—Libel—Gestures alone not constituting slander.

JUDGMENT of Mr. Justice Pedro (sitting without a jury):

"In this case Miss Hero Leonato, of Messina, claims damages from Mr. Borachio, of Arragon, and Margaret, his wife, the former for slander, under the Slander of Women Act, 1891, and the latter for slander and libel. The innuendoes in the Statement of Claim against each of the defendants are practically identical, namely, that the male defendant by spoken words, published of and concerning the plaintiff to persons other than the plaintiff, and the female defendant by signs, gestures, actions, and by an impersonation of the plaintiff, published as aforesaid, implied that the plaintiff was unchaste, that her behaviour and bearing were indecent and improper, that she was a woman of low moral character, and that she was unfit for and unworthy of marriage to Mr. Claudio, to whom she was affianced.

"The evidence which has been offered before me on behalf of the plaintiff, which remains for the most part unrebutted, discloses a sad story of human envy and malice. The plaintiff is the daughter of Mr. Leonato, the Governor of Messina, and belongs to a family which, both by descent and service to the State, bears the finest reputation. The lady herself is well known to be of the highest character and repute. Some six months ago she became affianced to Mr. Claudio, a gentleman of good family, and the marriage was to have been celebrated within a few weeks after the betrothal.

"The female defendant was at all material times a lady's-maid, in the service of the plaintiff, and the evidence shows that she is a person addicted to practical joking of a malicious kind. I have formed my own opinion of this defendant by observing her demeanour in the witness-box, and I will say at once that there is, in my opinion, as much of envy and malice in her character as of the sense of humour in which she takes so much pride. Be that as it may, the evidence incontrovertibly shows that she and her husband together concerted an arrangement calculated to render the plaintiff ridiculous and, worse than that, contemptible in the eyes of her future husband and of the world that knew her.

"The male defendant, whose motives in the matter are even more reprehensible than those of his wife, appears to have conceived an implacable hatred of Mr. Claudio, the plaintiff's future husband. Concealing this as best he could, and having first made all preparations with his wife to practise the deception I am now about to describe, he went to Mr. Claudio and, by specious protestations of sincerity, persuaded him to keep watch, with witnesses, the night before the wedding, on the plaintiff's sleeping chamber. The female defendant taking advantage of the plaintiff's temporary absence in the bath, assumed the plaintiff's clothing and, standing by the plaintiff's open window, received her husband, who had climbed thither by means of a ladder, with lively demonstrations of affection. The husband, addressing her as 'Hero' (the plaintiff's own name), with many endearing epithets and much show of a clandestine intrigue, eventually suffered himself to be invited into the room, the window being then closed and the curtains drawn. All this elaborate subterfuge was of course practised for the deception of the affianced husband and his witnesses, who were not unnaturally shocked and outraged by what they thought they had seen.

"If Mr. Claudio had there and then pursued his investigations and followed the male defendant to the plaintiff's room, the deception would have been discovered on the spot, and much subsequent misfortune avoided. That he did not do so is due to his friends who, with the best of motives, persuaded him to avoid an unseemly brawl, but to take a more subtle revenge. This took the form of attending the next day in the local church, where the marriage ceremony was to take place, and there, in the presence of a large and distinguished congregation, accusing the plaintiff of unchastity. The shame of such an accusation, made publicly in such circumstances, and the shock it caused to a lady of delicate sensibility, may well be imagined. I am happy to know that the subsequent disclosure of the truth has brought about a reconciliation, and that the marriage will shortly be celebrated; but the damage to the plaintiff's health, and the mental suffering which she has undergone, are matters which must weigh heavily with any Court which has to assess damages, always assuming that the causes of action are well founded in law.

"This question of law, unfortunately, is one which it is not easy to decide. So far as the male defendant is concerned, the words uttered by him, of which the plaintiff complains, are few and simple—'Hero, my darling! Hero, my sweet! At last we are alone!' It is clear that these words, taken alone, are not *primâ facie* defamatory of the plaintiff. The plaintiff, however, has assigned to these words the innuendo which I have quoted above, and the burden of proving that that innuendo is the true meaning lies upon the plaintiff to establish. (*Leng (John) & Co.* v. *Langlands*.) Since the language taken by itself does not establish the innuendo, it is for the plaintiff to show that there is extrinsic evidence to prove that the sense alleged is the sense in which the words were intended to be construed, and were in fact construed, by those who heard them uttered. (*Ibid.*) The defendant has put forward the defence that the words quoted are not in law capable of bearing the meaning ascribed to them and, further, that those words did not in fact convey that meaning to those who heard them. So far as the second part of the defence is concerned (taking upon myself for the moment the functions of a jury), I am in no doubt whatsoever that the words used in fact conveyed to Mr. Claudio and his witnesses precisely the meaning alleged. But the preliminary question which I have to decide is whether they are in law capable of such a meaning.

"I have been referred to a large number of authorities, and I think it will suffice for me to state shortly the principles which can be deduced from the relevant cases. These are as follows:—

"A statement, though literally true, may involve an innuendo which is defamatory and actionable. (*Chap-

man v. *Ellesmere*.) Even though the words complained of may (as here) be innocent or even laudatory of the plaintiff, he or she may assign to them, by innuendo, a defamatory meaning, if such meaning is justified by the circumstances of the particular case (*Boydell* v. *Jones*). If such an innuendo is alleged (as is the case before us), it is the duty of the Court to consider not merely the words complained of and the context in which they were spoken, but also the manner and occasion of the publication, the persons to whom they were published and all other facts which are properly in evidence as affecting the meaning of the words, in the particular circumstances of the case. (*Capital* & *Counties Bank* v. *Henty*.)

"Taking all the above-mentioned matters into account, can it be said that the words spoken and published by the male defendant were capable in law of (I use the statutory words) 'imputing unchastity' to the plantiff? I consider the context in which the words were spoken— a context, not indeed of words, but of acts—acts of affection and intimacy, embraces and the like. I consider the manner and occasion of the publication—the man on the ladder by the plaintiff's open window, the figure personating the plaintiff within the room, the apparently clandestine nature of the assignation, the subsequent entry and the darkening of the window. I consider also the persons to whom the words were— deliberately and maliciously—published—the plaintiff's affianced husband, the friends of her own circle, as witnesses. Taking all these matters into account, I am bound to hold that these seemingly innocent words are abundantly capable of bearing, in law, the meaning which the innuendo assigns to them. The male defendant therefore fails in both parts of his defence, and there will be judgment for the plaintiff against him in respect of the spoken words.

"I now turn to the case against the female defendant. The claim against her is again for slander *per se*, under the Act of 1891, and also for libel. The defence in this part of the case is that, in the absence in the Statement of Claim of any allegation of defamatory words spoken or written by the defendant, the Statement of Claim discloses no cause of action; alternatively this defendant pleads that the said signs, gestures, actions and impersonation on her part were harmless or equivocal and are not capable in law of bearing the defamatory meaning alleged in the innuendo.

"So far as the alleged signs, gestures and actions are concerned, the plaintiff is here placed in some difficulty, not so much under the substantive law of slander as under the established rules of pleading. In the days when the strictest adherence to these rules was insisted on, it was essential that the actual words alleged to have been used by the defendant, and not merely their substance, should be quoted *verbatim* in the Statement of Claim, and at one time proof of the actual words pleaded was regarded as essential (*Capital* & *Counties Bank* v. *Henty, supra*). Counsel has reminded me that the strictness of the old rule against variance in the language has long since gone by the board, and that nowadays proof of words substantially identical with those pleaded is admissible. This, however, does not resolve the plaintiff's difficulty, for it appears on the authorities that the actual words alleged to have been uttered must, as a matter of pleading, be set forth in the Statement of Claim. I am well aware of, and have already referred to, the rule that words not in themselves *primâ facie* defamatory may be explained and interpreted by accompanying signs, gestures or other circumstances to justify the innuendo which the plaintiff places upon them; but Counsel have been unable to refer me to any case where such signs, gestures or actions have been held to constitute a slander without any accompanying words. I am constrained, therefore, for technical reasons, to hold that the plaintiff fails in her action against the female defendant in respect of the alleged slander.

"But the plaintiff's claim against this defendant is entered also upon the ground of libel, in respect of the defendant's impersonation of the plaintiff. Here again no words are alleged in the Statement of Claim, but on this part of the question there is weighty authority in the plaintiff's favour. In the well-known case of *Monson* v. *Tussaud's, Ltd.*, the Court of Appeal dealt with the claim of a plaintiff alleging libel against defendants who had exhibited a wax effigy of the plaintiff in proximity to the so-called 'Chamber of Horrors' in their waxworks exhibition. In that case Lord Justice Lopes said:

"'Libels are generally in writing or in print; but this is not necessary; the defamatory matter may be conveyed in some other permanent form. For instance, a statue, a caricature, an effigy, chalk marks on a wall, signs or pictures may constitute a libel.'

"This *dictum* is well supported (if support be necessary) by a number of cases which have been cited in argument but to which it is not necessary for me to refer in detail.

"This, then, is the argument to which I must now address myself. If a lifeless thing like a picture, a statue or an effigy, either by reason of some intrinsic quality or characteristic, or (as in *Monson* v. *Tussaud's*, *supra*) by reason of the place and circumstances in which it is set up and exhibited, may constitute a libel on the person whom it purports to represent, does not the same apply to a living person who, by adopting the plaintiff's clothing, showing herself at the window of the plaintiff's room and otherwise by her behaviour, impersonates the plaintiff in a place and in circumstances which, if the plaintiff herself stood there, would reflect the gravest discredit upon her, bring her into hatred, ridicule or contempt, or depreciate the plaintiff in the eyes of right-thinking members of the community? I can find no distinction between the two cases. Indeed, I feel that I may adapt a well-known maxim from the law of criminal libel and say of the case before us—'The greater the likeness, the greater the libel.' Had the defendants been content to carry out their defamatory intention by a picture, a caricature, a statue or an effigy of the plaintiff, representing her in improper or equivocal surroundings, the authorities show that such representation would have constituted an actionable libel. It is impossible to say that they can escape that result because the defamatory portrayal of the plaintiff was through the agency of a living person, the female defendant, posing in the plaintiff's likeness.

"In the result there must be judgment, with costs, against the male defendant for slander and against the female defendant for libel. There will be judgment, without costs, for the female defendant against the plaintiff on the issue of slander. I assess the damages against the defendants at 1,500*l.* each, and I desire to add the comment that the female defendant may account herself fortunate that the plaintiff did not resort to criminal proceedings against her."

A CLOAK FOR DECEPTION

KING'S BENCH DIVISION

PYRAMUS *v.* BANK OF BABYLON, LTD.

Contiguous tenements—Fissure in party wall—Law of Property Act, 1925, s. 38 and First Schedule—Building Societies Act, 1939, s. 9(1)—Oral communications through fissure—Clandestine meeting—Cloak mauled by lion—Suicide induced by shock of discovery—Claim in negligence—Fatal Accidents Acts, 1846 to 1908—Law Reform (Misc. Provns.) Act, 1934, s. 1—No duty to take care.

Judgment of Mr. Justice Theseus:

"In this case Mr. Pyramus of 4, Ninus Avenue, Babylon, as administrator of the estate of his deceased son, sues the Bank of Babylon, Ltd., as executor of Miss Thisbe, late of 6, Ninus Avenue, Babylon, under sect. 1 of the Law Reform (Miscellaneous Provisions) Act and the Fatal Accidents Acts, 1846 to 1908. The plaintiff alleges negligence against the deceased, Miss Thisbe, and claims damages against her estate for loss of expectation of life of his deceased son, Mr. Pyramus, Jnr.

"The defendant denies negligence on the part of the deceased Miss Thisbe, or that the damage was caused by negligence on her part, if any; and says that the death of the plaintiff's son was due solely to his own act and default.

"The facts are not in dispute, and they tell a tragic

enough story. As the addresses of the parties indicate, the plaintiff, with his wife and son, occupied premises in Ninus Avenue adjoining those in which the deceased Miss Thisbe lived with her parents. The respective premises were divided by a party wall which (as counsel has informed me) has recently been the subject of litigation in another Court under sect. 38 and Part V. of the First Schedule to the Law of Property Act, 1925. (I mention this in passing only because of its relevance to what follows.) Shortly after the Pyramus family went into occupation of No. 4, a large fissure appeared in this party wall, running from ground level to a height of some twenty feet. This circumstance rendered it possible for a person in a ground floor room in No. 4 to communicate with another person in the corresponding room in No. 6.

"The families first became acquainted as the result of litigation of a different order. Both houses had been purchased from the local builder with the aid of loans from the Babylon First Equitable Building Society, who had omitted to give to their respective mortgagors the notice in writing required by sect. 9(1) of the Building Societies Act, 1939. Upon the appearance of the fissure, to which I have referred, the families joined forces for the purpose of bringing the actions to which this omission had given rise against the Building Society under the warranty implied by the subsection to which I have referred, which resulted in a judgment against the Society. (The case is reported in 12 Bab. Ch. at p. 292.)

"It seems that during the progress of this litigation the two young people, Thisbe and Pyramus, met a great many times and conceived a great regard for each other. As, however, the proceedings were prolonged, differences arose between the two plaintiffs and eventually led to the further litigation under the Law of Property Act provisions to which I have referred above (14 Bab. Ch. 108). The friendship between the families developed a certain coolness, which eventually deepened into hostility, with the result that they ceased to visit one another; the present plaintiff forbade his son to see Thisbe, and her parents prevented her from meeting the younger Pyramus.

"The evidence shows that, not unnaturally, the cause which had led to the estrangement of the parents became a means of communication between the young lovers. Day by day, while the parents were away interviewing their respective solicitors, or going about their usual avocations, the young people (confined to the houses of their respective parents under lock and key) conversed with one another through the fissure in the party wall. There appears to be no doubt, from the dying declaration made by the deceased Thisbe, that they eventually became affianced, and their resolve to elope and marry awaited only a favourable opportunity of evading their parents' watch. They arranged that, as soon as the opportunity arose, they would meet outside the city at the monument known locally as 'Ninus' Tomb,' and from there travel together to a remote part of the country where they would find accommodation until the marriage could be celebrated.

"The opportunity came a few nights later, when, Thisbe's parents had inadvertently omitted to lock the door of her room. Notifying young Pyramus of her departure, she left the house while he made his preparations to escape from a first-storey window. Thisbe arrived safely at the appointed *rendezvous*, where she concealed herself in the shadow of the monument to await Pyramus' arrival.

"The lovers, in the ardour of their passion, had forgotten one important matter. The country outside Babylon is infested with wild beasts—a fact which is common knowledge in those parts—and it is considered unsafe for any human being to go abroad, alone and unarmed, after dark. Of this fact Thisbe, to her mortal peril, was now forcibly made aware. A lion roaming at large had scented her, and now advanced towards her out of the darkness. She had (as she has described) sufficient presence of mind to fling at him the week's family ration of raw meat, which she was carrying as provision for the journey, before she turned and fled up the steps of the monument for safety. Shutting the door against pursuit she saw, from the small grill window, that the lion had paused and was ravenously devouring the meat which she had thrown. Having finished his meal she saw him sniff at and paw her cloak, which she had dropped in her flight, but he was apparently satisfied for the moment and made off into the darkness. Still terrified she resolved to remain in safety in the monument till dawn.

"I now turn to the evidence given in the statement of the younger Pyramus before he expired. He had succeeded in climbing out of the window of his room and arrived at the tomb in the expectation of meeting his betrothed. What was his horror at finding only her bloodstained cloak and the mangled remains of what, in the darkness, he mistook for portions of a human body. The shock and despair of this discovery were too much for his highly-strung and sensitive nature. Convinced that Thisbe had died a horrible death, he took out the large clasp-knife with which he was in the habit of travelling and gave himself a wound which, first rendering him unconscious for a period, eventually proved mortal.

"It is clear from Thisbe's statement that he lay there till dawn, when she emerged from her refuge and found him bleeding and apparently dead. The consummation of the tragedy followed: she stabbed herself mortally with the same weapon, and was found shortly afterwards in a dying condition by two members of the local police force, who with commendable promptitude obtained medical assistance and took statements from her and from Pyramus, who had recovered consciousness for a few moments before he died. Such are the tragic circumstances which have given rise to this unfortunate action. I must not, however, allow my natural sympathy with the bereaved parents on either side to weigh with me in considering this case, and I now turn to the legal issues involved.

"Counsel for the plaintiff has argued that nervous shock, caused by the defendant's negligence, and accompanied by physical injury, gives rise to a claim in damages, and has referred me to the well-known cases of *Hambrook* v. *Stokes Bros.* and *Owens* v. *Liverpool Corp.* I am bound to hold that this proposition, as far as it goes, is well-founded, and I am prepared to accept counsel's further contention that a good cause of action must arise *à fortiori* if the nervous shock results in the death of the person whom the plaintiff represents. But the issues which arise in cases of this kind have recently been subjected to the review of the House of Lords itself in the case of *Hay* (or *Bourhill*) v. *Young*, to which the defendant's counsel has exhaustively referred, and it is proper that I should be guided (as, indeed, I am bound) by the *dicta* there delivered.

"As is well established by the law of this country, and as was succinctly phrased by Lord Russell of Killowen in the case to which I have last referred, 'a man is not liable for negligence in the air.' Quoting Lord Macmillan in *Donoghue* v. *Stevenson*, the noble and learned Lord added: 'The liability only arises where there is a duty to take care and where failure in that duty has caused damage.'

"Applying these *dicta* to the present circumstances, can it be said (and this is the first point) that the deceased Thisbe was, in the full legal sense, 'negligent' in what she did? To go out in darkness, alone and unarmed, in country which you know to be infested by wild animals, would clearly be described in ordinary non-legal parlance as a 'negligent' act—negligent, that is to say, so far as you yourself and your own safety are concerned. But has there been a breach of the duty to take care *vis-à-vis* any other person? Again I quote Lord Russell in *Hay* v. *Young, supra*: 'In my opinion such a duty only arises towards those individuals of whom it may be reasonably anticipated that they will be affected by the act which constituted the alleged breach.' Can it be said here that Thisbe could reasonably have anticipated that a person, in the circumstances in which Pyramus was situated, could be affected by the serious danger in which she was heedlessly placing herself? I cannot think so. So far as concerns physical danger to him from the wild beasts in the neighbourhood, she would know that he was armed and that two persons in company are safer than one person alone. So far as concerns physical danger to him, if the need had arisen of rescuing her from an attack, the circumstances of his acquiescence in the arrangement would have brought him within the maxim *volenti non fit injuria*, as happened in *Cutler* v. *United Dairies*. So far as concerns the events which actually occurred, could the deceased Thisbe reasonably anticipate that, her cloak having been mauled by the lion and she herself being hidden, the resultant surmise in the mind of Pyramus, if and when he arrived on the scene, would cause him physical injury by shock? I cannot think so. True, she was 'negligent' (in the ordinary non-legal sense) in dropping her cloak in the lion's path, but it is well-established that imminent danger may, 'in the agony of the moment,' justify an unusual course of action; pursued by the lion she cannot be expected to have acted with ordinary prudence or to have contemplated in that instant the hypothetical surmise which her involuntary act might put into his mind.

"Holding as I do, and as the House of Lords held in *Hay's Case*, that the deceased Thisbe was not guilty in law of such negligence as to give the deceased Pyramus the right af action which his personal representative claims, it is probably unnecessary for me to deal with the further question which arose in *Re Polemis and Furness Withy & Co.*, but lest my decision on the question of negligence should be overruled by a higher Court I deem it my duty to deal shortly with this further question. It was held in the *Polemis Case* that, once an act is properly characterised as negligent, then the negligent party is liable to the person to whom the duty of care was owed for everything that directly follows from the negligent act, whether or not it could have been foreseen as a natural and probable result of such act. Assuming, for the sake of argument, that Thisbe was guilty of negligence towards Pyramus in the full legal sense; can it be contended that his death directly followed therefrom? I can see no justification for such a contention. Pyramus died by his own hand—no doubt (to use the words of the coroner's jury) 'while the balance of his mind was disturbed.' Does a suicide 'directly follow' from the death of a loved one? Suicide is a crime—a form of felonious homicide. It is not excusable by the law of England even under duress, as some crimes are. If it had been proved that Pyramus was actually insane when he committed the *felo de se*, it might be possible to trace a direct chain of causation between the supposed death of his betrothed, the shock taking away his reason and his self-inflicted mortal wound. But there is no such proof; the evidence in his dying declaration—'I did not want to live without her '—is to the exact contrary. With all sympathy for both the victims and their bereaved relatives, I must hold that the chain of causation was deliberately broken by Pyramus himself: the shock left him still the power of choice, and his choice was death.

"In all the circumstances I have only to add that the action must be dismissed, with costs."

MISTAKE OF FACT

Probate Divorce and Admiralty Division (Divorce)

SEBASTIAN v. SEBASTIAN.

Mistake—Twin sister of Respondent in man's attire—Mistaken for man by petitioner—Petitioner's matrimonial intentions—Petitioner misled by resemblance of Respondent—Marriage to Respondent while so misled—Annulment suit—Cy-près doctrine not applicable—Petitioner intending to marry person "present and identified by sight and hearing"—Validity of marriage.

Judgment delivered by Mr. Justice Malvolio:
"This is a petition for a declaration of nullity of marriage filed by Mrs. Olivia Sebastian of "The Towers," Illyria, against the respondent her husband. The grounds of the petition are that the petitioner was mistaken in the identity of the person with whom she went through the marriage ceremony and that the purported marriage is therefore void *ab initio*.

"The evidence given by and on behalf of the petitioner discloses a strange and unusual set of circumstances and it is difficult to find any authority directly in point. The history of the matter, so far as agreed by all the witnesses or admitted by both parties, is as follows:—

"Mr. Sebastian, who is a young man of some twenty-five years of age, has a twin sister, Viola (now the Duchess of Illyria) whose resemblance to himself in stature, physical appearance and features is strikingly close. This lady has been subpoenaed as a witness in the case, and I have myself had the advantage of observing the extraordinary likeness between them. The lady in question affects the *coiffure* known generally as the 'Eton Crop' which has the effect both of increasing her resemblance to her brother and of removing one important visual mark which normally distinguishes her sex.

"It appears that, just over three months ago, the brother and sister (who are on the most affectionate terms) were on a yachting cruise in the neighbourhood of the Illyrian coast. The sister, in conformity with the prevailing fashion among the athletic young women of the day, discarded those feminine garments which are considered inappropriate to active and open-air pursuits; and adopted the male attire described colloquially as 'shirt and slacks.' In these garments she was accustomed to pass her time not only on board the yacht but in her excursions to the mainland whenever the vessel cast anchor.

"It is stated that, on one such occasion, the lady in question had gone ashore alone to explore the neighbouring countryside (which in parts is desolate and sparsely inhabited) and failed to return to the place where she had left the yacht's dinghy until the night was far advanced. The weather had changed for the worse, and when she reached the shore a storm was raging, the dinghy was nowhere to be seen, and the yacht was standing out to sea. Except for some anxiety for her brother's safety, as she says, the predicament in which she was placed left her comparatively unconcerned. Sooner or later, she was convinced, her absence would be noticed and her brother would return to seek her.

"The lady has made it clear in her evidence that, in view of the wild nature of the country to which I have referred, she realised that a premature disclosure of her sex might expose her to certain risks which could be avoided if she passed herself off as a man. I confess to an old-fashioned prejudice against the prevailing habits of young women who go out of their way to unsex themselves in matters of clothing and *coiffure*, and the sequel may serve to warn the thoughtless against the latent dangers in such practices. I will not, however, go so far as to say that the lady in question was ill-advised in what she did. She is obviously a person of considerable common sense and courage, and I have no hesitation in accepting her evidence of the reasons for what has been described (somewhat uncharitably) as a ' masquerade.'

"Garbed as she was, and with her youthful and healthy appearance, she had no difficulty in securing a temporary position as secretary of the Air Raid Precautions services on the estate of the young Duke of Illyria, who himself took an active part in the organisation. She has made no secret of the fact that she rapidly developed for him a strong and affectionate attachment which, however, except in the way of friendship, was not for some considerable time reciprocated. The Duke appears to have had no suspicion that she was other than she appeared— a young and attractive male person.

"It is admitted, and candidly admitted, even by the parties most concerned, that the Duke's affections were at that time centred on the petitioner. He visited her and wrote her a number of affectionate letters, and had several times proposed marriage—proposals which, however, the petitioner was not disposed to entertain.

"It had by this time become usual for Viola (as she then was) to combine her duties in the Civil Defence organisation with the carrying of messages of an intimate nature from the Duke to the petitioner. She did so, she says, with mixed feelings. On the one hand, duty and affection alike induced her to carry out such requests as he made with cheerfulness and alacrity ; on the other hand, her feelings for him made her an unwilling instrument of his courtship of another woman. In this dilemma she was deterred from making a full disclosure of her sex and station in life by the thought of the embarrassment it might provoke.

"Among the victims of this innocent deception was the petitioner herself. Within a short time she found herself attracted to this (as she thought) presentable young man, and attraction developed rapidly into a passion which nothing could assuage. Finding that her (somewhat unwomanly) advances produced no result, she made all preparations for marriage, trusting that she would finally succeed (as she has expressed it) in ' sweeping him off his feet.'

"The brother (the respondent) who had meanwhile been searching frantically for his sister in all parts of the countryside now comes back upon the scene. Happening to pass the petitioner's residence at a moment when she was leaving it, and being dressed in similar costume to the sister whom she knew only in male attire, he was amazed to be accosted by the petitioner in terms of affectionate familiarity. He has explained in the witness-box how he forthwith experienced the sensations which he has graphically attributed to ' love at first sight,' and was nothing loth, though somewhat taken back, when the petitioner proposed an early marriage. The ceremony between them was performed a few weeks later at the local Superintendent Registrar's office. I pass over the details of notice and licence, as no issue has been raised thereon. As regards form, the validity of the marriage is not in question.

"The petitioner alleges that, both at her first meeting with the respondent, at all material times prior to the marriage ceremony, and at that ceremony itself, she felt no doubt that the man before her was the person she had so long known as the emissary of the Duke. It was not until some days after the marriage (which had been duly consummated meanwhile) that she saw the respondent and his sister together, and realised the mistake under which she had been labouring. I have no reason to disbelieve her evidence on these points, though the respondent and his sister, not unnaturally, endeavoured to rebut her allegations on various grounds which it is not necessary for me to detail.

"I now turn to the law upon the subject, and up to a certain point the authorities are clear. It is necessary that the partes to a marriage, with full understanding of the nature of the contract, should freely consent to marry one another. It follows that, if there is a *bonâ fide* mistake as to the identity of the person with whom the contract is made, the marriage is void. The principle is well-established in contract law, and in this respect a contract of marriage is like any other contract. Fraudulent misrepresentation or concealment of material facts, on the other hand, does not generally affect the validity of a marriage to which the parties freely consented with a knowledge of the nature of the ceremony. (*Moss* v. *Moss*).

"The facts of this case are unprecedented, and none of the learned counsel who appeared has been able to refer me to any authority directly in point. Mistake there has certainly been, but is it such a mistake as will justify annulment?

"It behoves me at this point to deal with an ingenious argument on behalf of the respondent which was ably put by his counsel. The suggestion was that, on the analogy of the law of charitable trusts, the *cy-près* doctrine should be applied to this case. The doctrine is the well-known rule that, if the settlor of property on charitable trusts specifies an object of his bounty, but that object is, or later becomes, impossible or impracticable of performance, the gift will not fail, but the property will be used for some similar purpose as nearly as possible resembling the specified object (*Re Cunningham*). The application of the doctrine depends upon the paramount condition that the settlor has expressed, or the Court is able to infer, a general charitable intention. And the argument in this case, by analogy, is that, the condition having been amply fulfilled, the doctrine should be applied. The petitioner, it is said, has already expressed, by words and conduct, a general matrimonial intention; so much is abundantly clear on the evidence. She early specified an object of her matrimonial desires—a union with the lady who is now the Duchess of Illyria, but whom the petitioner at all material times believed to be a man. That object was at all times impossible of performance, by reason of the sex of the other party to the proposed marriage. Her general matrimonial intention may therefore (so runs the argument), without impropriety, be deemed to have been satisfied *cy-près* by her union with the respondent, who admittedly so closely resembles his sister that all persons concerned, including the petitioner herself, were convinced that they were one and the same person.

"This is an attractive argument, attractively presented, but I must not allow my admiration for its ingenuity to blind me to the maxim that equity follows the law. The prerequisites of a valid marriage are in law those which I have stated, and I know of no authority which would enable me, much as I might desire to do so, to override a well-established legal rule relating to validity on mere analogy with the subject of charitable trusts, which are the creature of equity and where the rules of equity are paramount.

"In the absence of authority in marriage cases, I am, however, at liberty to seek an analogy in the decided cases on the common law of contract. Here there is better guidance and, in my opinion, guidance of which I am justified in availing myself. If an offer made by A. is accepted by B. in the belief that the offer was made by another person, X., or if an offer intended by A. to be made to X. is accepted by B., there is no contract if the identity of the offeror or the offeree, as the case may be, is material to the other party as an inducement to him to enter into the contract. Thus far the principle of the law appears to support the contention of the petitioner. But there is, as is well known, an exception (or, rather, an apparent exception) to the rule. I refer to the well-known case of *Phillips* v. *Brooks*, where A., representing himself to be B. (a person of credit and stability), whose name was well-known to the plaintiff, presented himself in person at the plaintiff's shop and bought, by means of a worthless cheque, goods which he afterwards sold to the defendant. The plaintiff sued the defendant for the return of the goods, alleging that in the circumstances he had never parted with the property therein. Judgment was given for the defendant, Mr. Justice Horridge citing with approval the following passage from an American case in which similar circumstances arose :—

The minds of the parties met and agreed upon all the terms of the sale, the thing sold, the price and terms of payment, the person selling and the person buying. . . . He (the plaintiff) could not have supposed that he was selling to any other person; his intention was to sell to the person present and identified by sight and hearing; it does not affect the sale because the buyer assumed a false name or practised any other deceit to induce the vendor to sell.

" In the well-known leading case of *Lake* v. *Simmons*, the decision went the other way. There the facts showed that the goods which A. delivered to B. were so delivered only because B. represented, and A believed, that she was the wife of C., on whose credit A. had reason to believe he could rely. Viscount Haldane, distinguishing *Phillips* v. *Brooks* (*supra*), emphasised that in the earlier case there was *consensus* with the person identified by sight and hearing; whereas in the case then before him the belief of the contracting seller depended wholly on identity of character and capacity.

" It appears to me that the facts now before me bear a closer analogy to those of *Phillips* v. *Brooks* than to those of *Lake* v. *Simmons*. The petitioner met the respondent on a number of occasions before the marriage took place, they conversed at length and the usual intimacies of courtship were observed. Can it be doubted that the man whom the petitioner intended to marry was ' the person present and identified by sight and hearing ' ? Can the contract of marriage, freely and voluntarily entered into with that identical person, with a full knowledge of its nature, be affected by the petitioner's belief that the man before her, whom she was freely choosing as her husband, was the person to whom she had over a longer and earlier period made unsuccessful advances ? I can see no justification for such a proposition. There is here not even any question of misrepresentation, whether fraudulent or innocent, on the part of the respondent ; he made in fact no representation of any kind whatsoever ; the petitioner took him for her husband as he stood. I hold that there is no such mistake as will justify me in declaring that the marriage was *ab initio* void, and the petition must be dismissed."

ADJOURNMENT ON MOTION

COURT OF CRIMINAL APPEAL

SHIPTON AND OTHERS v. THE KING

Criminal Law—Partnership firm engaged in sorcery—Registration of Business Names Act, 1916, s. 1—Illegal purpose—Witchcraft Act, 1735, s. 4—False pretences—Larceny Act, 1916, s. 32—Venue—Criminal Law Act, 1826, s. 13—Criminal Justice Act, 1925, s. 11(1)—Jurisdiction of Quarter Sessions—Defendants travelling on broomsticks—Whether British aircraft—Air Navigation Act, 1920, s. 14—Air Navigation Act, 1936, s.28—Defendants not " apprehended or in custody or having appeared "—Want of jurisdiction.

THE following are extracts from the judgment of the Court, read by Mr. Justice Matthew Hopkins, in this appeal against convictions under the Witchcraft Act, 1735, s. 4, and the Larceny Act, 1916 :—

" This is an appeal against conviction and sentence at Witch's Bridle Quarter Sessions in July last, when the three appellants were found guilty and sentenced to imprisonment with hard labour for one year. The grounds of the appeal are that the trial at Quarter Sessions was a nullity, the Court having no jurisdiction, and the appellants having been absent during part of the proceedings.

" The appellants are three females, of no fixed abode, who had for some time past carried on what purported to be a business in partnership, first in Scotland and, later, in various parts of England, under the style or firm name of 'Three Witches.' It does not appear that the name has been registered under s. 1 of the Registration of Business Names Act, 1916, and, indeed, in the circumstances which I shall relate, registration could hardly have been effected. This so-called firm was formed for purposes which, as the evidence at Quarter Sessions has shown, are clearly unlawful, and it is established law that no such association can constitute a valid partnership.

"The appellants were indicted under the Witchcraft Act, 1735, s. 4, which makes it an indictable misdemeanour to pretend to exercise or use any kind of witchcraft, sorcery, enchantment or conjuration; or to undertake to tell fortunes; or to discover stolen goods by skill in any occult or crafty science. They were also indicted under s. 32 of the Larceny Act, 1916, for obtaining by false pretences.

"The particulars of the indictment, which it is unnecessary for me to read in detail, relate to a number of offences committed since the appellants' previous conviction on similar grounds. They include the purported making of prophecies to and telling the fortunes of Mr. Banquo, Lord and Lady Macbeth and a number of other people. Under the Larceny Act the appellants were convicted of obtaining money by the sale of concoctions marketed under the names 'Hell's Brew,' 'Hecate's Love Potion,' and 'Elixir of Life,' under the false pretence that these concoctions possessed magical powers.

"It is unnecessary for me to deal with the details of the offences themselves, which do not arise on this appeal. The appellants' ground of appeal is that the trial before Quarter Sessions was a nullity for lack of jurisdiction.

"It appears that the venue of a number of the offences with which the appellants were charged was decided to be in the County of Endor, and counsel have referred me to the provisions of two enactments on the subject of venue. The first is sect. 13 of the Criminal Law Act, 1826, which states as follows:—

" ' The venue of an offence committed on any person, or on or in respect of any property, in or upon any coach, waggon, cart or other carriage employed on any journey or on board any vessel employed on any voyage or journey upon any navigable river, canal or inland navigation, may be laid in any county through or adjoining to or by the boundary of any part whereof such coach, waggon, cart, carriage or vessel passes in the course of the journey or voyage during which the offence is committed, in the same manner as if it had been actually committed in such county.'

" The second of the enactments on the subject referred to is sect. 11(1) of the Criminal Justice Act, 1925, which is far more comprehensive. By the terms of that subsection a person charged with any indictable offence may be proceeded against, indicted, tried and punished in any county or place in which he was apprehended or is in custody on a charge for the offence, or has appeared in answer to a summons lawfully issued charging the offence, as if the offence had been committed in that county or place.

" The common law rule as to venue, as is well known, is that the proper venue is the area of jurisdiction in which, on the evidence, the acts occurred which are alleged to constitute the crime. If those acts were done in several places, it is a question of evidence whether a complete criminal act has been performed in any one of those places, so as to constitute that place a proper venue under the common law rule.

"The nature of the crimes alleged in this case has rendered it impossible for the prosecution to rely on the rule of common law regarding venue, and counsel did not attempt to argue this point before us. What is contended, however, by the prosecution is that either the Act of 1826 or the Act of 1925 gave jurisdiction to the Court of Quarter Sessions at Witch's Bridle—a contention which is strenuously denied by the appellants.

"The evidence before the Court discloses an extraordinary state of affairs. It appears that the appellants, by a system which is as reprehensible as it is ingenious, have been in the habit of carrying on their business (if it can be called such) not in one place, or at a number of branch offices or works, but at a number of unascertained places in remote localities, far apart from one another, throughout the country. It was further stated in evidence by the witness Lord Macbeth, that a great part of their business is carried on while they are actually in course of travel from one part of the country to another, and, further, that for the purpose of such travel they do not proceed on foot or employ any of the usual means of locomotion, by train, motor car, carriage or boat, but resort exclusively to aviation. There would be nothing extraordinary, in this air-minded age, in such a method, were it not for the further sworn testimony of a number of witnesses that the appellants are in the habit of flying, not in an ordinary aircraft, but on what they describe as broomsticks—a type of contrivance which seems to me singularly ill-fitted for the hazards of aerial travel.

"The Court would have found considerable difficulty in giving credence to these allegations had it not been for the transcript of the evidence of Inspector Malcolm, of the Scottish Mobile Police, who had the initiative to pursue the appellants in his special C.I.D. aeroplane over a distance of several hundred miles, during which hazardous voyage he clearly observed their behaviour. That they were mounted on broomsticks he is quite certain, though he does not profess to be able to explain the mechanical devices by which such flimsy types of aircraft are able to fly for long periods at a height of several thousand feet, and even to out-distance a modern, high-powered 'plane. But he was able to state categorically, from his own observations, that during their journey the appellants, by means of messages dropped by parachute, by announcements by wireless telephony, and by the preparation, packing and despatching of their noxious mixtures, completed the commission of the offences charged.

"Did sect. 13 of the Act of 1826, then, confer the requisite jurisdiction on the Court of Quarter Sessions? It is not denied that the appellants, in the course of their journey, passed over or across the county of Endor, but can they be said to have passed ' through or adjoining to or by the boundary of any part ' of that county? And, if so, can the words ' coach, waggon, cart or other carriage . . . or vessel ' be deemed to include an aircraft of the type employed by the appellants? As to the latter point, it has been held that the Act does apply to a journey by railway and, in other cases, that the Act is not confined to public conveyances or the carriages of common carriers ; but counsel were unable to refer us to any case where it has been held to apply to an aircraft of any kind. As to the former point, it was strenuously argued by the prosecution, on the analogy of the law of real property, that, for the purposes of venue, as for those of ownership, the maxim, *cujus est solum ejus est usque ad caelum et ad inferos*, should be applied, and counsel has somewhat ingeniously put forward the proposition that there is no more reason to refuse to apply the rules of venue under the Act to an aerial journey by broomstick than to a subterranean journey by the Underground Railway. This Court does not, however, consider the two cases at all analogous; in any event, we know of no authority for the application of the maxim which I have quoted to matters of criminal jurisdiction, in which the accused person is traditionally entitled to the benefit of any doubt. After mature consideration this Court has come reluctantly to the conclusion that Quarter Sessions possessed no jurisdiction under the Act of 1826.

"Before I go on to deal with the Act of 1925, I must refer to another argument of the respondent's counsel, which is germane to what I have already stated. Counsel has drawn our attention to the provisions of sect. 14 of the Air Navigation Act, 1920, substituted by sect. 28 of the Air Navigation Act, 1936, providing that any offence committed on a British aircraft is, for the purpose of conferring jurisdiction, to be deemed to have been committed in any place where the offender may for the time being be. These sections have not so far been the subject of judicial interpretation, and it is unnecessary for us here to decide the wider questions of jurisdiction involved, for two reasons: first, we are unable to hold that the broomsticks to which reference has been made fall under the head of ' a British aircraft ' within the meaning of the Act; and secondly, because the words ' where the offender may for the time being be,' though in themselves clear, give rise to the same difficulties of application as the words ' in which he was apprehended, or is in custody . . . or has appeared ' in the Act of 1925. It will be convenient to deal with these two phrases together.

"The evidence discloses the serious difficulties in which the respondents are placed. Inspector Malcolm was quite clear that, at several stages of his flight, he observed the appellants to land on a heath in a remote part of the countryside, where they busied themselves (so far as he could see from a height of several hundred feet) with a round metal object resembling a large saucepan or cauldron. He descended as quickly as possible, but asserts that on every occasion, when he reached the spot, all traces of the appellants in person had vanished. He found at these various places a heterogeneous collection of objects which were taken to the laboratory at Scotland Yard. On examination these proved to consist of a number of animal remains—a newt's eye, a frog's toe, and the decomposed body of a toad—some sprigs of the herb known as 'hemlock', a waxen image or two, and with them, horrible to relate, a nose of human origin, together with the finger of a stillborn child. At the bottom of the cauldron was always found a black viscous liquid which, on a laboratory analysis, proved to be a mixture or solution of the same disgusting ingredients. There seems to be no doubt that this solution found its way into the phials or bottles which were posted to those gullible members of the public who were foolish enough to send postal orders, as requested in the pamphlets they had received, addressed to the appellants at the Forres Post Office ; there is no doubt of the commission of the offence of obtaining by false pretences. The difficulty is to apply to such elusive personages the words in the Air Navigation Act—' where the offender may for the time being be.' The place chosen by the appellants for their nefarious practices was always an open space or heath, affording no cover to a fugitive; they were, as the inspector says, kept carefully under observation from the air, and the spot where they had been was marked by the presence of the implements they had employed; yet on no single occasion was he able to see anything of them once he had reached ground level, nor can he offer any explanation of their disappearance. As he was quite unable to suggest any reasonable method by which they could have concealed themselves, he was compelled to admit, under cross-examination, to a serious doubt whether he had ever seen them at all—in other words, whether they could be said 'for the time being to be' in any of the places described.

"Turning to the Act of 1925 the respondents are in a similar dilemma. The police apprehended (or thought they apprehended) the appellants in a remote part of Endorshire, and, as they thought, handcuffed them securely before placing them in the police van for the journey to Witch's Bridle. Yet, within half an hour, the van on arrival was found to be empty, and within the same period the appellants were seen passing over Carlisle, setting their course in a northerly direction. Similar incidents happened on two subsequent occasions. On their fourth arrest they were brought up within six hours and placed in the dock, under guard, at the local police court; yet during the course of the hearing itself the learned magistrate drew the warders' attention to the fact that the dock was empty. A few minutes later the appellants were descried by observers outside the Court carrying on a kind of triumphant dance on the roof of the building and playing leapfrog over the weather-vane. Before ladders could be brought to secure them, they had again disappeared and were subsequently seen flying at great speed round and round the interior of the neigh-

SHIPTON v. THE KING

bouring Registrar's Court, to the great disturbance of business and the serious perturbation of litigants.

"Reprehensible and, indeed, contumacious as such proceedings may be, this Court must withstand the temptation to allow a conviction to stand where the Court of trial has exceeded its jurisdiction. How can it be said that the appellants were 'apprehended' or 'in custody' or 'had appeared' at any of the places mentioned? 'Avoided apprehension,' 'escaped from custody' and 'disappeared' would be the more appropriate expressions. And, even though we were to overcome the initial difficulties of venue, how is it possible to say, in face of the evidence of what took place, that the appellants were present during the whole of the preliminary examination? Their temporary absence alone, for whatever reason, would require this Court to refuse to allow the conviction to stand. The trial was a nullity, and the convictions and sentences must be quashed."

The appellants were thereupon ordered to be discharged, but it was shortly afterwards reported to the Court that they were not to be found either in their cells or anywhere in the precincts of the building where they had been confined. Proceedings for *habeas corpus* against the Governor of the prison are reported to have been commenced.

ACTION ON A BOND

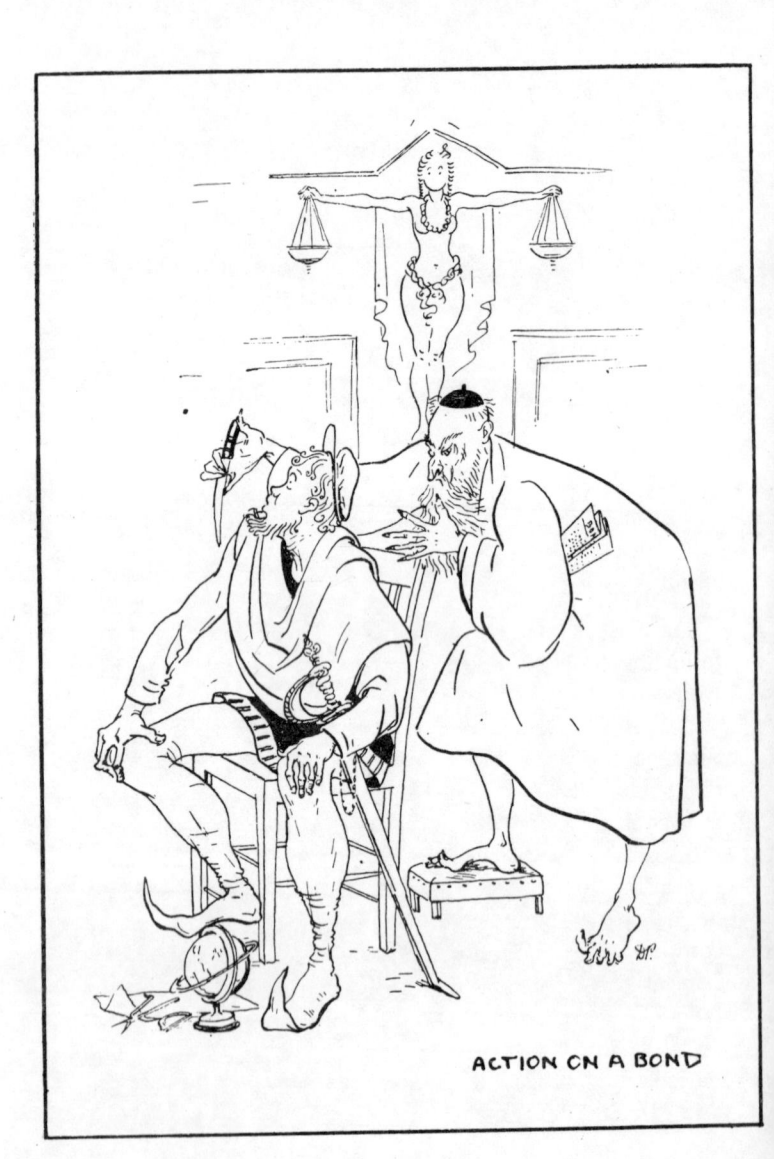

Court of Appeal.

SHYLOCK *v.* ANTONIO.

Conflict of Laws—Both parties domiciled in Venice—Bond to secure money lent—Penalty " one pound of flesh "—Not illegal by lex loci contractus—Whether illegal by lex fori—Public policy—No illegality—Whether res judicata—Irregularities of trial—Original trial null and void—No order for specific performance—Order for repayment of loan and interest.

INTERESTING questions of Private International Law were considered in this appeal from a decision of Shakespeare, J., in favour of the respondent. The following judgment was delivered by the Master of the Rolls:—

"This is an appeal from a judgment of Mr. Justice Shakespeare, who found in favour of the respondent on two grounds—first, that the subject-matter of the action is a contract of a kind which the policy of English law refuses to enforce, and, secondly, that it was not competent for him to rehear on its merits an action which (as he held) was already *res judicata*, a foreign Court of competent jurisdiction in Italy having already decided in respect of the same subject-matter in the respondent's favour.

"The appellant and the respondent are both Italian nationals, domiciled in Venice, but temporarily resident and carrying on branches of their businesses in England.

The appellant is a licensed moneylender, and the respondent is a merchant and exporter.

"The pleadings show that the foreign action which the respondent seeks to set up as a bar to these proceedings was heard in the ducal Court at Venice about a year ago. The matter there in issue was the enforcement by the appellant of a penalty clause contained in a bond, whereby the respondent undertook to repay to the appellant within three months a loan of three thousand ducats (equivalent, at the present rate of exchange, to 203*l.*), and representing money lent to him by the appellant without interest. The bond was conditioned by a penalty clause containing the somewhat unusual provision that, in default of payment, the respondent should forfeit to the appellant one pound of his flesh.

"There is no question that the proper law of the contract is the law merchant of Venice, and expert evidence has been given that such a contract is not illegal by that law. The respondent, however, has argued that this is a cause of action of a nature which the Courts of England would not entertain, as being contrary to public policy. He has reminded the Court that, notwithstanding the legality of a contract by its proper law—whether that law be the *lex loci contractus* or the *lex loci solutionis*—no civilised State will assist in enforcing terms which are contrary to its *ordre public* as understood by the *lex fori* (*Hope* v. *Hope*).

"Now, that is good law so far as it goes, and it is well established in this country that a contract, wherever made, to permit the commission of an act which is contrary to public policy, as understood in England, is illegal and unenforceable in our Courts (*Egerton* v. *Brownlow*). But public policy, as has been well said, is an unruly horse, and the Court will exercise extreme caution in applying so vague a conception to deprive a litigant of his legal rights (See *Hyams* v. *Stuart King*). There is always a presumption of legality in favour of the obligee, and it is for the obligor to rebut that presumption if he can. The Court will not presume an intention of illegality if it is possible to carry out the contract in a lawful manner. And when the legality of a contract is thus placed in issue, the Court is entitled to look beyond the express terms at all the circumstances—those in which the contract was made as well as those in which it is likely to be performed.

" Counsel for the respondent has attempted to rebut this presumption of legality by the argument that the taking by the obligee of a pound of the obligor's flesh constitutes an unlawful wounding, which is a crime by the law of England, and that a contract to permit the commission of a crime is illegal, consent or no consent. Were it possible to dispose thus shortly of the matter I should have had no hesitation in finding for the respondent on this issue. But in my opinion he has not succeeded in discharging the onus thus placed upon him. Conceptions of public policy must keep pace with the developments of science and social institutions in the world at large, and he would be a bold man who would assert that even so unequivocal an act as the taking of a pound of flesh from the body of a living person is necessarily a crime. Our newspapers, to give but one example, are full to-day of advertisements, addressed principally to the female part of the population, advocating the use of a variety of drugs and other remedies for the purpose of removing the excess of adipose deposit of flesh and tissue which too often disfigure the bodies and undermine the health of those who bear them, and it is beyond question that those who adopt these remedies, so far from suffering injury thereby, derive substantial benefit, physically and aesthetically, from their use. And not only so, but other and more drastic methods have from time to time been tolerated, and even encouraged, by the legislature. Parliament—whether wisely or not it is not for me to enquire—has licensed certain privileged persons—medical practitioners, surgeons and what-not—to excise from the living bodies of their patients such portions of the human anatomy as they, in their assumed wisdom, consider harmful or superfluous to a healthy life; it is alleged that they are accustomed at times to exercise that licence on the slightest provocation and with little or no justification whatsoever. Having regard to these established practices, can it be effectively contended that a contract whereby a man agrees to forfeit a pound of his flesh is necessarily and inevitably contrary to public policy? There can be but one answer, and that a negative one.

"I have observed the physical condition of the respondent, who has given evidence in this Court, and I will go no further than to say that he is a person of such rotund and corpulent physique that the loss of a pound of flesh could bring him nothing but lasting benefit. Moreover, there is evidence before us, unchallenged by the defence, that at the date when the bond was executed the respondent was about to enter a hospital for the removal of his appendix—an organ which, his physician advised him, was of abnormal size and in the most unhealthy condition. We are also told that the appellant's daughter Jessica—a young lady of brilliant attainments—was at that time studying medicine and surgery in the local medical school, and that she was anxious to acquire a human appendix for the purposes of medical research,

Viewed in the light of these facts, the flimsy character of the first part of the defence becomes at once apparent, and the Court has had no hesitation in finding for the appellant on this issue.

"I now turn to the second ground of the judgment in the Court below. The learned judge there found that it was not competent for him to rehear an action which was already *res judicata* in a foreign Court. This does, at first sight, confront the appellant with a more serious difficulty. The evidence of Dr. Bellario of Padua University, and other foreign experts, has established beyond all doubt that the decision of the ducal Court at Venice was a final and conclusive judgment by a Court of competent jurisdiction, and the respondent has quoted authorities designed to show that the matter must end there. The question is a difficult one, and the authorities are conflicting, but this Court, having given grave consideration to the matter in all its aspects, has remembered that, though every presumption is to be made in favour of a foreign judgment, and the burden of proof lies on him who impeaches it, yet, since no one is entitled to take advantage of his own wrong, a judgment obtained by fraud or misrepresentation, or a judgment arising out of proceedings which are contrary to natural justice, will be disregarded by the Courts of England (*Ochsenbein* v. *Papelier*). The burden of proof here lies on the appellant, and in the opinion of this Court he has successfully discharged that burden.

"The appellant, in the Court at Venice, was not legally represented, but appeared in person. Counsel for the respondent is stated in the Court records to have been a Dr. Balthasar, sponsored by that same Dr. Bellario whose evidence we have heard. It transpires, however, that by a most improper subterfuge Dr. Balthasar was impersonated at the trial by a young woman named Portia, who is not a member of the Italian bar, and had, by the *lex fori*, no right of audience in that Court at all. And as if that were not enough, not only did she succeed in cajoling the judge by her good looks and honeyed phrases, but the entire trial seems to have been conducted in an atmosphere of unreasoning prejudice against the appellant, which I can only describe as a disgrace to the Courts of any civilised community. It is well established in England (where, by a long tradition of tolerance and freedom since the days of Magna Carta, all men are equal before the law), that our Courts will not recognise a disability of a penal character imposing a status of a kind not recognised in England. What, then, are we to say of a trial which depended for its outcome, as here, on the prejudice created in the mind of the foreign Court on the grounds of the appellant's race and religion ? So far did that Court forget its duty that a trial which had begun as a civil action between two litigants was allowed, without protest, to degenerate into a form of criminal proceedings against the appellant, who, without the forms required by the *lex fori*, without warning or preparation, or the assistance of solicitor or counsel, was in those same proceedings suddenly confronted with a criminal indictment, convicted and sentenced to the confiscation of the greater part of his property. And what are we to think of a judge who, in open Court, invites counsel for one of the contending parties to celebrate at a banquet the victory of his client ? It is well known that our judges in this country are to some extent above the law, and that there is no positive rule, when their high duties are for the moment laid aside, to prevent their meeting members of the Bar

SHYLOCK v. ANTONIO

in an atmosphere of social cordiality. But the practice is in England safeguarded by those wholesome traditions of impartiality and independence from which, I am proud to say, our judiciary have never attempted to swerve. There can be no excuse for behaviour such as I have here outlined.

"Having regard to all these facts the Court has come to the conclusion that the purported trial of this action in Venice was a mere nullity from beginning to end. It follows that the learned judge below was wrong in holding that he was not competent to rehear the matter, which now resolves itself into a simple action by the appellant on his bond. No valid defence having been raised thereto, the appellant is entitled to judgment.

"It only remains for me to decide the form of the judgment, and here the matter passes into the realms of equity. The penalty clause in the bond, though not (as I have said) against the public policy of England, is not one which the Court will specifically enforce. Specific performance of a contract for the delivery up of a chattel or for the sale of goods (in which category it is, perhaps, possible to place this unusual transaction) will not be granted unless it is proved that the chattel or the goods have some peculiar property which makes it impossible to obtain things of a similar kind in the open market. No evidence has been adduced to show that the respondent's flesh is of a distinctive quality or that it differs in any marked degree from the flesh of any other obese and unhealthy individual. The respondent asks for relief against the penalty; equity will grant him relief, but only on equitable terms. He must repay to the appellant the full amount of the loan, with reasonable interest—at 4 per cent. per annum—from the date of the bond to the present time, and I give judgment accordingly for the appellant, who will have his costs here and in the Court below."

Lord Justice Marlowe and Lord Justice Jonson concurred.

TABLE OF CASES CITED

	Page
Alliance Bank v. Broom, (1864) 2 Dr. & Sm. 289	24
Attorney-General v. Seccombe, [1911] 2 K.B. 688	20
Boydell v. Jones, (1838) 4 M & W. 446	73
Brown, In the Goods of, (1910) 54 Sol. Jo. 478	53
Capital and Counties Bank v. Henty, (1882) 7 App. Cas. 741	73, 74
Chapman v. Ellesmere, [1932] 2 K.B. 431	73
Clark v. Molyneux, (1877) 3 Q.B.D. 237	35
Cunningham, Re, [1914] 1 Ch. 427	94
Currie v. Misa, (1875) L.R. 10 Exch. 153	24
Cutler v. United Dairies, [1933] 2 K.B. 297	85
Day v. Brownrigg, (1878) 10 Ch.D. 294	43
Donoghue v. Stevenson, [1932] A.C. 562	84
Egerton v. Brownlow, (1853) 4 H.L. Cas. 1	114
Hay (or Bourhill) v. Young, [1943] A.C. 92	83, 84, 85
Hambrook v. Stokes Bros., [1925] 1 K.B. 141	83
Hope v. Hope, (1857) 8 De G.M. & G. 731	114
Hyams v. Stuart King, [1908] 2 K.B. 696	115
Imperial Gas Light & Coke Co. v. Broadbent, (1859) 7 H.L. Cas. 600	45
Lake v. Simmons, [1927] A.C. 487	96
Leng (John) & Co. v. Langlands, (1916) 114 L.T. 665	72

	Page
McQuire v. Western Morning News, [1903] 2 K.B. 100	35
Merivale v. Carson, (1887) 20 Q.B.D. 275	34
Monson v. Tussauds, [1894] 1 Q.B. 671	33, 75
Moss v. Moss, [1897] P. 263	93
Ochsenbein v. Papelier, (1873) 8 Ch. App. 695	117
Owens v. Liverpool Corporation, [1939] 1 K.B. 394	83
Phillips v. Brooks, [1919] 2 K.B. 243	95, 96
Polemis & Furness Withy & Co., Re [1921] 3 K.B. 560	85
Robinson v. Kilvert, (1889) 41 Ch.D. 88	44
Rylands v. Fletcher, (1868) L.R. 3 H.L. 330	44
Sim v. Stretch, [1932] 2 All E.R. 1237	32
Sutherland v. Stopes, [1925] A.C. 47	34
Yates, Re, [1919] P. 93	51

TABLE OF STATUTES

	Page
Magna Carta, 1215	118
Witchcraft Act, 1735, s. 4	101, 102
Criminal Law Act, 1826, s. 13	103, 105, 106
Marriage Act, 1836, s. 10	54
Wills Act, 1837, s. 7	50
s. 18	53
Fatal Accidents Acts, 1846 to 1908	79
Bills of Exchange Act, 1882, s. 7	23
Slander of Women Act, 1891	69, 74
Finance Act, 1894, s. 2	18, 19
Mental Deficiency Act, 1913, s. 5	39
Larceny Act, 1916, s. 32	101, 102
Registration of Business Names Act, 1916, s. 1	102
Wills (Soldiers & Sailors Act, 1918, s. 1	51
Dangerous Drugs Act, 1920	65
Air Navigation Act, 1920, s. 14	106
Law of Property Act, 1925, s. 38	80, 81
s. 184	57
Fifth Schedule	80, 81
Workmen's Compensation Act, 1925	44
Criminal Justice Act, 1925, s. 11	103, 104, 105, 108
Age of Marriage Act, 1929, s. 1	55
Law Reform (Misc. Provns.) Act, 1934, s. 1	79
Air Navigation Act, 1936, s. 28	106
Building Societies Act, 1939, s. 9	80
Food (Rationing) Order, 1939	20
Acquisition of Food (Excessive Quantities) Order, 1939	20
Food (Restrictions on Dealings) Order, 1941	20
Meals in Establishments Order, 1942	20

GENERAL INDEX

Page

ACCIDENT
    Workmen's Compensation Act, meaning in, of .   44

ADMINISTRATION
    Montague, action by, for   49
    de bonis non, order for   57

AERIAL NAVIGATION
    broomstick, use of, for 104, 105
    Puck, pursuit of, by   27
    venue, rules of, applicable to . . .   106
    witches, method used by, for . . 104, 105

ALBANY
    Lear, deceased, administrator of . . .   17

ANTONIO
    bond, execution of, by   114
    flesh of, not of distinctive quality . .   119
    liability under bond, of   114
    Shylock, appeal by, respondent in . .   113

APPENDIX
    surgical removal of, legality of . . .   116

APPREHENSION
    accused's, effect on venue . . . 103, 109

	Page
ASPIRIN	
Juliet, administration to, overdose of	56
ASS'S HEAD	
defamatory implication of	29, 32, 33
BOND	
condition of	21, 22
curses as penalty in	21
Lear, daughters of, execution by	21
BORACHIO	
defamatory conduct of	71, 72
malice of, evidence as to	70
BOTTOM	
ass's head affixed on	29, 30
innuendo pleaded by	29
libel, action for, by	27
ridiculous situation of	31
BROOMSTICK	
aerial travel by	106
whether " British aircraft "	106
CALIBAN	
incapacity of	39, 43
nuisance, action for, by	39
Prospero, oppression by, of	43, 44
CAPULET	
Juliet, executorship of, whether valid	53
purported marriage of	53, 54, 55
tragic decease of	56

	Page
CAULDRON	
witch's, contents of, analysis of	107
CLAUDIUS	
acquittal of	66
evidence against, insufficiency of	65
CONFLICT OF LAWS	
contract, proper law of	114
res judicata, rules applicable to	113, 117
CONSIDERATION	
forbearance to curse, whether good	24
CONTRACT	
legality of	113, 114
proper law of	144
public policy, rules of, applicable to	114, 115
CONVERSION	
daughters, of, into toads	21, 24
equitable doctrine of	24
CURSE	
forbearance to, whether good consideration	24
paternal, whether legal tender	24
penalty in bonds, adequacy of	24
propensity of Lear to	18, 24
CUSTODY	
venue, in connection with	103, 109
CY-PRES	
marriage, application of doctrine to	94, 95
DEED	
execution of, validity of	22

Page

DEFAMATION

   ass's head constituting 29, 32, 33
   gestures, whether constituting . . . 75

DEVISE

   Romeo, will of, contained in 52

DONEE

   possession by, assumption of 18

DONOR

   exclusion from benefit of 18, 24
   mental incapacity of 22

DYING DECLARATION

   ghost, statement by, whether constituting . 64
   Thisbe, by, details of 81

ESTATE DUTY

   gift *inter vivos*, avoidance by, of . . 18
   crown, claim by, to 18

EVIDENCE

   dying declaration, admissibility as, of . . 64
   extrinsic, defamatory intention shown by . 32
   ghost's, hearsay nature of . . . 64, 65

EXECUTOR

   according to the tenor, implied . . . 53

FAIR COMMENT

   malice, vitiation by, of 35
   Puck, pleading by, of 34, 35

FALSE PRETENCES

   love-potions, sale of, constituting . . 102, 107
   witch, offence committed by, of . . 101, 102

	Page
FIEND, FOUL	
whether "fictitious person"	23
FLESH, POUND OF	
bond, penalty in, as	114
no specific performance as to	119
removal of, legality of	115, 116
FOUL FIEND	
(see FIEND, FOUL, *supra*)	
GERTRUDE	
acquittal of	66
hasty marriage of	65
GHOST	
attachment of, non-enforceability of	63
conflicting evidence as to	64
contumelious conduct of	63
evidence of, hearsay, inadmissible	64, 65
non-appearance of	63
subpoena, ineffective against	63
GIFT	
conditional nature of	24
Lear, execution of deed of, by	17
validity of, doubts as to	22
GOODFELLOW	
(see PUCK, *infra*)	
HAMLET	
deceased, alleged murder of	61
death of, how caused	62
junior, doubtful sobriety of	63
unsatisfactory evidence of	63

Page

HEBONA
(see POISON, *infra*)

IDENTITY
mistake as to, effect on marriage of . 89, 95, 96
nullity, relevance in, of 93

IMPERSONATION
defamatory implication of 76

INJUNCTION
jurisdiction for grant of 45, 46
Prospero, order against, for 47

INNUENDO
ass's head giving rise to 32, 33
Bottom, pleading by, of 29
gestures, sufficiency of, for 75

JUDGMENT
foreign, appeal against 113, 119
     enforcement of 114
     natural justice, contrary to . . . 117

JURISDICTION
ghost held to be outside 63
Quarter Sessions, of 101, 104
Vennetian Court, of 114

LEAR
advanced age of 18
curse of, as penalty 21
domineering temperament of . . . 18
estate of, duty on, liability to . . . 17, 24
followers of, difficulties of catering for . 20
gifts, deeds of, execution by . . . 17
mental condition of 22

LEONATO
Hero, defamation of 69, 71

LIBEL
ass's head constituting 29, 32, 33
circumstances relevant to 73
impersonation constituting 76

MAGIC
escape of accused allegedly due to . . 108, 109
exercise of, allegations as to 41
reliance on, relevance in nuisance of . . 42

MALICE
fair comment, effect of, on 35

MARRIAGE
minimum age of, rule as to 55
mistake of identity in 89, 95, 96
nullity of, action for 89
validity of 95
voluntary act, necessity for 93

MONTAGUE, ROMEO
decease of 56
extravagant testamentary language of . . 52
infancy of 50
military service of 51
nuncupative will of 51, 52
survivorship, evidence of . . . 56, 57
will of, validity of 53

NEGLIGENCE
nervous shock giving rise to 83
defendant's conduct, remoteness of . . 85

130

	Page
NEGLIGENCE *Continued*—	
duty to take care, necessity of	84
Pyramus, rights of, action for	85
whether death direct result of	86
NUISANCE	
Caliban, plea by, of	39, 43
defence to action of	40
Prospero, commission by	39, 43
PARTY WALL	
defect in, action in respect of	80
lovers, use by, of	81
statutory provisions as to	80
POISON	
Claudius, purchase by, of	65
PORTIA	
irregular appearance of	118
no right of audience of	118
PROSPERO	
alleged magical powers of,	42
oppressive conduct of	41, 44
personality of	40
PUBLIC POLICY	
contracts contrary to	114, 116
no extension of rules of	115
PUCK	
aerial exploits of	27
defamatory conduct of	29, 30
insulting behaviour of	31
practical joking, propensity of, for	36

Page

PYRAMUS

administrator, action by	79
deceased, death of	79, 83
elopement of	82
fatal result of shock to	83

REMAINDERMAN

grey cat, appointment of, as	23
euthanasia of	23

ROLLED-UP PLEA

legal effect of	34

SEBASTIAN

marriage of, validity of	89, 93, 96
mistaken identity of	93

SECURITY

pound of flesh, whether good as	115

SHIPTON

appeal against conviction, of	101
locomotion, method of, adopted by	104

SHOCK

nervous, whether basis of claim	83

SHYLOCK

appeal by	113
illegal conviction of	118

SLANDER

gestures, whether constituting	75
Leonato, action by, for	69
per se, when giving rise to action	74
words of, necessity for pleading of	74

	Page
Specific Performance	
decree, refusal of	119
Survival	
Juliet, of, evidence as to	56
implied	57
statutory provisions affecting	57
Sycorax	
intestacy of	40
personalty of	40
real estate of	40
Tenants for Life	
deaths in lethal chamber, of	23
trust for dogs as	23
Thisbe	
deceased, alleged negligence of	84
tragic death of	83
executor of, liability of	79
Trespass	
injunction as remedy for	46
User	
extraordinary, nuisance caused by	44
Venue	
Common Law rules as to	103
statutory rules as to	103
Viola	
disguise of, unfortunate results of	91, 92

WILL

	Page
infant's, validity of	50
nuncupative, evidence as to	52
provisions of, details as to	52
revocation by marriage, of	53
soldier's, validity of	50, 51

WITCHCRAFT

acts constituting offence of	102
potions concocted by	102, 107
prosecution for	101

WOUNDING, UNLAWFUL

appendix, excision of, not constituting	117
pound of flesh, removal of, not constituting	116

III
FINAL LEGAL FICTIONS

ENTERING A CAVEAT

See Page 15

FINAL LEGAL FICTIONS
A Series of Cases from Folk-Lore and Opera

TO MY SISTER,
CORNELIA JULIA POLAK,
H.M. VICE-CONSUL AT BERGEN, NORWAY.

TO MY SISTER

CORNELIA ADÈL POLAK

CONTENTS

Acknowledgments		*page* 5
Tema Con Variazioni		7
Cassandra *v.* Thymoetes	(K.B.D.)	13
Cio-Cio-San *v.* A.-G.	(Ch.D.)	23
Cupid *v.* Cupid	(P.D.A.)	33
De Ulloa *v.* Tenorio	(K.B.D.)	43
The Flying Dutchman	(P.D.A.)	51
Hansel & Gretel *v.* Pumpernickel	(K.B.D.)	61
Mephistopheles *v.* Faust	(Ch.D.)	69
Ogre *v.* Jack	(K.B.D.)	79
Rex *v.* Rigoletto	(C.C.A.)	89
Wotan *v.* Fasolt & Fafner	(Ch.D.)	97
Table of Cases		103
Table of Statutes		106
Index		108

ACKNOWLEDGMENTS

With the completion of the final volume of this series I desire once more to express my thanks to my Publishers, for their continued patience and courtesy; to the learned Editors of *Law Notes*, for their kindly interest and helpfulness, and to my friend A. Goodman, Esq., LL.M. (Lond.), LL.B. (Cantab.), for his work in reading the manuscript and making a number of valuable suggestions and criticisms.

My best thanks are also due to my Illustrator, Miss Diana Pullinger who, despite the exigencies of national service in distant Burma, has maintained the high artistic standard of her work which has formed a most attractive feature of this series. I am also grateful to my friend Mrs. Enid Dreyfus for her useful work in cover designing.

A.L.P.

St. John's Wood,
September, 1948.

Beware, then, of the introduction of new forms of music, which may imperil the whole of our system; for styles of music cannot be disturbed without affecting the most important institutions of the State. For the new style, gradually gaining an entry, quietly insinuates itself into manners and customs; from these it issues forth in greater strength and intrudes into the relations between man and man; and from these mutual relations it goes on relentlessly to attack laws and constitutions, until it ends by overthrowing every institution, both public and private.

PLATO, *The Republic*,
Book IV, 424 C

TEMA CON VARIAZIONI

VARIATIONS upon a musical theme have been a favoured form of exercise with composers from the eighteenth century to the present time. Bach, Haydn, Mozart, Beethoven, Schubert and Brahms, and (in recent years) Dvorak and Elgar, were masters of the art. The manifold restatement of the original theme delights the musical palate with the pleasures of repetition, while the spice of variety adds a refined flavour to the feast and prevents the cloying of the listener's taste.

With some such considerations in mind is presented this third and final set of variations upon the legal theme. To the reader who may have been tempted to stir restlessly in his seat, or even driven to stifle a yawn, at the implied *da capo* in the title of this volume, the first word of that title may (it is hoped) afford consolation and relief.

The courageous reader who persists beyond this point will discover that the events giving rise to this series of Reports are drawn (with one exception) from the operatic works of Lulli, Mozart, Berlioz, Gounod, Verdi, Humperdinck and Puccini, and from the music-dramas of Wagner. Lest it be suggested that there is a displeasing incongruity between the medium chosen in these pages for representation of the events and the original works in which they are recorded, a few reflections may not be out of place on the analogy between music and law.

Neither is an institution peculiar only to civilised communities; both appear as a spontaneous development in primitive society. The origins of the highly-developed arts of opera and ballet, and of the complex structure of the symphony orchestra, are to be sought in the ritual chants and dances and the metrical drum-beats of the savage tribe. In a similar way the complex systems of Mosaic, Mohammedan and Hindu law, of Anglo-Saxon law and equity and of the Code Napoléon, have evolved from the *tabus* and tribal customs of primitive man. The conception of order, upon which all communal institutions depend, is inherent in both, as it is in the cognate institutions of language, ethics and religion.

Not only so, but it is found that the social characteristics of a community at any time are reflected on the one hand in its music, on the other in its law. In the ancient Greek world the Dorian mode reproduced in the realm of music the stern and rugged characteristics of the Spartan system, which gave rise to a code of law of uncompromising severity. The Phrygian, Lydian and Aeolian modes had each its own moral significance, reflecting the character of the community that produced it, and the same character permeated that community's legal and political institutions. In the modern world the quickening of the critical faculty, which vitalised Europe in the Renaissance of Learning, was accompanied by a breaking away from the rigidity of the old and the development of new and revolutionary musical forms, and at the same time by far-reaching legal changes, of which the enormous growth in the power and activity of the Equity Jurisdiction in England was one manifestation.

In the present age the breakdown of manners and morals, in the chaotic political conditions of the nineteen-thirties and forties, has been reflected both in the revolutionary and anarchical experiments of modern musical composers and in the progressive deterioration of law and order in most countries of the world.

This post-war period is characterised by an impatience of all restraint, social and legal, a total lack of consideration for others and a cult of bad manners, masquerading as independence of spirit. In this country the confusion has penetrated not only into Broadcasting House, but even into our Courts of Law. The Divorce Division echoes to the tale of lives saturated with the emotional exhibitionism of Tchaikowsky, degraded by the cheap sentimentality of the "crooner"; the Old Bailey to the sensuality of Wagner, vulgarised by transatlantic blare; the Common Law Courts to the flamboyancy of Liszt, exaggerated by the cacophony of the modern school. Only, perhaps, in the Chancery Division is the calm atmosphere of the eighteenth century, the Golden Age of music, to some extent preserved. The weary practitioner must be grateful if he can sometimes escape from the turmoil to take refuge, in his leisure moments, with the sublime serenity of Johann Sebastian Bach, the genial humour of Franz Josef Haydn and the superb enchantment of that Master of the masters, the musician of musicians, - Wolfgang Amadeus Mozart.

INFLICTION OF A WAR INJURY

King's Bench Division

CASSANDRA v. THYMOETES AND ANOTHER

Negligence—Dangerous object abandoned by enemy—Interference by first defendant—Injury to plaintiff resulting therefrom—"Nominated defendant"—Duty owed by active participant—"War injury"—Personal Injuries (Emergency Provisions) Act, 1939, ss. 3, 8—Negligence—Non-Internment of "Fifth Columnist"—Defence Regulations, 1939, Reg. 18B—Discretion exercisable by Home Secretary.

JUDGMENT of the Lord Chief Justice:

"This is an action for damages for personal injuries brought by Miss Cassandra, of 'The Oracle,' Troy, described as a prophetess, against Col. Thymoetes, of the Royal Engineers, and Mr. Deiphobus, the former Home Secretary. The Statement of Claim sets out that, by reason of the negligence of the first Defendant in tampering with a warlike contrivance left by the enemy on the foreshore, and bringing the same within the city walls, and by reason of the statutory negligence of the second Defendant in failing to detain one Sinon, described as a fifth-columnist, in accordance with Regulation 18B of the Defence Regulations, 1939, the Plaintiff suffered a blow on the head from the butt end of a javelin at the hands of the enemy Commando Unit concealed in the said warlike contrivance, such blow causing her lesions of the brain and nervous shock, leading to the loss of her prophetic gift, with the result that she is unable to follow her employment.

14   FINAL LEGAL FICTIONS

"Before I go on to deal with the defence it is incumbent upon me, for reasons which will appear hereafter, to set forth in some considerable detail the circumstances of the case which the evidence has disclosed—circumstances of a nature which has become familiar to Judges of this Division as an aftermath of the recent war, with its tale of unexploded bombs, defective mines and military works of the nature of a trap. I am indebted to Counsel for referring me to a number of recent decisions which I am in a position to apply by analogy to the facts of this case, and to important *dicta* of the House of Lords by which I am bound.

"Many witnesses have been called in support of the Plaintiff's case, and the greater part of the evidence is clear and uncontroverted. I find the facts to be as follows:

"In the closing stages of the siege of the City of Troy the Intelligence Branch of the War Office observed and reported to the authorities certain indications tending to show the intention of the enemy to abandon the siege and to evacuate their base. Embarkation of the enemy's troops was going forward on an extensive scale and the camp was being dismantled. There came a morning when the Home Guard patrol found the foreshore deserted by enemy troops and the fleet standing out to sea. The only sign of recent enemy activity was an object which closer inspection by a detachment of Engineers, under the command of the first defendant, revealed as an enormous wooden structure, some sixty feet high and broad in proportion, roughly fashioned in the shape of a horse.

"The Plaintiff, who (as I understand) by virtue of her civilian employment occupied an important position at the War Office in the Psychological Warfare Branch, has told me in the box how emphatically she opposed any careless interference with this object, which she seems from the start, with considerable acumen, to have suspected of containing a concealed danger in the form of some variety of atomic bomb. Her advice, however, that it should be left in the comparative safety of the shore until it was broken up by the waves, or that it should be towed by a Bomb Disposal Unit into deep water and there destroyed by high explosive, was overruled. It is clear that the first Defendant, who had made a (somewhat perfunctory) inspection of this contrivance, was of the opinion that it was a structure of the nature of a platform or ramp for the discharge of rocket missiles against the city, and that its strange shape was to be attributed to considerations of camouflage. At any rate he pronounced it harmless, and he not only advised the High Command in his technical capacity, but also took an active part in supervising its transport within the walls. It was he who was in charge of the detachment which towed it, by means of a bulldozer, to the main gate; it was he who actually supervised the demolition of part of the fortifications to allow its passage within the city. The significance of these facts will appear in due course.

"I have now to consider the case against the second Defendant. It appears that, shortly after the first discovery of the wooden horse, a Home Guard patrol brought in a prisoner. On interrogation he gave his name as Sinon; he admitted his enemy origin, but asserted that he was a refugee from Argive oppression, an allegation which he supported with circumstantial detail. At the Home Office the view was taken that he was a friendly alien, and he was allowed to remain at large, the then Home Secretary (the second Defendant) merely directing that he must report periodically to the police. The Plaintiff's suggestion that he should be detained under Regulation 18B was overruled.

"The melancholy events that ensued are fresh in all memories.

"The wooden horse was hollow; the enemy Commando Unit concealed within it was released by the alien, Sinon, and emerged the same night, fully armed; raided and immobilised a number of strategic points and opened the gates of the city to the main enemy forces which had returned and disembarked meanwhile. The greater part of the city was destroyed and extensive casualties were involved. The Plaintiff, who was on fire-watching duty at the War Office, was one of the earliest victims of the enemy Commandos, and there sustained the injuries of which she complains.

"On these facts, which have been fully established, it is clear that the Plaintiff has suffered personal injury as a result of negligence on the part of some person or persons in positions of authority in the employment of the Crown. Negligence in the full legal sense there has certainly been; but is it such negligence as to give rise to an action framed, as here, in tort? And, if so, are the Defendants personally liable in damages in such an action?

"The defence, with which it is now incumbent upon me to deal, raises several issues of importance. The first Defendant pleads, in the first place, that the Plaintiff's claim discloses no ground of action against him, since he is merely what is called a 'nominated defendant' whose name has been supplied by the Crown as holding a position of authority in the armed forces and that, on *dicta* of the House of Lords to which I shall presently refer, the action is stultified *in limine*. Alternatively, and in the second place, the first Defendant pleads that if (which is denied) the Plaintiff suffered injuries, such injuries were 'war injuries' within the meaning of the Personal Injuries (Emergency Provisions) Act, 1939, and that claims in tort are barred by sect. 3 of that Act.

"The first plea of this Defendant refers to a device of convenience which has become all too familiar in recent cases, the purpose of which is to avoid the embarrassing effect upon a plaintiff's rights of the Rule of Law that 'the King can do no wrong'—in other words, that the Crown, who is in reality the responsible party, cannot be sued in tort. The meaning and effect of this device were considered by the House of Lords in the case of *Adams* v. *Naylor*, and the observations have been followed by the Court of Appeal in *Royster* v. *Cavey*. Referring expressly to this device Viscount Simon said in the former case:

" 'But it is to me somewhat surprising and, I think, misleading to refer to him, as the evidence does, as the "nominal" or "nominated" defendant. Such language seems to suggest that the issues at the trial are really issues between the plaintiffs and the Crown, and that the defendant is mentioned as a party merely as a matter of convenience. That is not the true position. The courts before whom such a case as this comes have to decide it as between the parties before them and have nothing to do with the fact that the Crown stands behind the defendant. For the plaintiffs to succeed . . . they must prove that the defendant himself owes a duty of care to the plaintiffs and has failed in discharging that duty.'

"The other noble and learned Lords expressed similiar opinions, by which I am of course bound in any case where similar principles apply.

"I have come, however, to the conclusion that the facts here proved before me in evidence are distinguishable from those in issue both in *Adams* v. *Naylor* and in *Royster* v. *Cavey*. In neither of those cases was any evidence given tending to connect the 'nominated defendant' with the commission of the negligent acts. In *Adams* v. *Naylor* the form of request by the plaintiff's solicitors to the War Office was: 'We should be obliged if you would furnish us with the name, rank and other particulars of the officer who should be made defendant,' and no evidence was given as to that officer's liability in negligence. No plea was there put forward that the officer in question either was under a duty to the plaintiff to take care, or that he had negligently failed to perform that duty. The House of Lords expressly left open the difficult question of 'the duty alleged to be due from the defendant, an officer in His Majesty's Army, to a member of the public in respect of acts done or omitted to be done in course of his military service.' For reasons which I shall shortly explain, it is equally unnecessary for me to express a final opinion upon this difficult question, though if it had become necessary for me to decide it I should have held that such duty of care may be owed, and not properly fulfilled, by an officer who, by personal participation, is responsible for bringing a hostile and lethal object such as this wooden horse within the confines of a populous town without first subjecting it to a meticulous technical examination.

"Equally in *Royster* v. *Cavey* the plaintiff failed because the name of the defendant was furnished by the authorities as the nominal occupier of the munitions factory where the accident occurred, though, as was pointed out by Scott, L.J., in the course of his judgment, 'as a matter of fact . . . the defendant so named had nothing to do with the matter. He was not the occupier. He had been guilty of no negligence and of no breach of statutory duty under the Act.' These words cannot be applied, directly or by analogy, to the facts before me; I will go no further at the present stage than to say that the present Defendant, Col. Thymoetes, cannot ask to be dismissed from the suit merely by reason of the principles enunciated in the two previous cases to which I have referred.

"I now turn to the second part of his defence, based upon sect. 3 of the Personal Injuries (Emergency Provisions) Act,

CASSANDRA v. THYMOETES AND ANOTHER

1939. That Act authorises the making of a scheme for payments out of public funds in respect of 'war injuries sustained by gainfully-occupied persons' and persons of certain other classes. There is no question but that the Plaintiff, who was a paid Civil Servant in the employment of the Crown, comes within a class of persons referred to in the Act and included in the scheme.

"The short effect of sect. 3 of the Act is to exclude the recovery of damages in tort by persons of the classes described who sustain 'war injuries.'" His lordship read the section, and continued: "If, therefore, the injuries which the Plaintiff has admittedly suffered can be brought within the statutory definition of 'war injuries,' the action in tort is misconceived and she will be driven back to her remedies, such as they may be, under the Act and the scheme made thereunder.

"The definition of these words is to be found in sect. 8 and (so far as relevant) is as follows:—

' "War Injuries" means physical injuries caused by (i) the discharge of any missile (including liquids and gas), or (ii) the use of any weapon, explosive or other noxious thing, or (iii) the doing of any other injurious act, either by the enemy or in combating the enemy or in repelling an imagined attack by the enemy.'

"It is clear that the injuries suffered by the Plaintiff were physical injuries; it is equally clear, on the medical and other evidence, that they were caused by the use of a weapon or the doing of some other injurious act by the enemy, within the definition which I have quoted. Once this is established, I think it is clear that the injuries are 'war injuries' within the meaning of the Act, and it is immaterial that one of the causes of such injuries was attributable to the *actus interveniens* of the Defendant or some other person. I would respectfully adopt the language used by Denning, J., in

Minister of Pensions v. *Chennell*, with which I find myself in complete agreement. Stating that the principles which he there lays down are applicable both under the Personal Injuries Scheme and the Royal Warrant, Denning, J., proceeds:—'If the discharge of a missile or other event may be properly said to be "a" cause of the injury, that is sufficient to entitle the claimant to the award ... notwithstanding that there may be other causes co-operating to produce it, whether they be antecedent, concurrent or intervening. It is not necessary that the discharge of the missile or other event should be "the" cause of the injury in the sense either of the sole cause or of the effective and predominant cause.'

"I therefore hold that, in consequence of the provisions of sect. 3 of the Act, the claim against the first Defendant must fail, and the Plaintiff must be remitted to any rights she may have under the scheme.

"The case against the second Defendant may be more shortly disposed of. The Plaintiff's claim against him is for statutory negligence in failing to detain the alien Sinon as a person of hostile origin or associations, under Regulation 18B of the Defence Regulations, 1939. It is not necessary for me here to consider the difficult questions of causation referred to by Denning, J., in the case to which I have referred. The short answer to the Plaintiff's claim is to be found in the wording of the regulation as interpreted by the House of Lords in the well-known case of *Liversidge* v. *Anderson*. It was held in that case that the words of the regulation—'If the Secretary of State has reasonable cause to believe any person to be of hostile origin or associations ... he may make an order against that person directing that he be detained'— leave the administrative plenary discretion vested in the Secretary of State; that it is for him to decide whether he has reasonable grounds or not and to act accordingly, and that the Court cannot compel the disclosure of or enquire into the grounds of his belief. Since this is so in a positive sense, it seems to me that it must also be so in a negative sense; I cannot think that it is competent for the Court to go behind the discretion clearly vested by the regulation in the Secretary of State and to hold that he ought to have exercised such discretion in favour of detention, but has failed to do so. In all the circumstances the Plaintiff's claim against both Defendants fails, and the action must be dismissed with costs."

(*Reporter's Note*—This case was decided before the coming into force of the Crown Proceedings Act, 1947).

SUICIDE WHILE BALANCE DISTURBED

CHANCERY DIVISION

CIO-CIO-SAN (otherwise PINKERTON) v. ATTORNEY-GENERAL

Legitimacy—American "husband" and Japanese "wife"—Birth of Applicant in British Territory—Remarriage of "husband" under American law—British Nationality Acts, 1914-1943, s. 1 (1) (a)—Supreme Court of Judicature Act, 1925, s. 188—Capacity of parties to "marriage"—Validity of "marriage"—"Marriage for 999 years"—Whether "marriage for life."

MR. JUSTICE PUCCINI delivered judgment as follows: "This is an application for a declaration of legitimacy under sec. 188 of the Supreme Court of Judicature Act, 1925, by Mr. Trouble Cio-Cio-San, otherwise known as Pinkerton. I find the circumstances of his parentage and birth to be as follows:

"His mother, Butterfly Cio-Cio-San, was at all material times a Japanese national, domiciled in the Empire of Japan. In 1922 this lady, then a spinster, became acquainted with a Lieutenant B. F. Pinkerton, of the United States Navy, an American Citizen, domiciled in the United States. His vessel was on a visiting cruise to Nagasaki, where the lady resided; relations between the two countries were at that time on a friendly basis, and Japan had been one of the Allied and Associated Powers in the First World War.

"A strong mutual attachment rapidly developed between Pinkerton and Butterfly, and it was not long before a contract of marriage was prepared. An active part in the negotiations was taken by one Goro, a Japanese national, who appears to have combined the *rôles* of family-lawyer and marriage-broker. The ceremony of marriage took place on the 20th day of February 1922, in the presence of several witnesses, including the said Goro; a Japanese lady called Suzuki, the personal attendant of the bride, and a Mr. Sharpless, then United States Consul at Nagasaki.

"The marriage was duly consummated, but a few days later the husband (as I will call him) was compelled by the exigencies of his naval duties to return to the United States. He promised the wife (as I may refer to her) that he would return the following spring. In October, 1922, the wife's relatives persuaded her to visit friends in the British Possession of Hong Kong, where the Applicant was born on the 18th November, 1922. She returned early in December to Nagasaki, where she continued to reside.

"At no time after his departure from Japan did the husband communicate with the wife, nor did she receive any allowance from him or from the naval authorities on his behalf. With traditional Oriental patience she waited and hoped for his return. Nor was she shaken in her faith in him when the spring of 1923 came and passed, and the year drew to a close without news of her husband. She was in serious financial straits, but she (in pleasing contrast to current notions of marital fidelity in some western countries) resolutely refused the advice tendered her by her friends that she should take divorce proceedings under Japanese law and accept one of the numerous proposals of other suitors, some of them wealthy and of high rank. She was convinced that her husband would return to her, and she appears (on the evidence) to have been strengthened in the discharge of her duties as a wife by the fact that she had, shortly before the date of the marriage, been received into the Christian communion.

"Three years elapsed without so much as a word from the husband. Early in 1925 the Consul Mr. Sharpless received a letter from him, as a result of which he visited Butterfly and attempted (without success) to prepare her for what was to follow. All that he was able to make her understand was that the husband was on his way back to Japan. So much was indeed true; but what the wife failed to realise was that Pinkerton, with the proverbial inconstancy of the seafaring man, had meanwhile 'married' an American lady in his native country, and she was accompanying him on his return.

"The closing events of this history were swift and tragic. Butterfly, overjoyed at the prospect of reunion with the man she loved, decorated her house and made all preparations to receive him with that love and affection which her faith (as she believed) had justified. By an unfortunate accident the first arrival at the house was the American 'wife,' Kate Pinkerton. At sight of her, Butterfly, with a woman's instinct, realised the truth at last. Retiring to her room she took her own life, Japanese fashion, with her father's sword.

"The child to whom she had (in memory of her long period of anxiety) given the name of 'Trouble', was sent by her family to England; he was brought up and educated here and is domiciled in this country. By virtue of his birth within His Majesty's dominions—*viz.* at Hong Kong—he is a natural-born British subject (British Nationality and Status of Aliens Acts, 1914 to 1943, sec. 1 (1) (a)), and he is therefore entitled under sec. 188 of the Supreme Court of Judicature Act, 1925, to make application for a declaration of legitimacy in this Court.

"In order to decide the question of legitimacy it is necessary for me to consider the circumstances of the union between the petitioner's parents; if that union was a valid marriage the Applicant's legitimacy will be established. The question is one of considerable difficulty.

"In the first place I have to consider the question of the capacity of the parties to contract a valid marriage. This matter is dependent upon the laws of their respective domicils at the date of the marriage in question. The law in both cases is foreign law—that of the United States and that of Japan. Evidence of foreign law is received in the Courts of England as a matter, not of law, but of fact (*Beatty* v. *Beatty*). Two affidavits have been placed before me—one by the Consul Sharpless and one by the said Goro, who states that he is a person entitled to practise in the Japanese Courts and is well acquainted with the law of Japan. Both affidavits make it clear beyond all doubt that the parties to the ceremony of 1922 had full capacity, by the law of their respective domicils, to contract a valid marriage.

"The next question which I have to consider is the essential validity of such a marriage as that into which the parties purported to enter. This question also depends upon the law of their respective domicils (*Ogden* v. *Ogden*). Here I am brought up against my first main difficulty. The affidavit of the said Sharpless makes it clear that the ceremony was not performed in accordance with the law of any State of the American Union, and that the attendance of the Consul Sharpless thereat was not in his official capacity, but as a friend of the bridegroom. No evidence has been adduced by the learned Attorney-General or by the Applicant as to the essential validity of such a marriage under American law. It was strongly argued by the learned Attorney-General that the invalidity of this Japanese union under the law of the United States might be inferred from the subsequent marriage, within the United States itself, between Pinkerton and the lady described as 'Kate.' But I cannot hold that this is conclusive; the second marriage, for aught I can tell, may have been bigamous so far as American law is concerned. I must leave this doubtful question for the time being as it stands and pass to other matters.

"The affidavit of the said Goro, on the other hand, establishes the essential validity of the marriage, by the law of the wife's domicil, beyond all doubt. The said affidavit deals also with the third question that I have to decide—the validity of the actual form of ceremony as a proper ceremony of marriage. This question, as is well known, is a matter for the *lex loci celebrationis*—the law of Japan (*Berthiaume* v. *Dastous*). It is clear to me beyond all reasonable doubt, from the affidavit of the said Goro, that the ceremony was duly performed in accordance with the forms required by that law—the reading of the contract, the presence of witnesses and the free consent of both parties. Subject therefore to the doubtful question of essential validity under American law, to which I have referred, I should have had no hesitation in coming to the conclusion that the union between the Applicant's parents was a valid marriage in all respects, but for two further matters to which I must now refer.

"In the first place the learned Attorney-General has argued that since, under the law of Japan, a wife deserted and left without financial resources by her husband—it matters not for what length of time—may divorce him and marry again, what is called a Japanese marriage is not such a marriage as the law of England can recognise as such. Whatever the law of the domicil of the parties—so runs the argument—whatever the forms required by the *lex loci celebrationis*, the law of England will recognise no union as a marriage unless it is a marriage in the Christian sense—'the voluntary union of one man and one woman for life, to the exclusion of all others' (*Hyde* v. *Hyde*). Now, that proposition is true of marriage in the Christian sense; but, as has been emphasised by the highest authority in this country in a recent case, the obligations of a civil marriage under the law of England are not in all respects co-extensive with those of a religious marriage (*Weatherley* v. *Weatherley*). The latter are unalterable; the former have to some extent been modified by statute—considerably modified in recent years. The law of England—as opposed to the religious law—recognises that the rights and duties of matrimony may come to an end during the lifetime of both the spouses if, and only if, a decree absolute of divorce is pronounced by a competent Court, by authority of law. Moreover, if authority is required, it was held in the case of *Nachimson* v. *Nachimson* that the circumstances in which under foreign law (in that case the law of Soviet Russia) a divorce may be obtained during the lifetime of the spouses do not, *ceteris paribus*, prevent a monogamous union, entered into in the first instance for life, with the consent of both parties, having full capacity, valid according to the forms of the *lex loci celebrationis* and recognised as essentially valid by the law of the domicil of each of the parties, from being recognised as a valid marriage by the law of England. That is the answer to the learned Attorney-General's contention.

"But, that being said, I must emphasise the final point. The foreign marriage which is being considered, in order that it may be considered by the English Court as a valid marriage, must be, at the time when it is entered into, the kind of union which has been described as a 'Christian marriage,' though not necessarily in the religious sense. That is to say, it must be monogamous—exclusive to one man and one woman—and it must be entered into, at the date of the marriage itself, for life. Here I am brought up against the second great difficulty of this case, for I am informed by the affidavit of the said Goro that this Japanese ceremony, valid in all other respects, purported to unite the parties (in Japanese fashion) for a period of nine hundred and ninety-nine years. I am not disposed to be swayed by the argument of the learned Attorney-General to the effect that I should apply the analogy from the law of property, nor do I propose to follow him in his expatiations upon the distinction under that law between a life estate before 1926 or a life interest since 1925, on the one hand, and a term of years absolute, on the other hand. Nor do I feel able, much as I regret it, to accede to the argument of Counsel for the Applicant that a marriage entered into, in the first instance, for a term of nine hundred and ninety-nine years—a period some fourteen times as long as the average span of human life—is for that reason, *a fortiori*, a marriage for life, if not for several lives to come. Nor, again, is the rule against perpetuities in question.

"The matter to be decided is one of principle. If I am to accede to the Applicant's request, and to hold that a marriage for the term of nine hundred and ninety-nine years is a valid marriage, where is the line to be drawn? If such a marriage is valid, so also is a marriage for ninety-nine years, or, in the case of parties who have attained their majority, for eighty years and upwards. If the status of marriage for a definite term is once admitted, what becomes of the principle? Is a Judge to hold that a marriage for a forty years term is valid for spouses in their sixties at the date of the marriage, but invalid for spouses under thirty years of age? I can see no justification for any such proposition. Human life is proverbially uncertain in its duration; with the progress of science it may well be susceptible of considerable extension. It is not for a Court of first instance to admit into the marriage law of England a principle so novel in its conception, so unpredictable in its implications.

"I venture to express the hope that a higher Court than this may have the opportunity of expressing an opinion upon this difficult question. Meanwhile I have come, with great hesitation and extreme reluctance, to the conclusion that, solely by reason that it was expressed to be entered into for a limited term of years, the said Japanese marriage was not one which ought to be recognised by the law of England, and that the Applicant's application must therefore be dismissed. The Applicant has all my sympathy, and leave to appeal, if asked for, will be readily granted."

DISCOVERY AND INSPECTION

Probate Divorce and Admiralty Division (Divorce)

CUPID *v.* CUPID (otherwise EROS)

Divorce—Husband's refusal to disclose identity—Disobedience of wife to husband's order—Alleged desertion by husband—Whether "without cause"—Matrimonial Causes Act, 1932, s. 2—Whether husband's order "reasonable"—Whether wife's disobedience justified.

THE President delivered the following judgment:
"This is a petition by Mrs. Psyche Cupid against her husband for dissolution of marriage on the grounds of his desertion. The marriage took place on the 10th August, 1942, and the petition, after giving particulars of cohabitation abroad and the subsequent establishment of a matrimonial domicil in this country, alleges that the Respondent has deserted the Petitioner without cause for a period of at least three years immediately preceding the presentation of this petition, the Respondent now being resident in Piccadilly Circus in the City of Westminster, and having failed to make a home for her or to cohabit with her since December 1943.

"The Respondent by his answer denies such desertion. He pleads, first, that the matrimonial home is in the house of his mother, Mrs. Aphrodite (better known as the leading lady in the beauty-chorus at the Mount Ida Theatre under her stage-name of Venus), and that his withdrawal from cohabitation with the Petitioner was not without cause, but took place by reason of the Petitioner's conduct in persistently disobeying his orders.

"The Petitioner's evidence discloses a relationship between the parties which, during the courtship and the early days of marriage, was of a strange and unusual nature. The Respondent, whose occupation is described as that of a toxophilist, never visited the Petitioner in daylight, and from the commencement of their acquaintance was insistent that they should meet only in a darkened room. The mystery was deepened by his refusal over a long period to give her any particulars about himself and his family—a refusal in which he persisted at and after the date of the marriage. Such a state of affairs would have been impossible in this country, where the marriage laws are designed to secure the utmost publicity as to the identity and matrimonial intentions of the parties, both prior to and at the ceremony itself; the evidence shows, however, that the ceremony in this case, which was held at midnight in a ruined and unlighted temple at Paphos, was valid according to the *lex loci celebrationis*, and no issue is raised thereon.

"It appears that the marriage was happy for the first few months, the Petitioner consoling herself for the mysterious comings and goings of the Respondent, and his refusal to allow her to see him in the light, with the reflection (perhaps not unnatural in a young and immature girl) that he was obviously a youthful, virile and considerate lover, and that (as she naively expressed it in the box) 'the whole thing was most romantic.' There came a time, however, when feminine curiosity began to get the better of discretion. She began to urge the Respondent to disclose his identity and family connections or, at all events, to allow her to see him in the light. To all such requests she received a brusque refusal, and she does not deny that the Respondent expressly forbade her at any time to make any attempt to see his features. His only explanation was that his mother would strongly disapprove of his marriage if she discovered that it had taken place.

"It does not appear to have occurred to the Petitioner, at first, that there was any other hidden reason for the secrecy with which the Respondent surrounded his personality. She has told me, and I have no reason to disbelieve her, that, so far as she was able to judge from tactile impressions, she could observe no physical deformity or malformation in her husband's body, except for a slight abnormality in the form of two small feathery excrescences in the region of the shoulder-blades, to which she herself attached little importance. When, however, she began to discuss the matter (as young wives will) with her sisters, in whom she was in the habit of confiding, they expressed considerable alarm at what she had discovered. Their curiosity expressed itself in importunities which at length persuaded her that the concealment insisted upon by the Respondent was due to some sinister motive connected with his physical appearance. At all events, she has explained how she at length succumbed to curiosity.

"On the 10th December 1943, the parties had retired to rest, as usual, in a darkened room. Satisfied from the Respondent's regular breathing that he was sound asleep, the Petitioner slipped from the marital bed and found and lighted an old oil-lamp which she kept in an attic; she has made it clear that, in pursuance of the precautions of secrecy which I have described, the Respondent had removed all electric light fittings from the bedroom. Returning with the lighted lamp, she held it over the sleeping figure.

"It is unnecessary for me to enter in detail into the naively ecstatic description of her husband's physical attractions, on which the Petitioner dilated, with many affecting details, during her evidence in the witness-box. It must suffice for my present purpose to say that his beauty of form and feature bewildered and overwhelmed her. The epithet 'godlike,' which, with the natural hyperbole of the very young, she applied to his personal appearance, graphically expressed her feelings when she thus looked upon him for the first time.

"It was unfortunate for the Petitioner that, in that moment of pleasurable agitation, her caution momentarily deserted her. Tilting the lamp to obtain a better view of her sleeping spouse, she inadvertently spilled a small drop of hot oil on his body. At the impact the Respondent awoke, and the recriminations which he hurled at her, and the language in which he expressed them, appear to have been anything but 'godlike.' I forbear to enter into these painful details, but it is clear that in that moment the Petitioner realised that her marital happiness had been irreparably shattered.

"With the stern admonition that, by her lack of confidence and disobedience to his orders, the Petitioner had forfeited his affection, the Respondent left the house there and then, without even staying to dress. He vouchsafed no information as to his future movements except to say that he was going to stay with his mother, whose name he now for the first time disclosed. The following day he entered into a contract to sell the matrimonial home with vacant possession; the title being registered, completion took place within fourteen days, and the Petitioner found herself homeless.

"Since that date there can be no question that the Petitioner has acted with sound commonsense and propriety. She consulted a Solicitor; as a result of his advice, and acting under a proper sense of her marital duty, though with serious misgivings, she sought out the home of Mrs. Aphrodite, the mother of her spouse. She has explained that her husband's last remark had given her to understand that he intended to make his home there for the time being; she felt it her duty as his wife to follow him thither, in accordance with the legal principle that it is within the husband's province to decide where the matrimonial home is to be.

"As might have been expected, however, the Petitioner's complaisance in her husband's high-handed conduct did not produce the desired effect. The Respondent segregated himself in one suite of rooms in the house, which is of extensive size, and refused either to sleep with her, to take his meals or his recreation in her company, or even to converse with her. The Petitioner has told me, and I believe her, that his silence and neglect were hard to bear; on the part of his mother it was certainly neither silence nor neglect that were matters for complaint. The Petitioner has described in affecting terms, no word of which rings falsely, how Mrs. Aphrodite displayed all that fretful arrogance towards her son's young and attractive wife which so often accompanies the attainment, by a once beautiful woman, of more than mature years. What has been called by one medical witness the 'mother-in-law complex' accounts for a fair proportion of the broken marriages which pass in review before the Judges of this Division, and this case is unfortunately no exception. From my observation of her demeanour in the witness-box it is clear that, in addition, Mrs. Aphrodite possesses more than the usual share of that combination of bad nerves and worse manners, sometimes misnamed 'artistic temperament,' which one associates with members of the theatrical profession. However that may be, it is clear that she treated the Petitioner in the most inconsiderate manner; menial tasks, rough words, shrill commands and even blows formed the treatment that fell to her lot during that unhappy period. It is unnecessary for me to go into details; the evidence has shown that the Petitioner's physical and mental health has been broken by the treatment she has received; and if the Respondent cannot be associated with that treatment in the sense of instigation or encouragement, there is no question that he was continually aware of it but remained aloof and callously indifferent.

"Counsel for the Respondent has argued that, since the husband has the privilege of deciding where and under what conditions the spouses shall reside, it was open to him in this case to transfer the matrimonial home to his mother's house if he so desired. Such a proposition is unexceptionable in law, but I was unable to follow Counsel in his statement of the corollaries which (according to him) follow from that proposition. His argument amounts to this—that there can be no desertion in the full legal sense where husband and wife, notwithstanding that they have ceased sexual cohabitation, are living under one roof; and further that, if this husband's attitude to his wife had become colder and more distant, this was an attitude which he had every right to adopt by reason of her disobedience to his commands.

"Even apart from authority I should have been disposed to hold that, on questions of desertion, every case must be considered on its own facts, and that there may be instances where both the *animus deserendi*, and the act itself, are clearly evidenced by the conduct of a spouse in cutting himself off from the society of and *consortium* with the other spouse even while they continue physically to reside in the same house, or even in the same suite of rooms. There is, however, ample authority on the point; although mere refusal of sexual intercourse does not, of and by itself, constitute desertion (*Weatherley* v. *Weatherley*), nevertheless a withdrawal from cohabitation and segregation (by a voluntary act) of one spouse from the society of the other in a separate part of the house, continued over the statutory period, has been held to amount to such desertion as the law requires for the granting of a decree *nisi* of divorce (*Powell* v. *Powell*). On the facts proved before me I have no hesitation in holding that the Respondent has been guilty of such desertion in this case." (His Lordship referred also to *Wilkes* v. *Wilkes*).

"The law however requires something more; sect. 2 of the Matrimonial Causes Act, 1937, lays down that such desertion must be 'without cause.' The Respondent pleads that this condition has not been complied with; he argues that his desertion, as I have held it to be, was not 'without cause'—the cause, in his view, being the disobedience of the wife to his order not to seek to discover his identity or to look upon his features. In deference to the able argument of the Respondent's Counsel I will accept, for a moment, the proposition that the withdrawal by the Respondent from cohabitation and *consortium* with the Petitioner was 'caused' by her act of disobedience in the full sense of the word. But can this be said to be sufficient to establish his defence?

"It is clear that the words in the section to which I have referred—'without cause'—must be construed (as so often in Acts of Parliament) as meaning 'without reasonable cause.' Let us suppose, for example, the hypothetical and extreme case of a husband of so perverse a disposition that he were to order his wife to show herself complaisant to a friend who desired her to commit adultery with him; suppose the wife were, quite properly, to refuse; suppose, in consequence of her refusal, the husband left her; could the husband in such a case be heard to say, in answer to a plea of desertion on his part, that he had left her not 'without cause,' and that his desertion was in the circumstances justified? Is there anybody who thinks that such a plea could possibly succeed? The cause—if such it were—would not be reasonable, and Parliament cannot have intended so absurd a result to follow from the omission of the word 'reasonable' from the section.

"What I have to determine, therefore, is whether it is a reasonable cause giving rise to a husband's desertion of his wife that the wife disobeys his order to refrain from trying to see his features or to ascertain his identity. Putting the question another way, was the husband's order in itself reasonable or unreasonable, and was the wife's disobedience of that order reasonable or unreasonable in the circumstances? These questions in my view admit of no possible doubt. The husband's order was unreasonable in the extreme; the wife behaved reasonably in disobeying it, and the husband's desertion, in retaliation for her disobedience, was without reasonable cause.

"In conclusion I would respectfully adopt the language of Morton, L. J., in allowing the appeal of the wife petitioner in *Meacher* v. *Meacher* (a cruelty case), the terms of which may be applied *mutatis mutandis* to the case before me. Criticising the judgment in the Court below, the learned Lord Justice said:—

'If this judgment is pushed to its logical extreme, it would seem to follow that a husband may issue unreasonable orders to his wife and beat her' (I would say here 'desert her') 'if she disobeys them; and the wife cannot obtain a divorce on the grounds of cruelty' (here 'desertion'), 'however often this happens, because she can prevent any further beatings' (or 'desertion') 'by obeying her husband in all respects. I cannot and do not believe that this is the law. . . I cannot agree that this Court is not justified in intervening where a wife is given an unreasonable order by her husband, disobeys it and the husband then violently assaults' (or 'deserts') 'her.'

"I pronounce a decree *nisi* in favour of the Petitioner with costs."

A STATUARY OFFENCE

King's Bench Division.

DE ULLOA v. TENORIO

Conflict of laws—Seduction abroad—Jurisdiction of English Court—Alleged death of plaintiff before action—Law Reform (Misc. Provns.) Act, 1934, s.1—No survival of action for seduction—Evidence of death inconclusive.

JUDGMENT of Mr. Justice Mozart:

"This is an action between two Spanish nationals in respect of a tort committed outside the jurisdiction of this Court. The Plaintiff is Major-General Don Pedro de Ulloa, sometime Military Commandant of the Spanish City of Seville, who claims damages against the Defendant, Don Juan Tenorio, in respect of the seduction by the Defendant of the Plaintiff's daughter, Doña Ana. The Defendant does not deny the allegations in the statement of claim, but pleads simply that the Plaintiff died before the commencement of these proceedings and that, in consequence, the action must fail.

"The case involves a number of difficult and doubtful questions, not the least of which is a conflict of evidence on the matter alleged by the Defendant on the pleadings. I propose in the first place to state the history of the matter, so far as it is uncontroverted, before I go on to deal with the questions in dispute and with the points of law to which they give rise.

"The Plaintiff's family is of high repute in Spain and has a proud record of outstanding military services to the State.

On his retirement from the Army, some ten years ago, the Plaintiff was appointed Military Commandant of the City of Seville, an office the duties of which he discharged with distinction, and which he still held at the time of the events which I am about to relate. His daughter, Doña Ana, was a lady of high repute in the aristocratic society of Seville; she was betrothed to a young nobleman called Don Octavio, but was not yet married. Her mother being dead, she spent her time in supervising the servants and undertaking the management of her father's household. No breath of suspicion had ever touched her virtuous reputation until the Defendant came upon the scene.

"The Defendant has also been a soldier; he is, I am informed, an expert swordsman and has achieved a reputation upon the Continent of Europe as a successful duellist in those 'affairs of honour' which, though illegal in England, are still tolerated by the laws of many foreign countries. His greater notoriety, however, as he was at pains to emphasise in the witness-box, arises from affairs of another kind. His own evidence and that of his valet, Leporello, has made it clear that he is one of those irresponsible young men who regard a reputation for sexual promiscuity as a tribute to their virility. The Defendant went out of his way to tell the Court, upon his oath, that in the past few years he has seduced no less than two thousand and sixty-five young women; his effrontery has gone to the length of annexing a detailed schedule to the defence which he has filed, divided into columns showing dates, places and the names of the victims. What the Defendant hoped to gain by this remarkable piece of exhibitionism I am unable to judge, but I observe that his 'affairs,' as he terms them, number two hundred and forty-five in Italy, two hundred and thirty-one in Germany, one hundred in France and no less than one thousand and three in his native country of Spain. I observe with some relief that the schedule contains no reference to England, which I should have taken to be a high tribute to the exceptional virtue of my fellow-countrywomen, had not the Defendant insisted on explaining that he has but recently arrived in this country for the first time in his life; he appended a number of other comments which I need not repeat, but which were calculated less to pay tribute to the native modesty of Englishwomen in general than to reflect upon their alleged emotional shortcomings.

"The evidence of the Defendant (if such it can be called) filled me with the utmost trepidation, which may serve to explain my digression from the immediate questions before me to comment upon a matter of high public policy. If I understand the defendant aright, this case is but the first of a series of some eighteen hundred similar actions, in which injured parents residing in seven or eight different continental countries of Europe are claiming damages against the Defendant for seduction of their respective daughters. As a Judge of the High Court I cannot but view with extreme perturbation the prospect of a high degree of congestion in the cause lists of this Division and the piling up of arrears which will, in my calculation, engage all the available Judges for several years to come. I can only trust that steps will be taken to consolidate such actions wherever possible. Meanwhile I desire to state in the most emphatic terms that I regard the continued presence of the Defendant upon our shores as a menace not merely to English womanhood, but to the entire fabric and machinery of English justice.

"I must not, however, be led by natural indignation and repugnance to shrink from the task of determining the issues before me in this action. The Plaintiff's statement of claim sets out, in the usual form, the facts to which I have referred and pleads that, by reason of the pregnancy of his daughter as a result of her seduction by the Defendant, the Plaintiff was deprived of her household services for a period of some six months. The nature of those services has been adequately proved by the Plaintiff and by the said Don Octavio; expert evidence of the law of Spain has satisfied me that seduction is not justifiable according to the law of that country. As it is also a tort by the law of England, this Court has jurisdiction to deal with the case (*Machado* v. *Fontes*). I find that the Plaintiff has amply proved his case. All that remains is to deal with the allegation raised by the defence to the effect that the Plaintiff is no longer a living person and that the action cannot therefore proceed.

"The importance of this issue is paramount. By the common law of England the maxim *actio personalis moritur cum persona* applies, *inter alia*, to actions of tort, in which class the action for seduction falls. It is true that the common law rule has to some extent been abrogated in recent years by the provisions of sec.1 of the Law Reform (Miscellaneous Provisions) Act, 1934, which provided that a cause of action vested in a person during his lifetime shall not lapse on his death, but shall be exercisable or enforceable by his legal personal representatives for the benefit of his estate. But the section expressly provides that certain types of action, of which the action for seduction is one, are excepted from the benefit of this change in the law; to this class of action the common law rule is still applicable. It is therefore incumbent upon me to consider the evidence as to whether the Plaintiff is alive or dead.

"That evidence is unfortunately of a conflicting nature. Early in the proceedings an application was filed on behalf of the Plaintiff for leave to give evidence on commission, on the ground that the Plaintiff was prevented by his public duties from leaving Spain. That application was granted by the Master and the evidence taken on commission is before me in writing. It states, *inter alia*, that the Plaintiff challenged the Defendant to a duel to avenge his daughter's honour, and that the Defendant seriously wounded the Plaintiff and escaped. The defendant alleges that the plaintiff died of his wounds before this action was instituted. The Plaintiff's daughter and Don Octavio have sworn that he is still living. No up-to-date medical evidence has been proffered by either side.

"In this conflict of evidence I must again meticulously examine the notes which I took of the testimony given before me. The Plaintiff's witnesses have sworn that, shortly after the duel to which I have referred, the Defendant, in a brazen spirit of bravado, sent a message, half in challenge, half in jest, to the Plaintiff's house, by which the Defendant invited the Plaintiff to dine with him on the following evening. Having regard to his physical condition, the daughter says (and I believe her) that she urged her father to ignore this fresh insult; but the proud old man was not to be deterred. Swathed as he was in bandages, he rose from his bed; stiff in every joint and tottering in his gait he proceeded to the house of his daughter's seducer and appeared punctually at the dinner-table. The Defendant (whose cool audacity is as remarkable as his moral worthlessness) sat through the meal opposite the Plaintiff in affected ease, left him to find his way home as best he could and departed the same night by the French Express for England. The Plaintiff, though his recovery was greatly retarded by this excessive exertion, eventually became convalescent and is no longer confined to his bed, though he cannot now attend to his public duties. This is the evidence of Doña Ana and Don Octavio.

"Cross-examined upon this episode, the Defendant told

a strange story, which was corroborated by the valet, Leporello. They were unshaken in the assertion that the Plaintiff, pierced during the duel by the Defendant's sword in a vital part, was dead when they left the scene. When the details of the invitation to dinner, and its acceptance, were put to them, they denied that the invitation was sent to the Plaintiff's house, but alleged that the Defendant, in contemptuous disregard of that awe and reverence with which the newly-dead are locally regarded, defiantly shouted his invitation at the statue of the plaintiff which the City Council, in recognition of his services, had erected during his lifetime in the public square. Such an act in this country would be a meaningless formality, but I can well believe that in some Mediterranean lands, where superstition is notoriously rife, it may (if it did in fact take place) have had a significance in adding to the Defendant's existing notoriety a reputation for defiance of supernatural, as well as moral, sanctions.

"Be that as it may, these two witnesses persisted in their story that their dinner-guest was not the live Commandant but his statue—the statue of a man already dead. They described, in almost identical words, the stiffness of his gait, the marble-like pallor of his countenance, the dead whiteness of his body and the cold touch of his hand. They both reacted strongly to Counsel's suggestion that they had invented the whole story. Nevertheless, I should have had no hesitation in committing them for perjury, but for two circumstances. The first is that they produced evidence (from respectable witnesses) of similar happenings of an allegedly miraculous nature in a town not far from Seville; superstition appears to be deeply ingrained in the character of the inhabitants of that part of the country. And, in the second place, both the Defendant and his valet, Leporello, agreed on circumstantial details; they have both described how the Defendant's invitation was followed and the arrival of the guest was heralded by a mysterious burst of music— 'the chord,' they insisted, 'of D minor and its dominant, played by unseen trombones and horns.' This delusion (for delusion it certainly appears) that affected their hearing seems to have extended to their other senses also, for both spoke of seeing the alleged statue surrounded by a reddish glow and of smelling the odour of burning brimstone. I am disposed to put a charitable interpretation on the matter and will conclude that the senses of the Defendant and his valet were deceived by the alcoholic liquor which they admitted they had been sharing, the effects of which no doubt manifested themselves in strange noises in the ears, unaccountable odours in the nostrils and an indistinctness of vision which led them to mistake the pale, bandaged and white-swathed figure of the Plaintiff, with his stiff joints and ungainly walk, for the coming to life of a marble statue.

"No credible evidence of the Plaintiff's death having been adduced, I accept the statements of his witnesses, and I give judgment for the Plaintiff in the action and award him one thousand pounds damages and costs."

INJURY BY MARITIME FAULT

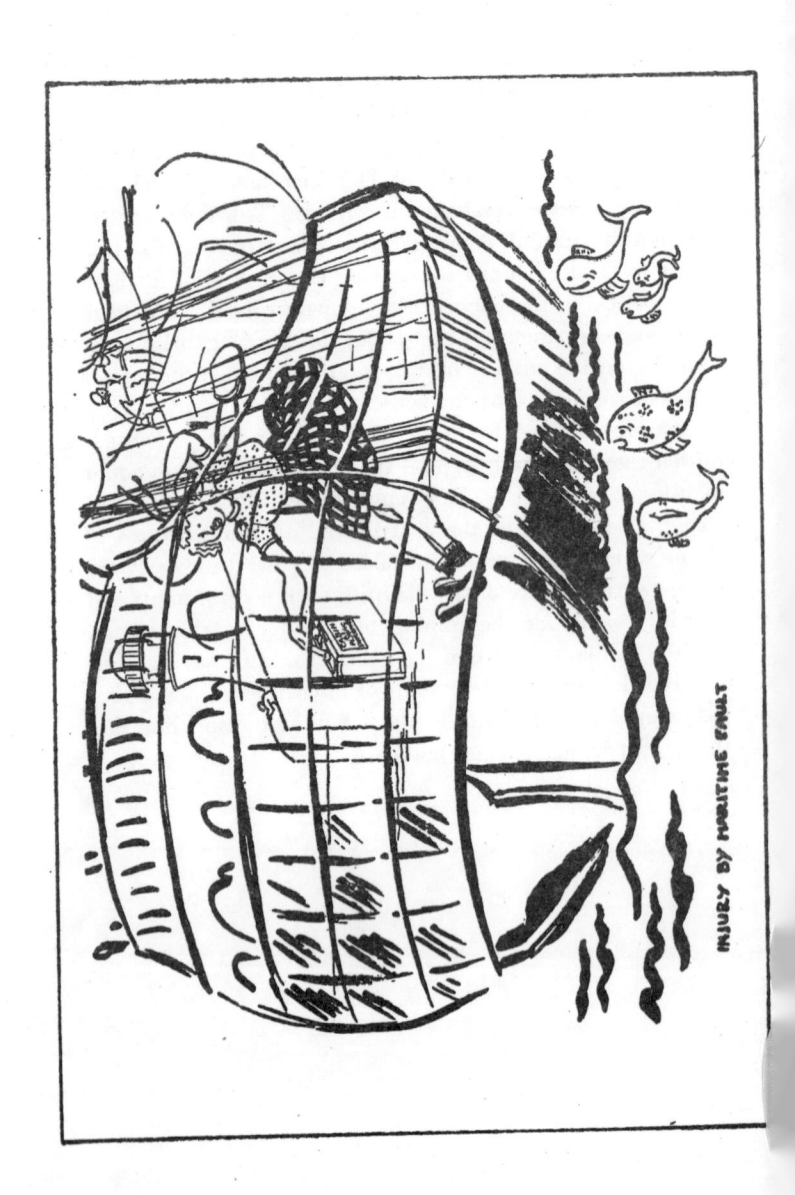

PROBATE DIVORCE AND ADMIRALTY DIVISION (ADMIRALTY)
THE FLYING DUTCHMAN

*Admiralty—Maritime lien—Loss of expectation of life—Alleged "phantom ship"—Law Reform (Misc. Provns.) Act, 1934, s.1—Fatal Accidents Acts, 1846-1908—Supreme Court of Judicature Act, 1925, s.22(1)—Jurisdiction—*Volenti non fit injuria*—Duty of shipowners—Claim by covenantee—Whether binding on subsequent owners.*

THE President delivered the following judgment:

"This is an action by Mr. Daland, a Norwegian National, as legal personal representative of his daughter, Miss Senta Daland, deceased, against the owners of the ship *Flying Dutchman*, for damages for loss of expectation of life of the Plaintiff's said daughter, who was drowned in boarding or attempting to board the said ship, owing to the alleged negligence of the said owners, their servants or agents. The Plaintiff also claims a maritime lien on the vessel, in accordance with the Admiralty rule that damage by a ship through its maritime fault *ipso facto* gives rise to such a lien in favour of the injured party.

"The Defendants raise the plea of *volenti non fit injuria*, alleging that the deceased lady was well aware of the fact that the said vessel was a 'phantom ship' and that she voluntarily acquiesced in the risk involved in boarding or attempting to board such a vessel. The matter is further complicated by the intervention of a third party, a Mr. Satan, who alleges that the vessel is subject to a restrictive covenant or obligation in his favour, of a nature which ought to be enforced by a Court of Equity; that the said restrictive obligation requires the defendant ship not to remain in port save for three days in every seven years, but subject thereto to sail the seas for an undefined period at his option, and that in the circumstances the Court should refuse to arrest the ship; alternatively, he asks for a declaration that the said restrictive obligation shall bind the said ship into whosesoever hands the same may come.

"The history of this case is in my experience unprecedented, but I will state the facts as best I may.

"The vessel which forms the subject-matter of the action is of a surprisingly great age, having been registered in 1621. She still sails however under the flag of the Netherlands, and appears to have been continuously in service since the date mentioned. Having regard to the enormous lapse of time since the date when the vessel was constructed, it is not difficult to understand that her seaworthiness and general condition must have left much to be desired. No attempt, however, appears to have been made by the appropriate Netherlands authorities to have her placed out of commission.

"In or about the month of January, 1947, the vessel called at the Norwegian port of Trondhjem, where the Plaintiff and his daughter resided. It is abundantly clear on the evidence that the identity of this ship, and the length of time she had been sailing the seas, were matters of common knowledge in those parts, and it is not denied by the Plaintiff that his daughter, the deceased girl, Senta, was well aware of the position. Undeterred, however, by the restless life in store for her, this misguided young woman lent an attentive ear to a proposal of marriage made to her by the master of the vessel; her father, the Plaintiff, was reluctantly persuaded to give his consent. For some reason, which I was unable fully to appreciate, the suitor, the master of the ship, appears the next day to have repented of his offer—whether from an understandable reluctance to expose the lady to the dangers of a voyage in a vessel so unseaworthy, or whether from the proverbial fickleness of his profession, does not appear. At all events the master set sail from Trondhjem the next evening at sunset, without her, and also, as it appears, without a word of explanation for his change of intention. The unfortunate young woman rushed to the quayside and, with more impulsiveness than discretion, leapt on to the deck of the moving ship.

"At this point there is a serious conflict of evidence. The witnesses for the Defendants have stated that the vessel was, and was well known to the deceased to be, a 'phantom ship'; pressed for further explanation they alleged that the vessel was of some insubstantial or incorporeal nature, designed or adapted only for carrying what they describe as a 'ghostly crew'; that she sailed the seas only under the impulse of a so-called 'accursed spell', and that she was unfit for and incapable of carrying human passengers and known to the deceased to be so unfit and incapable. One of the Defendants' witnesses, who stated that he was an expert in necromancy, went so far as to assert that the effect of an attempt by a natural person to board such a vessel would be that he would pass through the vessel as though it had no existence—that a leap (as I understood him) on to the 'notional' deck of this 'notional' vessel would be a leap into empty space.

"On the other side the witnesses for the Plaintiff have stated that the vessel was ostensibly a normal sailing ship, carrying red sails and a black mast, and that, apart from the presence of a profuse growth of barnacles on her hull and other similar indications of extreme age, there was nothing in her appearance to suggest that she was unfit for norm cargo and passenger service. These witnesses allege, however, that the events observed by watchers on the quayside indicate that the deceased, in leaping on the vessel, struck the deck at a point where the timbers were rotten; the weight of her body, and the force behind her leap, carried her through the flimsy structure of the vessel, and out amidships, on the starboard side, into the sea.

"I have carefully considered the evidence on both sides and I unhesitatingly accept that of the witnesses for the Plaintiff in preference to that for the Defendants. The classification of a vessel as a 'phantom ship' is one unknown to the Elder Brethren who have assisted me with advice during the hearing, and unrecognised by English maritime law or the law of nations; nor is such a classification to be found among the many vessels listed in Lloyd's Register. The Defendants have admitted that the vessel is over three hundred years old, and this fact in itself is sufficient at one and the same time to afford a perfectly natural explanation for the cause and manner of the accident and to convict the Defendants, the owners of the vessel, of negligence in a high degree. The application of the maxim *res ipsa loquitur* appears to be more appropriate to the circumstances than the maxim quoted by the defence, but on this point I shall have more to say at a later stage.

"One thing at all events is clear. Despite immediate efforts at rescue, the boat which was lowered to pick up this unfortunate girl was unable to do more than recover her lifeless body.

"The vessel, the crew of which appear to have been unperturbed by this terrible accident, continued on her voyage and is now lying in the port of London; the Plaintiff now sues the owners of the vessel for damages in respect of his daughter's death under s.1 of the Law Reform (Miscellaneous Provisions) Act, 1934, and the Fatal Accidents Acts, 1846 to 1908.

"Such are the melancholy circumstances giving rise to the plaintiff's action. A number of difficult questions of law are involved, and I must now turn to consider these in detail.

"The first question that arises is that of jurisdiction. The damage suffered by the plaintiff occurred in Norwegian waters; the delinquent vessel sails under the Netherlands flag. The Supreme Court of Judicature Act, 1925, sec. 22 (1), provides:

'The High Court shall, in relation to Admiralty matters, have the following jurisdiction................(a) ....(iv) any claim for damage done by a ship.'

"The meaning and effect of these words were recently considered in the Court of Appeal in the case of *The Tolten*. I cannot do better than quote the words used by Scott, L. J., in summarising the law on the subject:

'In my view the law maritime of damage, as administered in our Admiralty Court, vests a right of action in any person who suffers injury anywhere in the world, either to his person or to his property, whether moveable or immoveable, afloat or ashore, when caused by the maritime fault of the owner of a ship, he being responsible for the acts or defaults of his servants.'

"The learned Lord Justice went on to deal with one possible exception to the doctrine, which however does not apply to the case before me. I therefore come to the conclusion that this Court has jurisdiction to deal with the action before it.

"The next question that I have to decide is whether the defence of *volenti non fit injuria* can succeed. This doctrine, as is well known, lays down that the plaintiff in an action of negligence cannot succeed in recovering damages against the defendant if, with full knowledge of all the risks involved, he voluntarily acquiesces therein and exposes himself to dangers of which he knows or could be reasonably expected to have known (*Cutler* v. *United Dairies*). He is not however precluded from claiming if he is under a legal or moral obligation to undertake such risks (*Haynes* v. *Harwood*). In the case before me I am of opinion that the doctrine cannot be applied to deprive the deceased's estate of the damages claimed, and that for two reasons. In the first place there is no evidence before me that the deceased was aware of the rotten state of the timbers of the vessel which had sailed in an apparently normal manner into harbour, and which (as the witnesses have described), with her blood-red sails and black mast, appeared to the uninitiated eye of a landsman to be as trim and seaworthy a ship as any other in the roads. And in the second place I hold (if it is necessary for me to express an opinion on the point) that as the master's affianced bride the deceased was under such a moral or social obligation to take all reasonable steps to accompany him on his voyage as justified her in acting as she did on the impulse of the moment. Had she jumped short and fallen into the sea from the quayside, it is arguable that the *volenti* doctrine might have been applicable, for a person who attempts to leap upon a moving ship is well aware of the risk of missing his aim; the risk is within his contemplation at the time he undertakes it. But it is not within the contemplation of such a person that the vessel on which he succeeds in embarking is in so derelict a condition that his body will go through the timbers as though they were composed of matchwood.

"For the rest, the owners were clearly under a duty towards persons rightfully embarking on the vessel, whether as passengers or crew, to take care that the vessel was in a seaworthy and safe condition, and fit to receive them. They have clearly failed in that duty and there will be judgment for the Plaintiff for damages of £1,000 and costs.

"I now turn to the third party claim, which I confess has given me a great deal of anxiety. I have been at some pains to elucidate the nature of the restrictive obligation to which I have referred, but the evidence thereon is conflicting and ambiguous in the extreme.

According to one witness the vessel was, three hundred and more years ago, laid under 'an accursed spell,' a phrase which is beyond my comprehension and which is certainly unknown to equitable terminology. Owing to the antiquity of the matter direct evidence is difficult to come by, and I was constrained to have recourse to the Evidence Act of 1938 and, in my efforts at elucidation, to admit testimony on the borderline of hearsay. That evidence amounts to this: that the original master of the vessel, after being repeatedly driven back in his efforts to keep on his course, swore that he would round the Cape of Good Hope even though he were forced to sail the seas in perpetuity, and that he would achieve his end, if necessary, with the assistance of a personage bearing the same name as the third party in this suit, but (as I am asked to infer) that party's predecessor in title. In this manner, I am informed, the obligation arose. I have sought in vain to ascertain the identity of the obligee, his whereabouts at the time—whether on board the ship as passenger, supercargo or pilot, or whether at some port in the vicinity; the nature of the contract; the capacity of the master at the time, whether as agent of necessity or otherwise. Counsel for the third party has sought to convince me with a number of arguments more remarkable for their ingenuity, in some instances, than for their relevance. On the analogy of the law of property he has put forward the doctrine of a lost grant, but has been unable to refer me to any authority supporting the application of that doctrine to a case of this kind. At a subsequent stage of the argument he suggested that this 'spell' or 'curse', as it is called, could be considered as attaching to the vessel as a species of restrictive covenant, to which the principle of *Tulk* v. *Moxhay* might properly be applied, so that a purchaser of, or even a person entitled to a lien on, the vessel, taking with notice thereof, might be bound thereby. And, finally, he argued, somewhat plausibly (if I may use the word without disrespect), that what is called a 'spell' or 'curse' upon the vessel, requiring her to sail the seas in perpetuity on the terms described, might be regarded as of the nature of a charter-party—a form of contract—entered into between the owners and Mr. Satan (or his predecessor in title) and binding upon subsequent owners or incumbrancers in accordance with the law laid down in the *Lord Strathcona* case. The trouble with all these arguments is that none of them goes to the root of the difficulty—the ambiguity of the terms (if any) agreed upon at the time, the doubtful identity of the party or parties for whose benefit this obligation or 'spell' or 'curse'—call it what you will—enured, and the impossibility of classifying it under any of the kinds of interest recognised by equitable rules. In the circumstances I am constrained to hold that the third party has not substantiated his case against the arrest of the deliquent ship or for the declaration prayed for in his statement of claim.

"There will be judgment for the Plaintiff for £1,000 and costs against the owners and the vessel herself, with the usual consequences. The claim of the third party is dismissed, with costs."

TRESPASS WITH SPECIAL DAMAGE

King's Bench Division.

HANSEL & GRETEL (Infants) *v.* PUMPERNICKEL

Negligence — Trespass — "Gingerbread house" — Whether allurement to children—Duty of occupier—Whether children to be considered as licensees—Counterclaim for dilapidations.

JUDGMENT of Mr. Justice Humperdinck:
"This is an action by two infant Plaintiffs, suing by their next friend, Mr. Holzhacker, against Mrs. Bertha Pumpernickel, described as a witch, for damages for negligence. The statement of claim sets forth that the Plaintiffs, being invitees upon the premises occupied by the Defendant, were injured by a concealed danger thereon of the nature of a trap, of which the Defendant knew or ought to have known.

"The Defendant counterclaims for damages against the Plaintiffs for trespass upon the said premises and damage thereto and to the Defendant's fixtures and fittings thereon.

"The evidence discloses that the defendant is the occupier of a dwellinghouse situate within a wood at some little distance from the village where the Plaintiffs reside. The Defendant having (as she explained) experienced some difficulty in obtaining a licence from the local authority for the erection of a house by a building contractor in the ordinary way, successfully undertook the construction of the house with her own hands. Exercising more ingenuity than foresight, she decided, when faced with the current shortage of bricks and timber, to make use of substitute materials for the construction of what is known as a 'prefabricated' house, which she then transported to and placed upon the site she had chosen. Although, as she has told me, this site is well sheltered from the elements, one is tempted to remark that the dwelling can scarcely be one calculated to stand up to the inclement climate of these islands. The testimony of the eminent surveyors who have examined the structure shows that the walls are composed of gingerbread, the overhanging roof of chocolate and the joists and window-frames of barley-sugar.

"I am not called upon to speculate as to how, in these days of food-rationing, the Defendant succeeded in accumulating sufficient materials of this nature for the construction of even a small prefabricated house, of however flimsy and ephemeral a type. Nor has she made it clear, even if I accept her evidence that she has invented a secret process for the manufacture of the materials in question without recourse to rationed foodstuffs, whether she applied for and obtained the appropriate licence from the Ministry concerned. However, it is established on the evidence that the house is standing and that it is composed of the materials to which I have previously referred.

"Now, the Plaintiffs are infants of tender years; the boy Hansel is eight and the girl Gretel is seven years of age. From the time they learned to walk the wood has been their playground, and they have been in the habit of spending entire days wandering alone in its vicinity. From all I have heard their parents' conduct has been neglectful in the extreme, and I have deemed it my duty to bring the case to the attention of the appropriate authority for action under Sections 61 and 62 of the Children and Young Persons Act, 1933, since it is clear that these young people are in need of

HANSEL AND GRETEL (INFANTS) v. PUMPERNICKEL

care and protection thereunder. This, however, is a matter which is not relevant to the questions at issue in this action.

"On one of their recent excursions into the wood the infant Plaintiffs observed the house of the Defendant, a structure of a type and nature which were new to them. Impelled by the playful curiosity of the young, they entered the garden gate and approached the house itself. Naturally inquisitive, and hungry after their long tramp, they were at once attracted as much by the strangeness as by the edible nature of the structure they saw before them. It is regrettable that no considerations either of ethics or of caution (the inculcation of which appears to have been sadly lacking in their education) seem to have deterred them from inflicting serious depredations upon the external parts of the premises. The Schedule of Dilapidations which has been put in evidence shows that considerable portions of the roof, walls and window-frames were broken off and, I fear, consumed within a short space of time, and the photographs which have been laid before me leave no doubt of the very extensive nature of the damage. It is a lamentable fact that the shaped door-knocker made of marzipan is quite irreplaceable, and the best available substitute is one to be made of utility coconut-icing.

"Driven on by that same natural inquisitiveness to which I have alluded, the Plaintiffs then pushed open the door, which was ajar, and proceeded to explore the interior of the premises. Finding nobody within, they rummaged among the many strange objects which the living-room contained. Here it was not long before the trouble occurred which has given rise to the Plaintiffs' action.

"On one side of the living-room was a large oven, and in the far corner stood a large structure of wire-netting in the form of an enclosure or cage. Meddling, as children will, with these objects, the Plaintiff Gretel burned her hands severely on the handle of the oven-door (which she seems to have mistaken for a new variety of radio set) while the Plaintiff Hansel succeeded in shutting himself into the wire cage, the door of which opened on a spring and which the combined efforts of the girl and himself failed to reopen once he was inside.

"It was not until considerably after midnight that the Defendant returned home and discovered the intruders who, after a severe scolding, were restored to their parents the next day. I discount the fantastic story told by both Plaintiffs in the witness-box, that the Defendant not only threatened but made all appropriate preparations to cook and eat them for her next day's meal; such fancies are common enough among children of immature development, and exhibit a disregard for veracity which is regrettably in line with the Plaintiffs' deficiencies in moral education.

"I have now to deal with the legal issues raised by the claim and counterclaim. There is no question that the acts of the Plaintiffs were those of trespassers on the Defendant's premises; if the matter ended there the Plaintiffs' claim would be bound to fail, since it is established law that the occupier of premises owes no duty to a trespasser except the negative duty not to set a deliberate trap (*Hillen & Pettigrew* v. *I.C.I. (Alkali) Ltd.*). But it is well known that, where the persons committing the acts of trespass are children of tender years, other considerations may arise. There is a line of cases to which Counsel has referred me, the *dicta* in which show that, although there is no difference between the duty of an occupier towards trespassing children and trespassing adults, yet if the occupier of premises has brought on to and maintains on his premises dangerous objects which by their nature constitute an allurement to children of the naturally inquisitive temperament to which I have referred, and if the occupier has in the past permitted or tacitly acquiesced in the entry of such children upon his premises, he may be liable for injury arising from a child's natural propensity to intermeddle with such dangerous objects; and in such case the child, though actually committing acts of trespass, may be regarded in a position analogous to that of a licensee (or even, in some cases, an invitee) upon the premises (*Lynch* v. *Nurdin*; *Addie* v. *Dumbreck*). And it follows that, in such cases, the occupier is regarded by the law as under a duty to warn the child, as such licensee, of dangers which are more or less concealed, which he (the occupier) knew to exist upon the premises, or of which (in the case of an invitee) he ought to have known. In every such case it is material to consider whether the place is one which children do or are likely to frequent (*Angus* v. *Findlay*); the purpose for which they frequent it; the age of, and the means of control over, such children; and the extent to which the dangerous object is calculated to attract children to meddle with it (*Harrold* v. *Watney*).

"Applying to the facts before me the principles laid down in the decided cases I find, in the first place, that the presence, in the midst of a wood through which the public have rights of way, of an unguarded dwelling, the structure of which is composed of sweetmeats, constitutes an allurement to children of tender years and is extremely likely to attract them to meddle and (as occurred in this case) to do serious damage to the structure. If the Plaintiffs' activities had been limited to the exterior of the premises and if, for example, their gastronomic inclinations had led them to break off so large a portion of the walls as to lead to the collapse of the chocolate roof over their heads, with resultant injuries, I think the Defendant would have been liable under the principles to which I have referred. But the Plaintiffs went further; they actually entered the house, and I cannot think that in doing so they were actuated so much by the attractions of a naturally alluring object as by a propensity for mischief. In other words, assuming that the Defendant ought to have contemplated that assaults would naturally be made from time to time by children upon the external parts of her dwelling (assaults which the evidence shows she had been at pains to repel in the past), it cannot be said that it ought to have been within her contemplation that these infant Plaintiffs would go so far as to trespass upon the interior and to injure themselves by meddling with such objects as the oven and the wire cage in question. These do not in my view come into the category of things dangerous in themselves; the Defendant had a perfectly good right to have them where they were. The Plaintiffs were trespassers and knew that they had no right to be in the house. For these reasons it is unnecessary for me to deal with the elaborate argument of the Defendant's Counsel to the effect that, even if their tender years entitled these Plaintiffs to be regarded as licensees upon the premises, the misfeasance they had committed in the form of their depredations to the structure of the house had rendered them trespassers *ab initio* (*The Six Carpenters' Case*).

"The Plaintiffs' claim must therefore be dismissed with costs.

"Turning to the Defendant's counterclaim, it is clear that she is entitled to claim both general damage for the trespass itself and also special damage in respect of the injuries to the property. The latter class of damage falls to be estimated upon the basis of compensation for the deterioration in value caused by the wrongful acts of the Plaintiffs herein and for all the natural and necessary expenses incurred by reason of such acts (*Liesbosch* v. *Edison*). I accept the evidence offered on the Defendant's behalf in regard to the cost of making good the dilapidations to the premises, and assess the special damage at £150; in addition the Plaintiffs must pay a nominal sum of £5 in respect of general damage for the trespass. They must also pay the costs of the action.

"It does not fall within my province to deal with the Defendant's claim for a further supply of personal points under the Food (Rationing) Orders, 1939-1942. She must make her application therefor to the local Food Office and substantiate her case in the ordinary way."

RECEPTION OF A PATIENT

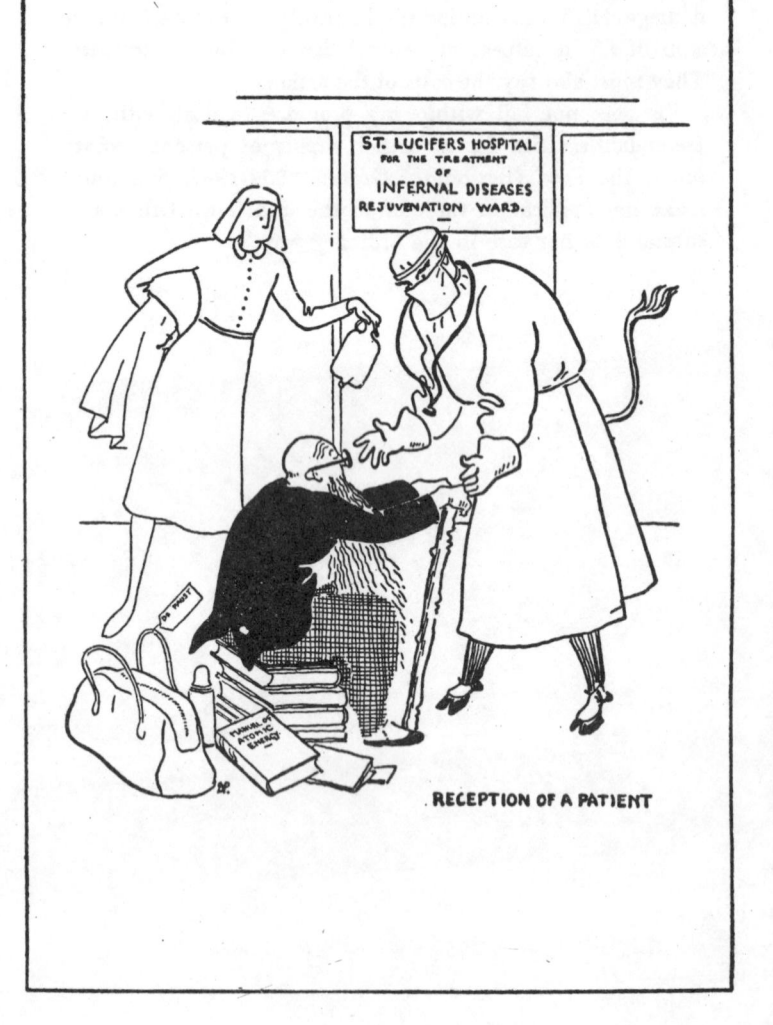

CHANCERY DIVISION.

MEPHISTOPHELES v. FAUST

Contract—Rejuvenation of Defendant by Plaintiff—Consideration—Delivery up of defendant's "soul"—Undisclosed principal—Statute of Frauds, 1677, s.4—Application of lex fori—"Soul"—Whether personal property of reversionary nature—Whether chose in action—Subject-matter of contract insufficiently defined.

IMPORTANT questions of contract law fell to be decided in this case, in which Mr. Justice Gounod delivered the following considered judgment:

"This is an action brought by Mr. Mephistopheles, of Gehenna, described as a Fuel Contractor, against Dr. Faust, a German scientist resident in the United Kingdom under the licence of the Crown. The Plaintiff claims (1) specific performance of an oral contract alleged to have been made, within the German Reich, between himself of the one part and the Defendant of the other part, (2) delivery up of the subject-matter of the said contract, namely, the 'soul' of the Defendant, to the Plaintiff or such person or persons as he may nominate, or in the alternative (3) the execution by the Defendant of a deed (to be settled by Counsel nominated by the Court) transferring all the Defendant's property in and title to the said 'soul' to the Plaintiff or to such person or persons as aforesaid.

"The Defendant raises a number of defences with which I

shall deal in due course. The facts disclosed by the evidence are as follows:—

"The parties met in 1930 in Germany, where the Defendant was at that time residing and where he was engaged in scientific and psychic research. He was then a man of some seventy years of age. His lifelong studies and researches were about to come to fruition. He was, as I understand, on the verge of an important discovery connected with the release of atomic power. His great regret was that, at his advanced age, he feared he would not live to put the results of his discoveries to practical application.

"The Defendant discussed his problem with the Plaintiff, who represented to him that he (the Plaintiff) was in possession of the secret of a medical or surgical process which would have a thoroughly rejuvenating effect and would give the Defendant a further thirty or forty years of vigorous life. On the basis of these representations the Defendant orally agreed with the Plaintiff that, in consideration of the Plaintiff's giving him the appropriate treatment by the process described, the Defendant would, if the treatment was successful, surrender, transfer and assign all the Defendant's property in and title to his 'soul' to the Plaintiff or to such person or persons as aforesaid.

"In pursuance of this agreement the Plaintiff gave the Defendant the required treatment, which appears to have been entirely successful in its rejuvenating effect. Having seen the Defendant in the witness-box, where he admitted that he is now in his eighty-eighth year, I have been able to form my own conclusions, and I have no hesitation in finding that he has the physique and vitality of a man of forty.

"The Defendant has not denied that his physical rejuvenation has been brought about by the intervention of the

Plaintiff, or that the agreement between the parties was substantially in the terms alleged. Nor has he attempted to deny that he has so far failed to carry out his part of the contract. He has, however, put forward in his defence a number of procedural and legal arguments, the validity of which it is now incumbent upon me to examine.

"The first of these is that the Plaintiff entered into this oral contract merely as agent for a principal who should have been made a party to these proceedings, but who has not appeared therein, though his identity was disclosed at the time when the contract was made. This mysterious personage, whom the Defendant admits he has never seen, and whose address he does not know, is said to have been mentioned under a variety of aliases which are so numerous as to leave in my mind a most vague and ambiguous impression. The Defendant alleges that the Plaintiff referred to him at different times under the names of Satan, Lucifer, Beelzebub, 'Der Teufel,' 'The Evil One,' and even 'Old Nick.' His residence, he says, was at no time disclosed and, except that he was alleged to be engaged in some occupation connected with central heating, no hint of his profession was vouchsafed. In the absence of some more definite evidence of the existence and activities of this alleged principal, I regret that I am driven to the conclusion that he exists only in the Defendant's imagination, and on this part of the defence I hold that the Defendant was contracting and intended to contract with the person (the Plaintiff) present and identified by sight and hearing (*Phillips* v. *Brooks*). I am fortified in this conclusion by the fact (which the Defendant does not deny) that it was the Plaintiff solely who conducted the negotiations throughout and who personally carried out the rejuvenating treatment which I have described. In the circumstances this part of the defence must fail.

"The second line of defence may be equally shortly disposed of. The Defendant pleads that, whatever may be the proper law of the contract (a matter to which I will revert), no action thereon can be entertained by the Courts of England in view of the provisions of sec. 4 of the Statute of Frauds, which provides (*inter alia*):—

'No action shall be brought whereby to charge any person..............................upon any agreement that is not to be performed within the space of one year from the making thereof................unless the agreement................or some memorandum or note thereof shall be in writing and signed by the party to be charged therewith or some other person thereto by him lawfully authorised.'

"I will admit that the Defendant is right to this extent— that the matters dealt with by the Statute of Frauds are matters of evidence and procedure and must be governed by the *lex fori* (the Law of England) of which the Plaintiff is seeking to avail himself. But, that being said, I am by no means convinced that this oral contract falls within the statutory words 'not to be performed within the space of one year from the making thereof,' as interpreted by the decided cases. These words have been limited by authority to such contracts as appear by their terms to be incapable of complete performance within the statutory period (*Boydell* v. *Drummond*); had the parties stipulated that the treatment to be given by the Plaintiff, the successful outcome of which was a condition precedent to the performance by the Defendant of his part of the contract, must continue for more than one year, there might have been more merit in the Defendant's contention. But no such stipulation was made. The further argument of the Defendant—that the term of the contract for the delivery up of his 'soul' contemplated, by the very nature of the transaction, that performance must be postponed until the end of his life (of which I shall have more to say anon) cannot avail him either. For even if the Defendant is right in his allegation that performance was to be so postponed, yet the promise of the Plaintiff to carry out the rejuvenating process amounted only to this—that it would confer upon him the vigour and vitality of a man in the prime of his life, *capable* of living for another thirty or forty years; it implied no warranty or guarantee that his life would unquestionably be so prolonged and that he would assuredly escape those risks of sudden death from accident or disease which are inevitably associated with human life—'what he may have to pass through—its normal vicissitudes, with all its joys, all its sorrows, with its hardships and its various burdens and duties' (*Rose* v. *Ford*). For these reasons I cannot hold that the Defendant has made out his plea under this Statute. It thus becomes unnecessary for me to deal with the argument of the Plaintiff's Counsel putting up the doctrine of part performance—the carrying out by the Plaintiff of his side of the bargain—or to consider whether the acts done by the Plaintiff were or were not unequivocally referable to the terms of the contract in issue. On this matter I have grave doubts, but fortunately I am not called upon to express a final opinion thereon.

"The only merit that I can observe in the Defendant's pleas is to be found in his third line of defence—that the subject-matter of the contract is of an ambiguous and unidentifiable nature, and that the acts which he is required by the contract to perform are not defined with sufficient accuracy. Here the Defendant is on surer ground. The evidence of Dr. Goethe has established only that the contract is not illegal or invalid by the *lex loci contractus*—the law of Germany; but neither this careful witness nor any of the other experts have succeeded in making clear to me under what class of property the 'soul' of the Defendant can be said to fall, or whether, indeed, it can be descrbied as 'property' in any sense of the word.

The difficulty is this. The remedy of specific performance—the delivery up of the Defendant's 'soul', or the execution of a document purporting to transfer to the Plaintiff the title thereto—is sought from the English Court, the *forum* where the action is being tried. I will assume in the Plaintiff's favour that the proper law of the contract is the law of Germany. I have it on the authority of the experts that the contract is valid and legal by that law. But the grant of a decree of specific performance by the English Court is limited to the case where the Court is in a position to enforce its decree. That is not this case.

"Whether the oral contract in its original terms was for the Defendant to perform forthwith after the Plaintiff had performed his part, or whether performance was intended to be postponed until after his death (as the Defendant contends) and to be binding upon his legal personal representatives, makes little difference to the elucidation of the main difficulty. It is clear that the Defendant's 'soul' is not a chattel, to be transferred by manual delivery. It has not been produced for inspection, and no description thereof by form or substance, size, weight or colour has been given. It is clearly not a *chose* in possession. I am not therefore in a position to make an order for delivery up of the Defendant's soul as the statement of claim requires.

"As to the alternative claim, Counsel has suggested that the subject-matter of the contract is a *chose* in action, analogous to a share in a joint stock company, conferring on the owner certain rights and duties during his lifetime and certain benefits and liabilities on his death or dissolution, and that I should order the Defendant to execute a deed of transfer.

MEPHISTOPHELES v. FAUST

This argument, ingenious as it was, left me profoundly unconvinced. There are, it is true, certain similarities between a natural person and a legal or artificial *persona*, such as a corporation, but the analogy, if pressed too far, breaks down. The rights and duties of the Defendant in respect of his 'soul' are not dependant upon any documents in the nature of a company's Articles of Association, which are susceptible of legal construction, either while he remains (if I may be permitted the metaphor) a going concern or upon his winding-up, whether compulsory or voluntary; and I have yet to learn that the conduct of his affairs is regulated by ordinary, extraordinary or special resolutions, or that he can effect a transfer of his 'soul' by writing under seal.

"Counsel's endeavours to bring the subject-matter of this contract within other classes of property recognised by the law of England were equally unsuccessful. Can the Defendant's 'soul' be classed as a species of reversionary interest? I have the gravest doubts. In what sense can it be said to be vested in him in reversion rather than in possession, and under what recognised type of interest can it be classed? Counsel was unable to enlighten me, and could only suggest that it was an equitable interest in the nature of a trust. This, however, takes us no further. For a trust implies a trustee and a *cestui que trust*, and if it be said that the Defendant stands in both capacities there is no trust subsisting, and consequently no equity to be enforced.

"I am therefore unable to make the alternative order asked for, that the Defendant do execute a deed of transfer, surrender or assignment. I was not impressed by the evidence that a writing by the Defendant on a piece of human skin, signed in his own blood, would be valid to effect the necessary transfer by the *lex loci solutionis*. This Court, as the appropriate *forum*, can do no more than order the execution of documents recognised by the *lex fori*, viz., simple contracts or specialities under seal. The law of England does not recognise any special validity as attaching to a further class of documents which are alleged to depend for their validity upon the material with which, or upon which, they may be inscribed.

"In all the circumstances I am bound to hold that the subject-matter of the contract is of a nature not recognised by the law of England; that in consequence the contract is void for ambiguity and that this action for specific performance must fail. There will be judgment for the Defendant, with costs."

EJECTMENT OF A TRESPASSER

King's Bench Division.

OGRE v. JACK AND ANOTHER
JACK v. SPROUTING SEEDS LIMITED

Nuisance—Contiguous hereditaments—Plant of excessive height—Deprivation of light—Abatement of nuisance—Whether notice necessary—Assault—Negligence—Sale of Goods Act, 1891, ss.13, 14—Non-compliance with description of goods—Fitness for purpose—Duty of supplier to Plaintiff.

THE following are extracts from the Judgment of Hans Andersen, J.:

"In these consolidated actions the first Plaintiff, Mr. Ogre, of Giant's Castle, claims damages and an injunction against the first Defendant, Mr. Jack, of Sea View, Erewhon, for nuisance, assault and negligence, and against the second Defendants, Sprouting Seeds, Ltd., for negligence. The first Defendant counterclaims in the former action for damages for trespass, and as Plaintiff in the second action for breach of warranty on the sale of goods. Both actions arise out of the same events, which are briefly as follows:—

"The first Plaintiff and Defendant occupy adjoining properties, and until recently, it seems, good neighbourly relations were maintained between them. Both properties are unrestricted freeholds and no question of title arises on the pleadings.

"In February last, Mr. Jack, who is an enthusiastic gardener, purchased from the second Defendants (to whom I shall for convenience refer to as 'the Company') a packet of seed, described on the packet itself and in the invoice as 'Common or Garden Broad Bean.' No express warranty was given other than the description on the packet.

"Mr. Jack proceeded to plant the seed in his garden, at a distance of some three feet from the fence separating his property from that of the Plaintiff. Evidence, which is not disputed, has been given by gardening experts to the effect that the broad bean plant ordinarily takes from one to two months to sprout, and grows to a maximum height of about four feet. The fence between the two properties is six feet high.

"The first Defendant is a gardener of experience, and he was not a little astonished to find, early on the day following the planting, that the seeds had already sprouted. By sunset that day the plants had already overgrown the top of the fence; by the next morning they were 15 feet high, and by the end of that week they had attained the extraordinary size of 118 feet, and showed every sign of growing higher. Nor was this all, for the stem or stalk which, I understand, ordinarily has a thickness of half an inch at most, was no less than 14 inches in diameter, and the leaves were proportionately large. An added feature—and the one calculated to arouse the gravest disquiet on the part of a property-owner— was the spread of the roots of this prodigious growth. As may be expected (if anything connected with this amazing episode could be expected) the roots were of a size proportionate to the remainder of the plant. They spread outwards beneath the surface of the ground to an unexampled distance and at an unprecedented speed. There is no doubt on the evidence that the stability of the Plaintiff's house has been permanently impaired and its restoration is a matter of great expense and labour, for which the grant of a building licence has several times been refused.

"While the Defendant was naturally astonished and alarmed at this sudden excrescence of exotic *flora* at the bottom of his garden, the Plaintiff was justly indignant. His house was erected some forty-two years ago, and there is no doubt on the evidence that his windows had long since acquired, under the Prescription Act, an indefeasible right to light. Some necessary diminution of light, as Counsel for the Plaintiff has admitted, is a matter to which no man who enjoys the advantages of living in a society can reasonably object; he is entitled to a sufficiency of light according to the ordinary usages of mankind, no more and no less." His Lordship here referred briefly to *Colls* v. *Home & Colonial Stores*, and continued:—

"But could anyone for a moment describe what the Plaintiff has suffered as a 'reasonable diminution' of light? Counsel for the Defendant has quoted to me authorities showing that minute and ingenious methods of calculation have from time to time been applied to measure such diminution and its effects, but when the light has been diminished to vanishing point the application of such methods must needs appear supererogatory. Mathematical and even legal niceties must yield to considerations of fact and common sense, and fact and common sense tell me that Mr. Ogre's rooms are dark—that even in broadest daylight they are, to use a homely expression, 'as dark as night.'

"In these circumstances I have had no difficulty in coming to the conclusion that I ought to grant the injunction prayed for. Where damages will not provide an adequate remedy, an injunction will be granted as of course.

"The Plaintiff also asks for damages for the infringement of his ancient lights, and to these he is entitled—*Leeds*

Industrial & Co-operative Society v. *Slack*. I assess the damages under this head at £20.

"Now, it appears that Mr. Ogre is of an impulsive and adventurous disposition and, as he has told me quite frankly in the witness-box, he was rather glad than otherwise when his Solicitor advised him that he was entitled to take the law to some extent into his own hands. With an agility surprising in one so corpulent (he weighs, as he told me, some nineteen stone), he set himself to climb the stalk, and after one or two false attempts succeeded in reaching a bough which sprouted from the main stem and overhung his garden at a height of some thirty feet from the ground. Here he sat himself astride a smaller bough overhanging the Defendant's garden and began to cut through the veritable jungle by which he was surrounded.

"It was unfortunately at this precise moment that the Defendant, who had hitherto refused to accede to the Plaintiff's request to abate the nuisance, but had consulted his Solicitor now that the growth had begun to take on unusual dimensions, came out into his garden and, with an axe, commenced hewing at the massive stalk. The Defendant has sworn that, though he had seen the Plaintiff enter his garden, he was unaware of his presence on the stalk itself and, hidden as the Plaintiff was by the dense foliage around him, I have no reason to doubt the Defendant's word. Before the Plaintiff realised what was happening there was, as he has described, a loud cracking sound and he himself, with the stalk to which he clung, was precipitated earthwards, sustaining serious, though happily not fatal, injuries. His very bulk, though it must have accelerated the fall of the stalk, afforded a certain resilience to the impact.

"The Plaintiff's second claim falls first under the head of assault, and on this head I think he cannot succeed. An assault has been defined as an attempt or offer to do violence to the person of another, but such attempt or offer must be intentional, so that, although this definition extends to the act of a defendant who intentionally withdraws support from the person of a plaintiff (as by deliberately removing a chair on which he is about to sit) no less than to the act of one who offers to strike or hurl a missile at another, it is a good defence to establish, as the Defendant has, that the support had not been deliberately withdrawn or the injury intentionally inflicted.

"But the Plaintiff claims also under the head of negligence, and here he is on surer ground. The Defendant's reply alleges merely that the Plaintiff was, at the time of the accident, a trespasser. Counsel for the Defendant has enlarged upon this part of the case by arguing that, since the Defendant is the owner of his land and everything upon it *usque ad caelum*, the Plaintiff was trespassing in sitting on the bough thirty feet up no less than if he had installed himself in the same posture on the Defendant's favourite bed of nasturtiums, which lay immediately beneath him, and on which in fact he subsequently reposed. There can be no doubt that in ordinary circumstances an individual who sees fit to perch on his neighbour's branches within his neighbour's land is a trespasser pure and simple. On the other hand the Plaintiff was possessed of certain rights in attempting to abate the nuisance by lopping off the branch which overhung his land (*Lemmon* v. *Webb*). And it is settled law that subject to certain qualifications he was entitled to go on to the Defendant's land for this purpose. The qualification is the increasing tendency of the Courts to require that, prior to any such entry, due notice thereof should be given to the owner of the land where the nuisance is situate. In the ordinary way notice is requisite, and its absence would deprive the Plaintiff of any higher status than that of a trespasser. Nevertheless, there is authority for dispensing with notice where the adjoining owner is the original wrong-doer who created the nuisance and I might have been prepared to hold, although with some uncertainty, that this case fell within this principle. I am fortunately absolved from deciding this point in view of the well-recognised principle that entry without notice is justifiable in a case of emergency. In my judgment such emergency existed here. This monstrous growth showed every disposition to continue growing until it entirely obliterated the sky above, the light of the sun, the song of the birds, and created a vast and impenetrable canopy under which the Defendant would live in dismal, dank darkness for the rest of his days.

"Moreover, the Plaintiff has another answer, which is equally effective. It is well established that the occupier of land is under a duty not to do anything which makes a dangerous change in the condition of his land, without giving warning even to trespassers whom he knows to be present and likely to be injured." His Lordship here referred in detail to *Mourton* v. *Poulter*, *Addie* v. *Dumbreck* and *Excelsior Wire Rope Company* v. *Callan*. "The case is analogous to, though not identical with, these authorities quoted; in my opinion it is sufficient for this purpose to say that the Defendant ought to have given warning to the Plaintiff, a possibility of danger to whom, by the lopping off of the bough, he must have contemplated. I therefore find for the Plaintiff on this part of the claim and assess the damages at £200. It follows from what I have said that the Defendant's counterclaim for trespass must fail.

"I now turn to the claims of the first Defendant and of the Plaintiff against the Company. I will deal with them in that order, since the latter involves questions of greater complexity than the former.

"The first Defendant's claim against the Company is for damages for breach of condition under ss. 13 and 14 (1) of the Sale of Goods Act, 1893. The statement of claim alleges, first, that the goods failed to correspond with the description and, secondly, that the goods were not reasonably fit for the purpose for which they were required.

"As to the first part of this claim, non-compliance with description is a breach of condition, going to the root of the contract, such as would have justified the Purchaser in repudiating the contract had he known of it in time. The fact that he actually used the seed and thus rendered himself incapable of treating the contract as rescinded, before he became aware of the breach, arouses difficulties which are more apparent than real. *Wallis* v. *Pratt* is an authority for permitting the exercise of the remedy appropriate for a breach of warranty, that is, suing for damages, in cases where the other remedies for breach of a condition are no longer exercisable. As to the merits of the claim itself, there is plenty of evidence available. 'Common or Garden Broad Bean' is scarcely an apt description for a plant which grows five yards in twenty-four hours and rises in a week to a height of one hundred and eighteen feet.

"As to the second part of this claim, it is equally clear that the seeds which produce a plant of the type I have described are not reasonably fit for the purpose for which they were required. Such seeds may well (for aught I know) be eminently suitable for clothing with luxuriant verdure the arid plains of Brazil, or for providing shade and sustenance to man in the trackless wastes of Central Africa. But they were not required for this purpose. They were required for the purpose of planting in a suburban kitchen-garden, and there is evidence before me that this purpose was made clear to the Company when the seed was bought. Nor is there any doubt in my mind that the purchaser relied upon the skill and judgment of the vendor. The Company's Memorandum of Association shows that one of its principal objects is to carry on the trade or business of a seedsman, and it is not disputed that the first Defendant relied on the Company's skill in that capacity.

"I find for the first Defendant (the Plaintiff in the second action) on both parts of his claim against the Company and I assess the damages at £200.

"I now finally turn to the first Plaintiff's claim against the Company, a claim based on the Company's alleged negligence in delivering to the first Defendant a dangerous chattel. Counsel has, in an able and elaborate argument, drawn an analogy between the duty owed by the supplier of such a chattel to persons who, as he must have contemplated, might be injured thereby and the duty owed in this case to the occupier of neighbouring premises by the vendor of the seed to the gardener next door. This doctrine is of comparatively recent origin and is still in process of development." His Lordship here referred at length to *Heaven* v. *Pender*, *McAlister* v. *Stevenson* and *Grant* v. *Australian Knitting Mills*, and concluded:—"It may be said, and said rightly, that none of these cases is on all fours with this action, but the analogy is a reasonable one, and the principles to be deduced from the cases quoted are equally applicable to this. The Company, if it gave the matter consideration at all, must have contemplated the possible effect on the amenities of neighbouring properties of plants one hundred and eighteen feet high. They gave the first Defendant no warning, nor was the unusual character of the seed apparent on inspection by an amateur gardener, though expert analysis might have revealed its nature. Having regard to all the circumstances I am of opinion that the Plaintiff's claim against the Company has been made out, and I assess the damages at £50.

"I accordingly give judgment for the first Plaintiff against both Defendants, and for the first Defendant against the second, with costs. I also find for the first Plaintiff against the first Defendant on the counterclaim, with costs."

DISPOSAL OF THE CORPUS

COURT OF CRIMINAL APPEAL

REX v. RIGOLETTO

Criminal Law—Appellant counselling or procuring principal felon to murder A—Murder of B—Whether Appellant accessory to murder of B.

THE Lord Chief Justice, delivering the judgment of the Court, made the following comments:

"This is an appeal against a conviction in the Central Criminal Court, before Mr. Justice Verdi, where the Appellant was found guilty of the charge of being an accessory before the fact to the murder of his daughter, Gilda, and sentenced to death. The Appellant was, with one Giovanni Sparafucile, convicted on an indictment setting forth that, on the 12th day of January 1947, in the County of Middlesex, he did counsel, procure and command the said Giovanni Sparafucile to murder the Duke of Mantua, and that the said Giovanni Sparafucile did on the 19th day of January 1947, murder Gilda Rigoletto.

"The Judge at the trial, in a very careful summing-up, explained to the jury, and directed them upon, the law relating to accessories before the fact to a felony, in the fullest possible manner. No complaint is made by Counsel for the Appellant of any particular passage in the summing-up, but it is contended that the learned Judge ought to have withdrawn the case from the jury altogether; and should have directed them, as a matter of law, to find a verdict of 'not guilty'.

"The evidence at the trial disclosed a story of base intrigue and revengeful passion. The Appellant was employed for many years in the household of the Duke of Mantua, a young man who has acheived an unenviable notoriety as a betrayer and seducer of young women. How far the Appellant may have been concerned in these nefarious activities is not relevant to the issue of this appeal, and attempts by the prosecution to bring up such matters at the trial were very properly repressed by the learned Judge. One piece of evidence, however, relevant because it throws light on the question of the Appellant's motive for what he did, was duly admitted. The witness Ceprano deposed that one of the latest victims of the Duke's amorous activities was the murdered girl, Gilda, the Appellant's daughter.

"There was no doubt on the evidence adduced by the prosecution, and it was not denied by the defence, that the seduction of his daughter preyed upon the mind of the Appellant and inspired him with a bitter hatred of his late employer, who betrayed her. It is beyond question also that the Appellant's love and affection for his daughter were sincere and profound—a fact which, while it was made much of by defending Counsel in his closing address to the jury as tending to rebut the guilty motive of the accused, also afforded an opportunity to the prosecution to emphasise the deep malice with which the Appellant regarded the man who had seduced her, the intended victim.

"In this state of mind the appellant approached one Giovanni Sparafucile, the licensee of the 'Black Horse' public-house, known to the Appellant to be frequented by the Duke, and by a gift of money procured, counselled or commanded him to murder the Duke on his next visit to the said public-house. An elaborate conspiracy was concocted. The Duke was to be stabbed as he entered; his body was to be placed in a sack which was to be handed to the Appellant the same night; the balance of the money promised for the deed was then to be paid to the murderer, and the Appellant was to throw the sack into the river. The Appellant was to take no part in the actual murder; it was in fact proved by the defence that he was several miles from the scene of the crime when it was committed, and the prosecution made no attempt to connect him with the actual deed as principal in either the first or the second degree. Nor was it denied by the defence that, if the crime had in fact been carried out as planned, the Appellant would have been liable as accessory before the fact.

"At this point however, arose *a nova causa interveniens*. The Duke, having tired of the unfortunate girl Gilda, was by now paying his attentions to Madellena, the sister of the innkeeper, Sparafucile. This young woman was originally charged, together with her brother, as an accomplice in the actual crime which was eventually committed; but at the commencement of the trial it was intimated that no evidence would be given against her and she was discharged. Appearing subsequently as a witness for the prosecution, she testified how, knowing the details of the conspiracy but being too terrified of her brother to go to the police, she endeavoured to prevail upon him to halt upon the threshold of the crime. Accepting the Duke's advances at their face value, and believing him to be honourable in his intentions, she had conceived a tender regard for him and, as she explained to the jury, set herself at any cost to save his life. She failed, however, to persuade her brother to refrain altogether from the crime of murder, but after a stormy scene he promised her he would modify his course of action. He would not murder the Duke, her lover, but he was already too deeply involved in the plot to withdraw completely. The inn was in a lonely place; the first benighted way-farer who might chance to enter that night would be murdered in the Duke's stead; his body would be placed in the sack, and the Appellant would fling it into the river in the belief that his wishes had been accomplished.

"Evidence of the movements of the girl Gilda during the fatal evening established clearly that she was seeking everywhere for her faithless seducer. Her search led her to the inn; she gained admission and was immediately stabbed, repeatedly and brutally, to death by Sparafucile. The murderer placed her body in the sack which, on the arrival of the Appellant two hours later, was handed to him. The money was paid over; the Appellant was commencing to drag the sack to his waiting car when he heard, from an upstairs window, a voice drunkenly singing the well-known air *La donna è mobile*. The appellant told in his evidence, with much emotion, how he recognised the song as a favourite song of the Duke's, and how he recognised the voice as the Duke's voice. Sick with horror and apprehension he tore open the sack and found therein the lifeless body of his own murdered daughter. He was found on the spot, in a state of unconsciousness, by the local police who, on information given by the inn-keeper's sister, arrested the Appellant together with the murderer himself, who has since been convicted and executed.

"Such are the tragic and sordid circumstances of this crime which has led to the conviction against which the Appellant appeals. It is now for the Court to apply itself to the law, which has been ably argued by Counsel on both sides.

"A person who procures, counsels or commands another to commit a felony, but who is not present when it is committed, is an accessory before the fact (*R.* v. *Gordon;*

R. v. *Soares*). The felony may be either a felony at common law or a felony created by statute. It is immaterial whether there is any direct communication between the accessory and the principal felon; it is sufficient if the accessory direct an intermediate agent to procure another to commit the felony without naming the person to be procured (*M'Daniel's Case; R.* v. *Cooper*). The Court need therefore attach no importance to the weakness of the evidence on the actual method by which the Appellant in the present case communicated his wishes to the murderer; the evidence has established clearly that those wishes were so communicated, whether directly or indirectly, and that money was paid over to the murderer by or on behalf of the Appellant, both before and after the crime.

"By statute an accessory before the fact to a felony may be indicted, tried, convicted and punished in all respects as if he were a principal felon (Assessories and Abettors Act, 1861, ss. 1, 5.).

"So much is common ground, but Counsel for the Appellant nevertheless contends that the conviction was wrongful in law. We have been referred at length to many authorities of great weight and antiquity, including Foster's Crown Cases, Hale's Pleas of the Crown, Hawkin's Pleas of the Crown and Blackstone's Commentaries. The Court regards the following propositions as established:—

"If the principal felon substantially complies with the directions of the instigator, but makes some variation in circumstances of time or place, or in the manner of execution, the instigator is liable as an accessory equally with the principal felon (*Foster*, 369, 370; 2 *Hawkins P.C.*,c.29,s.20). Thus if A. counsels B. to murder C. by poison, and B. kills C. by some other means, or if A. counsels B. to murder C. at one place and B. commits the murder at another place, A.

H

will be liable as accessory; for the murder of C. was the object principally in contemplation (*Ibid.*) Nay, more; if the principal goes beyond the terms of the instigation, yet if the advice of the instigator is substantially followed, and the felony committed was a probable consequence of what was advised, the instigator is an accessory to that felony (*Foster*, 370). Thus if A. counsels B. to rob C., and in committing the robbery B. kills C. in such circumstances that the killing of C. is in the ordinary course of things the probable consequence of the robbery, A. is accessory to the murder of C. (*Parkes* v. *Prescott.*)

"If however the instigator procures the principal felon to commit a felony of one kind, and the principal knowingly and wilfully commits a felony of another kind, the instigator is not liable as an accessory (*Foster*, 369). Thus in *R.* v. *Saunders and Archer*, Saunders, desiring to kill his wife, was counselled by Archer to mix poison in a roasted apple, which he gave her to eat, but she, having eaten only a small part, with non-fatal results, gave the remainder to her child, who died of it. 'It was ruled, without much difficulty, that Saunders was guilty of murder of the child (though he had dearly loved it), but with regard to Archer it was agreed by the judges upon conference that he was not accessory to this murder, it being an offence he neither advised nor assented to.'

"Counsel for the Crown has been unable to refer us to any case where an instigator, who procured the principal felon to murder A., has been held guilty as an accessory to the murder by the principal felon of B. It has indeed been suggested in the books that an exception may arise where the crime actually committed was one which was itself likely to arise out of the instigation to commit some other crime not actually committed, as where A. counsels B. to murder C.

but B. by mistake murders C's twin-brother D., who resembles him so closely that B. is deceived (*See Foster*, 370, *supra*). But those are not the circumstances of the case before us, where not only was there no likelihood that the appellant's attempt to procure the murder of the Duke would lead to the murder of his own daughter, but that murder was committed principally owing to the *nova causa interveniens* of a third party, the sister of the murderer himself.

"In these circumstances we agree that the Judge, as a matter of law, ought to have withdrawn the case from the jury. The appeal is allowed and the conviction must be quashed."

TRANSFER OF ENEMY PROPERTY

CHANCERY DIVISION.

WOTAN v. FASOLT and FAFNER.

Contract—Breach—Counterclaim for quantum meruit—Building Agreement—Consideration—Custody of infant—Illegality—Parties in pari delicto—Property belonging to alien enemies—Trading with the Enemy Act, 1939, s.7.

JUDGMENT of Mr. Justice Wagner:

"This is an action by Mr. Wotan, of Valhalla, described as a war-god, for the recovery of certain security given to the Defendants to secure payment of the consideration payable by the Plaintiff for work to be done by the Defendants under a building contract. The Defendants are Messrs. Fasolt and Fafner, carrying on the business of builders and decorators as a firm under their own names at Riesenheim. The Defendants counterclaim for specific performance of the said contract by the Plaintiff and for the handing over to them of the custody and control of the infant Freia, aged eighteen months, of whom the Plaintiff and his wife Fricka are said to be the lawful guardians by adoption. The Defendants contend that the consideration therefor has been duly executed by them, but that the Plaintiff refuses to perform his part of the contract. In the alternative the Defendants claim payment for the work done by them at the request and by the authority of the Plaintiff on the basis of *quantum meruit*.

"The evidence which has been given before me discloses the following facts:

"By a building agreement dated the 10th April 1944,

made between the Defendants of the one part and the Plaintiff of the other part, the Defendants jointly and severally agreed to erect and construct a dwellinghouse, to be known as 'Valhalla', as a residence for the Plaintiff and his family. Subject to the obtaining of the necessary licences the work was to be carried out in accordance with the plans drawn on the said contract and the specifications set out in the Schedule thereto and subject to the approval of the Plaintiff's Surveyor, Mr. Loge. The licences were duly granted and it is not denied that the work has been carried out by the Defendants in accordance with the said plans and specifications, that the work has been approved by the said Surveyor, and that the Plaintiff and his family are now residing in the said dwellinghouse.

"The sole question at issue between the parties relates to the consideration to be given by the Plaintiff for the carrying out of the work. In lieu of the usual provisions for payment of a fixed sum of money for the building work, to be discharged in instalments as the various stages of the work were completed and approved by the Surveyor, this contract contained the unusual term that, on such completion and approval, the Plaintiff should hand over and grant custody and control of the said infant to the Defendants or one or either of them.

"For the sake of convenience I will deal first with the counterclaim. It is scarcely necessary for me to point out that such a contract as this is clearly void and illegal as against public policy. It is apparent that the Defendants are ignorant men, of little or no education, and I am satisfied that when they entered into this Agreement they had no idea that they were making a stipulation which was likely to prove completely abortive. Their evidence has also convinced me that they made this stipulation with no nefarious motive, but that each of them sincerely intended to enter upon an honourable courtship of the lady with the view that she might ultimately be persuaded to marry one or other of them. No such excuse is available to the Plaintiff and his wife, who are persons of sagacity and education; indeed, I am informed that the wife is a member of the Bar. There is no question but that they have taken advantage of the Defendants throughout this transaction and that their conduct merits the strongest reprobation.

"Early in the hearing the Defendants' Counsel conceded, with commendable frankness, that the Defendants' counter-claim for specific performance must necessarily fail. It is elementary law that, in any proceedings before the Court in which the custody of an infant is involved, the Court must regard the welfare of the infant as the first and paramount consideration, and must treat any rights, priorities or preferences of the parents or either of them as subordinated thereto. This is a principle which is deeply rooted in the jurisdiction of this Division, and arises from the maxim that the King is *pater patriæ* and exercises a special measure of protection over those who cannot help themselves. 'The comfort, the health and the moral, intellectual and spiritual welfare of the infant are the matters for consideration' (*Re Mc Grath*), and the general principle has now received statutory confirmation in sect. 1 of the Guardianship of Infants Act, 1925.

"That being an established principle of equity and statute law, it is clear that the right of custody to an infant cannot be bargained away as an incidental term in a commercial or other contract. A father cannot by contract deprive himself of the right of custody, control and education of his children, and such a contract has been held void as against public policy (*Agar Ellis* v. *Lascelles*). I have no hesitation in holding that an adopting parent is subject to the same disability. The Defendants' counterclaim for specific performance must therefore clearly fail.

"Now, since this contract is not merely void but actually illegal, no rights can arise on either side thereunder. If therefore the Defendants had failed to complete the building work which they purported to contract to carry out, the Plaintiff would have been unable to compel them to do so or to recover damages from them in default. The evidence shows, however, that the Defendants have performed their part and that the Plaintiff is in possession of and enjoying the fruit of their work and labour performed by his authority and at his request. The Defendants, who carried out the work in ignorance of the illegal nature of the consideration, are not *in pari delicto* with the Plaintiff, and are entitled to be paid for such work and labour on the basis of *quantum meruit* (*Clay* v. *Yates*), and this part of the counterclaim will be remitted to one of the Official Referees for assessment. I give judgment in favour of the Defendants for the sum found to be due to them on such assessment. The question of costs is reserved for further argument.

"This disposes of the counterclaim, and I now turn to the more difficult question of the Plaintiff's claim for recovery of the security which he gave. The evidence shows that, shortly after the date when this purported contract was made, the Plaintiff handed over to the Defendants (for the purpose of securing the due carrying out by him of the consideration which I have held to be illegal) a substantial quantity of gold bars and jewellery, which are still in the Defendants' possession. And the Plaintiff claims to recover the said property or to set off the same or some part thereof against the payment which may be found to be due to the Defendants under their counterclaim.

"Now, it is clear, on the principle *ex turpi causâ non oritur actio*, that as a general rule money paid, securities given and property transferred under an illegal contract are not recoverable. 'No Court ought to enforce an illegal contract, or to allow itself to be made the instrument of enforcing obligations alleged to arise out of a contract or transaction which is illegal, if the illegality is duly brought to the notice of the Court, and if the person invoking the aid of the Court is himself implicated in the illegality. It matters not whether the defendant has pleaded the illegality or whether he has not. If the evidence adduced by the plaintiff proves the illegality, the Court ought not to assist him' (*Scott* v. *Brown, Doering & Co.*) The only exceptions to this highly salutary rule are two—first, that where the parties are not *in pari delicto* the innocent party may recover money or goods which he has handed over in pursuance of the contract; such circumstances may arise where the party who has given the property is an ignorant man who has been taken advantage of by a man of sagacity and education (*Hughes* v. *Liverpool Insurance Co.*) That is not this case, where the *rôles* are reversed; the Plaintiff, who has parted with the property by way of security, is the morally guilty, not the innocent party. The second case, in which the law permits the recovery of such security, is where nothing more has been done than the payment of money or the handing over of property, and no part of the illegal purpose of the contract has been carried out (*Taylor* v. *Bowers*). At first sight this proposition appears to support the Plaintiff's claim, since the illegal act—the handing over of the infant into the custody of the Defendants—is still executory. But here another principle comes into play. It has been held (*Harse* v. *Pearl Life Assurance Co.*) that, even if both parties act under a mistaken view of the law, and make an illegal contract without knowing that it is illegal, they must be regarded as *in pari delicto*; in such cases the principal rule applies and the security or other property cannot be recovered. The principal rule must apply *a fortiori* in the case before me, where the Plaintiff who seeks to recover the property is morally more blameworthy than the defendants. The Plaintiff's claim must therefore be dismissed.

"That disposes of the main action, but the matter does not end there. The property in question is claimed by the Custodian of Enemy Property, who has been represented before me. Counsel for the Custodian has adduced evidence to show that the gold and jewellery to which I have referred is not the property of the Plaintiff at all, but belongs to three female aliens of German nationality, resident in Germany, whose names are given respectively as Wellgaude, Woglinde and Flosshilde, and described collectively as 'Rhine-maidens.' How the property came into the possession of the Plaintiff is a matter which has not been explained, but he has failed to establish any *bonâ fide* claim of right thereto; on the other hand, sufficient evidence has been given on behalf of these alien persons to support their claim. And on the principle *nemo dat quod non habet* it must follow that the Defendants cannot be entitled to retain the property, which was handed over to them as security, as against the rightful owners, for whom the Custodian stands in the position of a trustee under the terms of the Trading with the Enemy Act, 1939, and the Regulations made thereunder.

"I therefore make an Order for the handing over by the Defendants of the said property, transferred to them as security by the Plaintiff, to the Custodian of Enemy Property, within seven days."

Judgment was entered accordingly.

TABLE OF CASES

	Page
Adams v. Naylor [1946] A.C. 543	17, 18
Addie (Robert) & Sons Collieries Ltd. v. Dumbreck [1929] A.C. 358	65, 84
Agar-Ellis v. Lascelles (1883) 24 Ch.D.317	99
Angus v. Findlay (1887) 24 Sc. L.R. 237	65
Beatty v. Beatty [1924] 1 K.B. 807	26
Berthiaume v. Dastous [1930] A.C. 79	27
Boydell v. Drummond (1809) 11 East. 142	72
Clay v. Yates (1856) 1 H. & N. 73	100
Colls v. Home & Colonial Stores Ltd. [1904] A.C. 179	81
Cutler v. United Dairies (London) Ltd. [1933] 2 K.B. 297	56
Excelsior Wire Rope Co., Ltd. v. Callan [1930] A.C. 404	84
Grant v. Australian KnittingMills [1936] A.C. 85	86
Harrold v. Watney [1898] 2 Q.B. 320	65
Harse v. Pearl Life Assurance Co. [1904] 1 K.B. 558	101
Haynes v. Harwood [1935] 1 K.B. 146	56
Heaven v. Pender (1883) 11 Q.B.D. 503	86
Hillen & Pettigrew v. I.C.I. (Alkali) Ltd. [1934] 1 K.B. 455	64
Hughes v. Liverpool Victoria Legal Friendly Society [1916] 2 K.B. 482	101
Hyde v. Hyde (1866) L.R. P. & D. 130	28

		Page
Leeds Industrial & Co-operative Society Ltd. *v.* Slack [1924] A.C. 851.		82
Lemmon *v.* Webb [1895] A.C. 1		83
Liesbosch, Dredger *v. Edison*, S.S. [1933] A.C. 449.		66
Liversidge *v.* Anderson [1942] A.C. 206		20
Lord Strathcona Steamship Co., Ltd. *v.* Dominion Coal Co., Ltd. [1926] A.C. 108		58
Lynch *v.* Nurdin (1841) 1. Q.B. 29		65
McAlister *v.* Stevenson [1932] A.C. 562		86
McGrath, *Re* [1893] 1 Ch. 143		99
Machado *v.* Fontes [1897] 2 Q.B. 231		46
Meacher *v.* Meacher [1946] 2 All E.R. 307		40
Minister of Pensions *v.* Chennell [1946] 2 All E.R. 719		20
Mourton *v.* Poulter [1930] 2 K.B. 183		84
Nachimson *v.* Nachimson [1930] P.217		28
Ogden *v.* Ogden [1908] P.46		26
Parkes *v.* Prescott (1869) L.R. 4 Exch. 169		94
Phillips *v.* Brooks Ltd. [1919] 2 K.B. 243		71
Powell *v.* Powell [1922] P. 278		39
R. *v.* Cooper (1833) 5 C. & P. 535		95
R. *v.* Gordon [1789] 1 Leach 515 C.C.R.		92
R. *v.* M'Daniel (1755) 19 State Tr. 745		93
R. *v.* Saunders & Archer (1573) 2 Plowd. 473		94
R. *v.* Soares (1802) Russ. & Ry. 25 C.C.R.		93
Rose *v.* Ford [1937] A.C. 826		73
Royster *v.* Cavey [1946] 2 All E.R. 642		17, 18
Scott *v.* Brown, Doering, McNab & Co. [1892] 2 Q.B. 724		101
Six Carpenters, The (1610) 8 Co. Rep. 146 a		66
Taylor *v.* Bowers (1876) 1 Q.B.D. 291		101
Tolten, The [1946] 2 All E.R. 372		55

	Page
Tulk *v.* Moxhay (1848) 2 Ph. 774	58
Wallis, Son & Wells *v.* Pratt & Haynes [1911] A.C. 394	85
Weatherley *v.* Weatherley (1946) 62 T.L.R. 362	28, 38
Wilkes *v.* Wilkes [1943] 1 All E.R. 433	39

TABLE OF STATUTES

	Page
Statute of Frauds, 1677, s. 4	72
Prescription Act, 1832	81
Fatal Accidents Acts, 1846-1908	55
Accessories & Abettors Act, 1861	
s. 1	93
s. 5	93
Sale of Goods Act, 1893	
s. 13	85
s. 14(1)	85
British Nationality & Status of Aliens Acts, 1914-1943	
s.1(1)(a)	25
Guardianship of Infants Act, 1925	
s.1	99
Supreme Court of Judicature Act, 1925	
s.22(1)	55
s.188	23, 25
Children & Young Persons Act, 1933	
ss.61, 62	62
Law Reform (Misc. Provns.) Act, 1934	
s.1	46, 54
Matrimonial Causes Act, 1937	
s.2	39
Evidence Act, 1938	57

	Page
Personal Injuries (Emergency Provisions) Act, 1939	
s.3	16, 18, 19, 20
s.8	19
Trading with the Enemy Act, 1939	
s.7(1)	102
Defence Regulations, 1939	
Reg. 18B	13, 15, 20
Food Rationing Orders, 1939-1942	67.
Crown Proceedings Act, 1947	21

GENERAL INDEX

	Page
ACTION	
personal nature of, prevents survival	46
right to, survival of	46
ADMIRALTY	
jurisdiction of	55
torts committed abroad, triable in	55
AGENT	
position of, where principal undisclosed	71
ALIENS	
property of, disposal of	102
Rhine-maidens held to be	102
BEAN	
excessive growth of	80
nuisance constituted by	81
stalk of, deprivation of light by	81
BUTTERFLY	
death of	25
domicil of	23
fidelity of	24
marriage of	24
religious conversion of	25
status of	23

Page

CASSANDRA
action by	13
advice of, ignored	15
assault upon	16
evidence of	14
personal injuries of	13, 16
prophetic gift of, loss of	13
psychological war-work of	14

CHILDREN
allurement to, gingerbread house constituting	65
care and protection of	62
inquisitiveness of	63, 65
welfare of, paramount	99
whether licensees or trespassers	66

CIO-CIO-SAN
application by	23
birth of	24
domicil of	25
nationality of	25
legitimacy of	25, 26
parentage of	24

CONFLICT OF LAWS
contract, legality of	73, 74
lex fori	72, 76
lex loci contractus	73
lex loci solutionis	75
marriage, applicability to, rules of	26

CONSIDERATION
illegality of	98
infant, in respect of	98

	Page
CONTRACT	
building, provisions of,	98
foreign law appicable to	74
illegality of	98
performance within year of	72
soul, delivery up of, as to	70
subject matter of, identification of	74
CRIMINAL LAW	
accessories in	95
murder, as to	96, 97
CUPID	
animus deserendi of	38, 39
conduct of, whether constituting desertion	39
features of, disclosure of	35
identity of, concealment by	34
marriage, conditions in regard to	34
mysterious behaviour of	34
order, reasonableness of, by	39
whether desertion without cause	40
wife, desertion of, by	36
CUSTODIAN	
rights of, as to enemy property	102
DISCRETION	
Court, non-interference by, in	20, 21
Home Secretary, by, exercise of	20, 21
statutory, under Defence Regulations	20, 21
DIVORCE	
desertion, when sufficient to justify	39
Japan, law of, as to	24, 27

	Page
DON JUAN	
dangerous character of	45
delusions suffered by	49
duels fought by	44
military reputation of	44
musical details alleged by	49
promiscuous conduct of	44
scandalous behaviour of	45
seductions by, particulars of	44
sobriety of, doubted	49
DON PEDRO	
action by	43
alleged death of	43, 48
courageous behaviour of	47
daughter of, action in respect of	43
services to State of	44
statue to, alleged vivification of	48
survival of, conflict of evidence as to	47
FASOLT	
building activities of	98
contract made by, illegal	98
counterclaim by	97
FAFNER	
(See FASOLT)	
FAUST	
contractual obligation of	70
defences raised by	71, 72, 73
rejuvenation of	70
soul of, disposal of	75
specific performance claimed against	69, 74

Page

GINGERBREAD HOUSE
   an allurement to children 65
   construction of 62
   damage caused to 63
   occupier of, liability upon 65
   trespass in respect of 63

GRETEL
   (*see* HANSEL)

HANSEL
   dilapidations caused by 63
   trespass on part of 63, 64
   whether regarded as licensee . . 66

HORSE WOODEN
   concealed danger in 16, 18
   destruction of, suggestions for . . . 15
   emergence of commandos from . . 16
   negligent inspection of . . . 15, 18
   removal of 15

HOME SECRETARY
   alleged negligence of 13
   attitude to alien of 15
   discretion of, upheld 20, 21
   emergency powers of . . . 13, 20

HOUSE, GINGERBREAD
   (*see* GINGERBREAD HOUSE)

HUSBAND
   desertion of Japanese wife by . . . 24
               Paphian wife by . . 36, 37

HUSBAND *Continued—*

   identity, concealment of, by 34
   matrimonial capacity of 26
   mysterious conduct of 34
   orders to wife by, disobedience of . . 36
                  reasonableness of . . 40

JACK

   alleged nuisance committed by . . . 81
   horticultural activities of 80
   rights of, against trespassers . . . 83, 84

JAPAN

   matrimonial law of 26, 27

LICENCE

   child trespassers, when implied for . . 65

MARRIAGE

   capacity for 26
   Christian, meaning of 27, 28
   form of, law as to 27
   Japanese, validity of . . . 26, 27, 29
   term of years, for, whether valid . . 29, 30
   United States, validity of . . . 27

MEPHISTOPHELES

   agency of, alleged 71
   contractual rights of 70
   medical treatment provided by . . 70
   rights under contract 70

MURDER

   accessories in 92, 93
   counselling and procuring, what is, in . 93
   liability of accessory for . . . 93
   where different victim . . . 94

Page

NEGLIGENCE
    alleged, against adjoining owner . . . 79
                    Engineer Officer . . . 13, 18
                    Home Secretary . . . 13, 20
                    supplier of goods . . 85, 86
    Crown servants, liability-of, for . . . 18
    failure to intern, whether constituting . . 20, 21
    nominated defendant not liable for . . 17
    statutory, alleged 13

NOMINATED DEFENDANT
    allegations as to 16, 17
    device as to, disapproval of . . . 17
    meaning of 17, 18
    non-liability of 17, 18

NOTICE
    nuisance, abatement of, necessity for . . 83, 84

NUISANCE
    abatement of 82, 83
    claim in respect of 79
    light, in respect of 81
    serious nature of 80
    support, in respect of 81

OGRE
    abatement of nuisance by . . . 82, 83
    ancient lights of 81
    corpulent physique of 82
    injuries sustained by 82
    negligence, claim in respect of, by . . 79
    nuisance, claim in respect of, by . . . 79

		Page
PHANTOM SHIP		
category not recognised		54
curse upon, whether incumbrance		58
injury caused by, whether actionable		55
maritime lien, application of, to		51
owners of, liability of		54, 56
restrictive covenant attaching to		58
spell upon, whether enforceable as covenant		57, 58
unseaworthy condition of		52, 54
PINKERTON		
(*see also* CIO-CIO-SAN)		
marriage, Japanese, validity of		27
United States, validity of		27
naval duties of		23, 24
wife, desertion of, by		24
QUANTUM MERUIT		
Fasolt, claim by, for		97
when permissible		100
RHINE-MAIDENS		
held to be alien enemies		102
property of, disposal of		102
RIGOLETTO		
conviction of, quashed		95
prosecution of		89
SALE OF GOODS		
breach of condition, remedy for		85
of warranty, remedy for		85
compliance with description		85
fitness for purpose		85
statutory provisions as to		85

Page

SENTA
   fatal accident to 51
   impulsive behaviour of 53
   tragic death of 54

SHIP, PHANTOM
   (*see* PHANTOM SHIP)

SOUL
   whether *chose in action* 74
        personal property 74
        reversionary interest . . . 75

STATUE
   alleged lifelike behaviour of . . . 48

TROY
   destruction of 16
   fortifications of, breach in 15
   Home Secretary of, alleged negligence by . 13, 15
   seige of 14

VOLENTI NON FIT INJURIA
   application of doctrine 55
   knowledge required for 56
   phantom ship, application of doctrine to . . 56

WAR INJURY
   definition of 19
   effect on plaintiff's action of . . . 16, 20
   statutory provisions as to 19

WAR OFFICE
   Trojan, attack upon 16
        defendant representing . . . 18
        military policy of 14

		Page
WITCH		
action for trespass on behalf of	. .	61
alleged cannibalistic inclinations of	. .	64
gingerbread house built by	. .	61
how far liable to child trespassers	. .	65
WOTAN		
party to building agreement	. .	98